The Key: Identity

The Key

Identity

Kenneth George Mills

Sun-Scape Publications
Stamford • Toronto

© 1994 by Kenneth George Mills

All rights reserved, especially the right of reproduction in whole or in part in any form without written permission except in the case of brief quotations utilized in critical articles and reviews.

Canadian Cataloguing in Publication Data
Mills, Kenneth G., 1923 -
    The key : identity

ISBN 0-919842-18-6   (bound)   ISBN 0-919842-16-X   (pbk.)

1. Identity.   I. Title.

BD236.M55 1994   126   C94-932258-X

Sun-Scape Publications
A Division of Sun-Scape Enterprises Limited
P.O. Box 793, Station "F"
Toronto, Ontario M4Y 2N7, Canada

65 High Ridge Road, Suite 103
Stamford, Connecticut 06905, USA

Cover design: Concept by Kenneth George Mills; art by Robert Withstandley

Printed in the United States of America

TABLE OF CONTENTS

FOREWORD
PREFACE

I	THE BEAUTY UNFOLDMENT	1
II	HOW THE GARDEN GROWS	19
III	PRINCIPLE POINTS	37
IV	NEAR TO THE FIRE	59
V	THE ESSENCE	79
VI	FUNDAMENTAL QUESTIONS	93
VII	THE EFFICACY OF JOY	107
VIII	BE THE STAR	123
IX	THE SEAL OF APPROVAL	149
X	THE NEED OF CHANGE	163
XI	SEEDING	175
XII	CORRECT WORDS	195
XIII	FREEDOM IS FOUND	213
XIV	A REFLECTION OF THE WORDLESS	233
XV	THE PRISTINE DROP OF CLARITY	247
XVI	WORDS SEASONED WITH SALT	257
XVII	THE NEWNESS OF THE UNCHANGING	285
XVIII	ROBOTERY	301
XIX	THE UNLIMITED VIEW	321
XX	GREEN STUFF	333
XXI	THE MAGICIAN	351
XXII	THE MALADY OF FALSE IDENTITY	363
XXIII	LIFE — FORCE OF LOVE	381
XXIV	THE QUICKENING SPIRIT OF RADIANCE	393

FOREWORD

IDENTITY: INTRODUCING A NEW PARADIGM

"Who am I?" is a question that has been asked, we can easily imagine, ever since the dawning of self-awareness. Certainly a look at written history reveals many and varied forms of this inquiry. The answers given have been equally varied, and it is particularly interesting to see that the answers reached by the greatest philosophers and wise men have often differed greatly from the everyday opinions of the masses.

What *is* our true identity? And why does this question seem to be so difficult to answer?

Identity, from the Latin *idem,* "the same," has as its primary meaning "the quality of being the same or identical, oneness." By extension it has come to refer to what remains the same about a person or thing at all times and in all circumstances. Therefore, properly speaking, the identity of an individual refers to the qualities of that individual that never vary. Everyday usage has gone far beyond the original meaning and would now admit a statement like "My identity is a young American musician." But all three of the attributes mentioned (age, nationality, and occupation) are subject to change and therefore are not properly attributable to *identity.*

Kenneth George Mills is a contemporary philosopher and poet of broad vision and great wisdom who since 1968 has given over 30,000 hours of public lectures, called *Unfoldments,* where he has sounded a universal standpoint from which to view self, experience, and world. A cornerstone of his offering is the correct understanding of identity and the active living of that understanding. The living of it he has called *right identification,* and his own life reveals its viability.

Mr. Mills' view of Man embodies a radical return to the root understanding of *identity* as that which is unchanging. As he has said, "Man is a Conscious State of Being. It has nothing to do with being men and women." Addressing what is real in each one of us, he states, "You are not a man of a nation. You are a Light experience, or a Conscious experience, and only secondarily a person with a nationality. You are Conscious Experience primarily."

This provocative statement introduces the ideas of person and of Conscious Experience. *Person* refers to the common, everyday understanding of "who I am": an individual of a particular sex consisting of a body and a mind, existing in a certain place and exhibiting certain traits — in short, "a person with a nationality." The Romans used the word *persona,* which means "to sound through," for the mask worn by an actor in a play, which contained a small megaphone to amplify the voice. Then it came to mean a character acted, a part played. These overtones are present when Mr. Mills uses the word. The person is the part played on the world stage by an individual whose True Identity is Conscious Experience or Light Experience.

What is that? *Consciousness* is commonly thought to be a mental state of being awake or aware. Mr. Mills uses the word *awareness* to define that mental state and the word *Consciousness* as synonymous with the ultimate Reality, the metaphysical Ground of Being, That which exists in and of Itself. Consciousness can be conceived as the true fabric or substance of all the specific things, seen and unseen, that constitute experience. Think of a movie screen. The mental screen never seems to move or change, yet the pictures, which have no separate existence of their own apart from the screen, appear to move. We never say that we are going to the theater to watch the screen, but without it there could be no picture show!

Without Consciousness there could be no awareness of objects, of subjects, of universe. Yet, like the movie screen, it remains unchanged at the heart of all experiences, constant yet rarely recognized. Because Consciousness is unchanging, unlimited, and undifferentiated, any attempt to describe it — including this analogy of the movie screen — can never capture its Essence, since the description tries to compare the Infinite and Unlimited with the finite and limited. Any description, any metaphor or simile for Consciousness can do no better than *point to* what it is. Consciousness is the Substance to the perception of all that is, and it cannot be found in a box made of words or concepts. As Mr. Mills has said, "To be Conscious transcends your thoughts of what Consciousness is."

This view of Man's true Nature, this Absolute or Unitary Standpoint, is the one that has been sounded by the Great Ones of our race. From Jesus and the Buddha to the present this has been the common thread of inspired prophecy. But many contradictory belief systems have been accepted by the mass of humanity. Isn't each person entitled to his opinion about who he is? And what about other philosophical standpoints? When René Descartes posited his well-known formula "I think, therefore I am," he sounded the keynote for what has been called the Age of Reason. Unfortunately, his assertion of the equivalence of thinking and being has gained in strength as it has continued to resonate from the 17th century to the present. This helps to explain how we have swallowed such a huge lie about our Nature, for it has impeded the understanding of metaphysics and has narcotized mankind into the belief of mortality and separateness. The words of wisdom from the lips of Mr. Mills that have been transcribed and set forth in this book are a wake-up call for us to emerge from such a slumber.

If Man's real identity is One with the Source of Being, then that must be everyone's identity! To have a practical meaning, this must be able to be experienced. Where is the bridge between the Absolute and the everyday understanding of "What am I"? How do we experience the qualities that never change regardless of circumstances?

Every morning, upon waking, we can witness a facet of the answer when we emerge from what we call sleep and we have no question about who we are. Even if someone has moved us to a different bed while we slept, we have no doubt that our life is continuous, that we are the same individual as when we went to sleep. There is something in our experience that is so obviously continuous that we are *incapable* of doubting its continuity. This Something has nothing whatever to do with the objects or subjects of what we call our physical world or with the experiences that make up our mental world. How do we know this? Because all those objects, subjects, and experiences vanish in the dreamless sleep state, yet we still exist.

The very fact that we are willing to go to sleep, to abandon ourselves to what is usually called "unconsciousness," shows that we know innately that we are sustained by a power that is not dependent on the fluctuations in our mental state or level of awareness. Some have called this power God or the great Life Force, but even those who profess to be atheists do not fear to lose "consciousness" in sleep, because they know beyond doubt that the Essence of their Being is never touched! This unshakable conviction points directly to the existence of That.

We leap to a new standpoint when we recognize that all of us, both non-believer and believer, demonstrate in our lives our faith in the continuity of Identity, regardless of a fluctuating awareness, and in the sustaining presence of a higher Power that does not require our attention in order that we continue to live and move. Even more radical is the unifying leap of re-cognition that Mr. Mills asks of us when he says, "God, the Source, and you are inseparable." And he has said, "I and my Father are One *here-now* and not 'shall be.'" Suddenly that higher Power, which we have just acknowledged, is revealed as not other than what we are in essence.

Having revealed the universality of this experience of Identity's continuity, we must wonder why there seems to be so little recognition of our innate knowingness of who and what we are. The answer lies in the education, both explicit and implicit, that bombards each individual born into this world, almost from the moment of birth, an education rooted in the beliefs of the Age of Reason. We have been taught to identify ourselves with our bodies and with our thoughts. We have been educated to think that we are nothing but persons living in an objective world. Indeed, a large portion of our lives does appear to be played upon this stage, but since Identity is a constant, then constantly It is present at every moment of our waking and sleeping. It doesn't take the sleep state to reveal Its omnipresence.

How is Identity experienced, yet unrecognized, as we move upon this planet?

Our experience consists of events within the field of our awareness. Awareness disappears in sleep (at least to a very great degree) and along with it disappear our physical and mental worlds. During the waking day awareness is always ebbing and rising, and it seems to move from object to object, from thought to thought. One moment we are aware of one thing; the next moment it is something else.

What is the source of awareness? How do we perceive that the objects of our world are changing and that our awareness is changing? There is a Constant Presence, an unchanging Consciousness, right where we appear to stand. This is our reference Point, whether we realize it or not.

How can you know that this is so? Pay attention and see! *Attention* is the name given to the faculty of awareness that allows it to be focused on different objects, and that allows it to expand and contract. "Pay attention!" is a familiar admonition, heard frequently in childhood from parents and teachers. But to what did our childhood mentors wish us to pay attention? To physical objects and mental objects. Thus proceeded our education in being persons.

What if our ability to explore our inner landscape has been dwarfed by our upbringing? And what if the world that we truly inhabit is infinitely vaster and richer than we have been led to believe? Kenneth George Mills offers this discovery. His Unfoldments invite us to engage a vision, take the key, and discover that the New Landscape revealed is none other than the Essence at the heart of our very Being. What a Wondrous Adventure to engage!

Stephen M. Diamond

Editor's Note

Notes on the use of "I," "you," and "me."

Mr. Mills uses the words "you," "me," "I" and "I AM" in a very specific sense. The you and the me, especially when stressed, refer to the imaginary entities that we have created in our minds and claimed to be the identity of both ourselves and others. The you and the me represent the state of thought that believes itself to be embodied physically and thus part and parcel of a material world. It is our conceptual identity; it is a limited corporeal self-image that we have been educated to construct on the premise of duality and materiality. In short, it is the human personality that parades one way one minute and another way the next.

The I AM is the Infinite, the Eternal and the Unchanging. The I or the I AM is our true Identity. The I AM is what we really are. It is beyond any thought that can be identified with the finite. It is not a conceptual identity for it cannot be conceived, yet it is the Light to all conception. The I AM is synonymous with other terms appearing in the text: Consciousness, the Source, the Self, Christ, Truth, Life, Love, the Light, That Which IS. Yet, we cannot think in terms of being That personally, because that would impose a limit on the I AM, which is limitless.

Mr. Mills gives this very clearly in the following statements:

> "I" points to Being.
> You call it "you" or "me"
> when you think in terms.

> The I AM permits man to assume
> an "I am" identity;
> but the I AM isn't *in* the identity.

PREFACE

This world needs somebody who is going to give it back to the Arms of Love by recognizing the incredible objectification that has taken place in the generic form of creation, and what has happened as a result of adulterated teaching is confusing the issue of precipitated verification and Generic Essence. Consequently, there has been a tremendous divulgence of information that has been misconstrued and misconceived, and the conception therefore is confined to a limited state and is held there by false education. This false education is causing the alacrity of thought to be considered the epitome of accomplishment, instead of perceiving that the immediacy of thought and perception is the way the vehicle operates in its episode upon the surface of this planet, which has been precipitated solely to enjoy experiencing — a form of the Formless!

People have fallen in love with the form instead of Being the Love Energy of the Formless, which would embrace all forms and give them back to a world of peace, harmony, and love where people could live and have families and be whatever they wished. But it has to be done from the Standpoint of Unity and not diversity.

Nationality is the drug that has taken the place of LSD or cocaine. It has become the drug of false identity, which carries with it a vicarious pleasure in a false basis of energy.

All of the discord, which is arising from the chromaticism that comes about as a false pitch, needs to be resolved. The only way it can be resolved is by restoring the key of Identity to the crisis of time. The key of Identity is found in the framework of associating with the *generic* Sense of Being, not the hereditary sense of being.

The hereditary sense of being needs a root system to offer mothers, fathers, sons, daughters, to perpetuate the tree of life. But the Tree of Life, in Essence, is not from the roots up; its top is in the ground and the roots go up! Every branch of heredity should be seen as an evocation to the Divine. You might say it's backwards: the Tree, really, is standing on its head, but we don't see it that way. We see it buried in the ground of delusion; the branches of that tree could never bear healing to the nations. As long as the tree sheds its leaves as a result of seasons, it can never bear healing — it fluctuates.

The Tree of the Revealed State is the one that shares the Jewels faceted to bear the refracted Light to the people who can perceive them in their Glory.

Bonfires will exist all over the world, because by keeping conflict alive, you crank the Wheel of Return. That is why bonfires are started in Canada, in the United States, in Israel, in Russia, in Poland, in Italy, in Yugoslavia, in the Middle East, in Africa. Every time a bonfire starts, it takes combustion, which means what? The explosion as a result of elements coming together as a result of compression. What's more compressed and more isolated than the belief that each person has a right of his or her own! The only thing that each person has within his cognition is a question that he isn't "this." What is his own? The Answer.

This is how the Wheel of Return has to be stopped; otherwise, the wheel is kept going.

Kenneth George Mills

You are the inheritors
of the entire Kingdom
because you have the code: Identity.
That's the Key.

Kenneth George Mills

I.

The Beauty Unfoldment

Beauty does not fade,
only when it is thought timed.

I say, "Exalt one another
as I have exalted One to you!"

THE BEAUTY UNFOLDMENT

This evening we are gathered with the old and new that make up any suggestion of civilization. The picture that is being scanned is one of beauty, and yet if you see beauty all about, it is well to move to a different level of observation because you are not perceiving beauty all about, any more than you are perceiving Divinity *without* (outside yourself). Beauty is not without; beauty is not about, a gadabout, runabout, or turnabout!

Everyone feels, and feels differently about beauty. Some who feel that they are ugly this time were beautiful another time. Those who are beautiful this time are doing everything in their power to sustain their beauty in case another time they are not! It does seem as men and women look over the horizons, that they recede (the horizons, or men and women?) according to the clear seeing of the one . . perceiving! And the one who perceives that there is no limit perceives beauty not all about, but perceives perception beauty clad. That is why it can be said to be about. But you see, if you tend to observe the perceived without worshiping the Source of the perception (the Self, the I AM, or God), the perceived perception changes, and you say beauty fades as does a rose. But you see, what you are seeing fading is what has been holding space apart, or holding the gates of possibility open, for you to adore until your own beauty is perceived beyond the confines of a limited approach to your incarnation and to the suggested incarnation of That which is termed Altogether Lovely. (It is only belief that has suggested that the Infinite or the Divine was or could ever be limited to incarnation.)

Unto the power of perception man has given all types of thought-structures and thought-forms to substantiate the perception. Few there be who have walked across the picture book of time and have said to the pageant unfolding, "Stop right where you are, and see what is behind the act of

---

This Lecture is available on cassette, Sun-Scape Publications ISBN # 0-919842-50-X

movement, for if you can stop it, it is obvious that it must have started somewhere. But if you can't stop it, it is obvious it never started somewhere — it always has been!" There cannot be too much movement; there can only be undirected movement. There cannot be too much action; there can be only unbridled action. There cannot be too little action; there can only be the suggestion that act depends upon actor.[1]

We can stem the great tide of entropy through the great outpouring of the Eternal Truths, because they are the only things that are not known objectively but are known subjectively. When the subject, the aspirant, has no object for verification, then the subject collects its subject material unto itself and finds in the subjective situation that the object was only an act for those who perceived the subjective experience objectified, until space was swallowed up and time was thwarted in its attempt to divide or limit the Eternality surrounding the Eternal Garment of Truth. Those who parade across the picture book of time bear the Torch that shall never be snuffed out because the Source of the Flame was never found in a well of oil or in an oil that could possibly be dissipated, for it springs as it is said to have sprung, right from the very Center of Being.[2]

As men and women say, "Oh, you are beautiful," we are so grateful to hear the declaration. Why? Because somewhere within the heart there is a chamber that responds to the accuracy of declaration in spite of the suggested limits, "you."[3]

> *Beauty does not fade, only when*
> *it is thought timed.*

---

1. The false notion that act depends upon person, instead of upon the Divine; this personalization limits and reduces the efficacy of act.

2. "Oil" is symbolic of consecration; "springs" conjoins with the idea of the Spring that gushes forth from the mountainside mentioned in the poem on p. 13.

3. Essence ultimately recognizes only Essence, in spite of dualistic appearances.

What are we about in our day-to-day experience upon this trip called Earth? It is so fascinating, it is so productive to consider your visit to Earth as such. In the entanglement of minutes we get bound in their garments called hours, and their flowing robes called days and months. And a minute wearing such a train must find that the train is chained with such links of ineffable beauty that they clasp the wrist of the mind[4] so that when it comes to dance with the rhythm and the music of a timeless experience, the train of thoughts that the moment wears can never trip one into believing that the Dance of God is limited to a trip on Earth.

Now it is in the great frequency of blue [Mr. Mills was wearing a blue suit, and blue is a color often associated with adoration] and it is in the great frequency of adoration that man may perceive through the closed lids of time the great opportunity that awaits when the mind is freed from entertaining the beauty of objects and the objects of beauty, and finds in so doing that the objects of beauty are enhanced as the beauty of the objects is magnified beyond their limited nature, and thus reaches out and touches the responsive chord sometimes dormant in the eyes of the perceiver.

As the Masters of Eternal Light have always said, as the door opens it is not the door of a great cave, it is not the door of a hidden vault. *It is the door that is hinged upon the impulses that are forever ready to move into a service role when the call goes out unto those who would be given to praise!* As the door swings open, it seems so simple. If you are without, standing on the street side (objective attitude) of your habitation and would ask to enter into the inner side (subjective attitude) of your dwelling place, or state of consciousness, if it is yours you know *the key* and you also know that whether or not you have *the key*, if it is yours there will be, there must be, there shall be the Keeper of the

---

4.   This image refers to a wrist-chain that once gave women in formal dress control over the long, flowing trains of their gowns. "By wearing this chain attached to the wrist of the mind, the trailing thought-fields are not permitted to enter into a position outgrown and thus are unable to trip one who dances in rhythm with an unearthly prompting." K.G.Mills.

door ready to open it unto you. For all you have to do is say, "I am here; let me in," and the door swings open, for you have gained the right of entrance, having fulfilled the act whereby the hinges, the impulses, are forever kept honed to the demand of Home.[5]

A house vacated soon interiorly deteriorates. A house that is occupied bears the possibilities of becoming translated in spite of its limits into a conscious experience called Home. *Now, a home is where the heart is; a house is where it should be occupied by a heart. A house calls out for a heart to come home; a home opens its door unto a heart that knows it is.*

Now you say, **"What in God's name has this got to do with me?"** And I would say on behalf of you, but in the name of One, that it has everything to do with you, just as beauty does, for the God of you is the Light of you *thought* outside the Home of All-inclusive Being.[6] The whole question that arises when men and women say, *"Why?"* arises from being on the street side of life instead of resting in the Home Center of Life.

What has this got to do with you? It has all to do with you, and yet you cannot touch the All-Doingness! For as long as you persist in perceiving existence from your bias you will never perceive conception unconfined, and therefore *you can never experience a new birth in the Light of the Risen Light of Cognition bearing fruitage only of the knowingness that Life IS, Truth IS, God IS, Man IS freed from the train of your thoughts, for they have been bound to the wrist of the mind in the scintillating chain of perpetual knowingness.*

Do not think in parts! Whoever heard tell of a chain being thought in the terms of a link? Whoever heard tell of Beauty being thought of in terms of a stone? Whoever

---

5. Home — True Identity as God-Being; Being found All-inclusive.

6. God is usually considered to be a Supreme Entity *separate* from man, or "outside the Home of all-inclusive Being."

heard tell that Truth bears no link, but is the Perpetual Act never repeating but forever reappearing because men and women have thought through the framework of perceivers and perceiving perceptions, instead of dropping this train of limits and finding the train of thoughts commensurate to the God That IS and forever found in the sparkling cognition that I and My Father are One, because I cannot separate my *I* from conscious knowing.

Integrity is friends with few and should be the bosom pal of everyone, for it is indivisible and found part of the great tapestry of God-Being. *You will never wear a gown of adoration if you find not integrity hemming it and adorning it and shining forth in whatever way men and women evaluate integrity and how they perceive integrity.* Will it be gold plated, silver plated, sterling . . or gold? Will it be solid or will it be plated? I tell you now, if it is plated it is quite acceptable, knowing full well that if it can be plated it can be genuine[7] because anything holds space apart to be cognized in a great intuitive leap with no train of thoughts, and in that cognition lies the fourteen carat, the eighteen carat gold or the sterling silver or whatever symbol you perceive as pointing to That, which is untarnished by space and *untouched* by a moment wearing a gown of minutes and days, months and years, strung into your gown of limits. And yet some may say, "I perceive your coming and your going," and others will say, "I have perceived that I never come or never go but I AM invested in the Vestment of Eternal Light." Just as four is the eternal truth, mathematically, of two and two, so **my knowingness that I and My Father are One is eternally experienced in the knowing that I and my Father cannot be other than the Father and I in the bosom of That which is termed the Source.**

---

7.   In other words, if integrity (or any garment of Realization) were held as an image or an ideal to be experienced (i.e. symbolized by "gold-plating"), regardless of it being on an intellectual level at first, the promise of it becoming an actual experience or state of mind is immediately instilled!

*"You who are called out," means this: you
are called to step out of the rank situations
of the mind and file in rhythmic procession
before what you know to be true, for you
have lived in this age and under the aegis of
the Light for you know that you of yourself
couldn't have done it, do not do it, cannot
do it even if you thought you might!
Because with God there is no question, "I
can or I can't, I will or I won't, or I would
if I could."*

Be quiet, you who have worked through the minutes strung endlessly into days, and find it is all said and done in the perfected moment when I AM ALL and you are swallowed up in the awestruck power of the Light. Creation ceased (the notion of doing or creating *personally,* fades) for the Act was One, done, and IS.

Men and women may write about, gad about, and ride about but few can talk about what IS and give a jab to an ass in time to see it skip over the moon![8] And few there be who can find the joy of being stung and reaping the joy of the Great Dance staged when the hive of action all points to the Nectar (Heart) of the Light.[9]

You are well organized. You have a skeleton, you have what constitutes the required elements to give you a visibility. And yet no man can perceive what is the Operator, for when under the magnification of the great X-Ray, no picture will show who is inhabiting such a station!

---

8. "Few can give a point that can cause those men and women who are caught in the play of life to jump over the suggestions of life's game and see in the directed Life, in the directed Light, What IS. There are few who can give this point and cause those who are not prepared to leave the reflective nature (the moon, which is often associated with the psychic or mediumistic: that which shines by reflected light) and see the subjective experience of Life and Its acts." K.G.Mills.

9. The few who find their actions "dancing" as it were, in rhythm with the Divine, involuntarily pointing to and magnifying the Divine. This can often be initiated by a conscious "jab" or "sting" by the Master, or a given experienced Truth.

Salt, water, chalk, protoplasm or slime
Are held together in your bag of time.
But who is there perceiving such situation?
No picture is taken of such act on location.

Do not look to find
What you are in body timed.
Body timed gives likes of "you"
Trip in time on Earth to do.
Earth[10] became place of act;
Thought went out,[11] forgot I AM THAT.

I AM THAT heraldic might
Broke the lids of limited sight.
Opened wide the Door of Light,
And found the Fields of promised Might.

▼▼▼

Buzzing bee gave space a start,
Dived right through it, found nectar at Heart.

Bird in flight saw branches dance,
Claimed a branch and thus embraced dance.

Branch's dance with partner breeze
Gave freshness to nest, and bird you see?

Wind blew, branches bend,
All bowed to Omnipotent Friend.

To look for the Wind
is to search . . without realizing
IT is the very Power
that is behind the looking!

---

10. Duality consciousness.
11. Thought became objectified.

You who have taken the Earth on a visit, don't leave it littered with your debris, the residue of incomplete and personalized actions. Don't pass over its highways or its byways and use its parks of amusement, its places of entertainment to leave your messes! *For you came not to bring a mess but a message to a mass, for the Great Message that must be amassed is how it is possible to be part of a dimensional pageant and enjoy the freedom beyond the limits of the planes perceived and unperceived.* Just as you do not see any further than anyone else if you are walking with them on the same street, you cannot stay on the level of your biases if you are to look beyond them. To look beyond them means to rise above the suggestions of them! You cannot be inclined and so weak-kneed that you bow down to your predispositions when you are now disposed to find the Place of refuge.

The Great Message that is being massed and being amassed for the mass is to enable the mass to be given to praise and the great chants of bondage be seen as a theological hoax to chain people to a religious framework that can do nothing but leave the heart crying after the Living Heart. No man or woman born bearing appreciation of beauty whenever it is seen about is devoid of perceiving beauty — not about, not within, but *Beauty as all there is to the Source when it is seen as part of the great garment of the Eternal Figure of Flame.*[12] You cannot perceive the passing of the Flame and expect to see that which it utilized in the passing remain the same. Yet you would be damned and *you are damned by thinking that you can be the receivers of the Flame for a Friday evening or a Sunday evening, and the rest of the week be charred remains and only occasionally showing an ember of the Flame having been around when you are fanned by a moment of dis-ease or a moment of unrequited love!*

---

12. "Beauty is a garment that the Source might be said to wear — find it apart from IT if you can!" K.G.Mills.

The Great Teachings may appear, to those who do not know, to be achieved in many different ways. The Great Truths are never achieved in many different ways, for the Great Truth is only One, and the many ways to It is the propaganda offered by the mind, for *the mind hates in hell to change its garment and live in Heaven sponsoring Truth.*[13]

Do not fall for the suggestion that you can claim the Kingdom of your Divine State through drugs, because there is no possible way to be one with God and a drug! You will never gain God-Being through the God-damning of a drug! What kind of teaching would permit a student to be on drugs and suffer the delusion that he was entering the Kingdom of God-Sonship? Can't be!

So, may these few words that have been given to you from this Plane of rare Beauty, and rare Force, and rare Experience, be found acceptable to you, and in the Sight of the One Altogether Lovely. *For I am only a servant, and may Earth become the footstool for my rest and may it become the stage where you may be blessed in accomplishment and offer your lot, as I have offered mine, at the foot of the altar of the Eternal Flame where the great Door opens and man enters, for he knows that he never did leave Heaven for Earth.*

Now as I quit this Plane[14] of sound modifiers of a Heavenly State, may we find, through the adjectives and adverbs that you will find in the transcription, may we find in the living experience of having heard that your mind was freed from forming a sentence, from creating a verb and its tense, and may you find that in the simplicity of having heard, *a leap was intuitively made right into the lap of Beauty.* May you find as you come to bear the great gifts

---

13. "The many Paths offered by the mind have to do with the ritualistic and mystical approaches when the mind still wishes to *entertain* Truth, but not to be Its servant. The Mind as the servant can appear as the Truth appearing as a mind servicing. When God is All, where is mammon to be found?" K.G.Mills.

14. "Quitting" is only used figuratively, for the Plane of Consciousness as it IS can never be approached or left; it only appears to the relative consciousness that different levels are experienced.

of the God of Eternal Light that you too may find a precious jewel set in a precious setting, for in the simplicity of being set, a jewel unrecognized may be seen as one of great beauty. They all came from the Earth, but:

> *Someone realized that a rock could be filled with fire and knew that if it only could be struck right, one would strike it rich and find no longer any need of a sixty-four thousand dollar question, for the answer was the imperishable awareness that in the Heart of All I AM the Flame.*

It is of unearthly Beauty, because with the flick of my lid the door is opened, and with the waving of my hand recognition dawns, and in the act of experience I AM embraced, and in the act of embracing I AM found. Few know what is transpiring in Its transforming, and in Its transforming few know the form that *I* take. In the taking few know the Transcendent Nature, and yet a few may perceive that in experiencing the sound, the nature transformed is apparent. And in experiencing the transformed apparent sound, the Source of it must be known either it could not have appeared to have translated the vocabulary of limits into one that is limitless.

There is no one greater or lesser in the Kingdom unless he makes it so, for the Kingdom knows no greater or lesser among the sheep; they're all a miracle and *it is unfortunate that some choose to be rebels because no matter how much they rebel, they are still part of the fold. They can become "black" if they want to, but their lot is the sheepfold!*

You are damning yourselves by thinking in secret and thinking no one suffers from your thoughts. You must not hold one another in adjudications that you will not speak to another's face, and before doing so, find them not in you! If you do speak to others of their faults, or behind their backs speak of the faults, for God's sake go to the one you have spoken of and say, "I'm speaking to you of your faults; I am not faultless. I see yours, and I am offering this to you just with the hopes that by my telling you, you will be freed and in your love free me from my imperfection."

Whenever I make an adjudication on a situation, if you will note, it is done with great care, because it is never to pin a weight on anyone; it is to expose what it is that is binding them from the Lightness that could be theirs.

Very few people know Mr. Mills because they *think* Mr. Mills, but they don't *know* Mr. Mills. For if they knew Mr. Mills, they couldn't think about Mr. Mills, they would experience Mr. Mills. And no one wants to experience Mr. Mills because if they experience Mr. Mills the mills of this Mills don't grind slowly, there is no time! A long time ago a trance medium said to me, "Remember, beloved son, the mills of God grind slowly." And I thought, "No, damn it, they don't. I haven't got time!" I never have. I don't believe[15] . . and that is why some of you find it so difficult to be with me, because you think it is going to take time to change. Not on your life!

How you divide your action is appalling. How you divide it is just so limited. *Just the division of your action is the limit of your accomplishment. You cannot divide it!* If I thought I was just a talker and not capable of doing anything, what would be the value of it? You are the evidence of what this is and whether or not people will enjoy it. Your lack of authentic response is so common, it is so frequent. You don't respond naturally; I can see the egotistical inflation so quickly. And so often you are so inebriated with my realization for you! You suffer such hangovers because you do not know the Wine which you quaffed when you were with me. If you did, your response would be so different. *This is what happens with so many of you: you are given this Unfoldment, you are given this embrace, this Enfoldment, and you don't secure it within your own experience! You*

---

15. The implication is that of *knowing* rather than *believing*.

become a pawn for all the rest of the world and all the other world teachings if you do not utilize what you find of value. This is the only thing that will stem it and stop it from running right through you like a sieve. It can't help but bless you. It is just like the little boy who took the baskets of water to his father. You know the story . . .

> You know there was this father who had a
>   son in time,
> And as he grew up to be a helper, the father
>   took him to the fields and not to the
>   mines.[16]
>
> He took his son maturing unto the fields
>   where he worked,
> And as the day was dawning, and the sun in
>   the sky ne'er did shirk
> Its work, of ever shining upon the fields in
>   time,
> The father said unto the son, "Son, I thirst.
> Find water to quench it for me, your father
>   in time."
>
> And the son, he knew where to go; a Spring
>   gushed forth
> Right from the mountainside of the field
> And he said, "Father, what will I fetch the
>   water for you in? I have no can."
> And the father said, "Oh, yes, you can. You
>   have found this fact:
> That I brought my lunch for you and me,
>   and in the basket may you find that."
>
> And the son he took the basket and went
>   unto the Spring,
> And from its depths it offered refreshment
>   for servant and for king.

---

16. The fields represent the Light of awareness; the mines represent the darkness of limited ego-consciousness, and the subconscious.

The son, he ran unto the father and said,
  "Here is water, Father of the Light!"
And the Father said, "My son, the basket's
  empty! Run and fetch me more in
  Light."

The son took the basket and ran unto the
  well,
And ran right back to the Father, and the
  basket was empty.
And the Father said as well, "Run right back
  unto the well and fetch me water for
  my thirst."
And the son, being obedient, said, "I will
  run, for I know you thirst."

And then he reached the Father again with
  empty cup,
For you see, it was made of weaving and it
  was not tightly woven and the water
  ran through as such.
And then the son burst into tears, and the
  Father said, "Cry not, my son in time,
For you see, in your act of service my thirst
  is quenched, 'twas Act Divine."

And the son knew not the meaning and
  said,"Tell me, Father, what have I
  done?"
And the Father said, "Look at your basket,
  son, it's sparkling in the Sun!
For it has washed clean by *doing*, it is
  washed free in *act*,
Of all the debris that collected by being
  useless."

And then the son matured in wisdom and
  found in a clap of Light,

And said, "Oh, I see my Father!" and the
Father said, "See what, my son in
Light?"
And the son said, "Oh, my Father, it's just
like my mind of time.
The basket is like my thoughts which make
it up, and they must be woven to the
Thread Divine."

And the Father said, "Well done, my son,
you see the Teaching of my Light
You ran to service me with water, and now I
give you the Baptism of the Light."
So the Son, He waxed in glory, and the
Father never waned in Light,
And the Son reached the stage of Knowing,
and the Father declared, "Thou art my
beloved Self, insight."

Are there any pertinent questions? Yes.

Bill C.) Sir, I am seeing that the ability to
criticize and to see faults in others in one
way is good and it is very helpful, but to be
able to turn that criticism into positive seeing, yet with the same awareness, takes a lot
more energy and a lot more ability.

*Yes, and it takes a lot more dying, because it is so easy
to see the faults in others because invariably what you are
seeing is from your own level. The best way to see a fault
in another is by flying so high that you don't even see the
other (as being separate from, or "other" than oneself) to
see the fault in until you approach the plane of limits. But
you remain flying at the altitude at which you see no limits,
no duality, and then you might speak to the limits, but you
do not enhance them!*

Some people get as much kick out of criticizing as they do out of drinking too much, eating too much, or doing something they shouldn't be doing too much . . and you can put yourself anywhere you like! *You have to look very carefully at this area of criticism. You have to look very carefully at the area of why you criticize. Are you criticizing to make someone greater than you are, or are you criticizing to make someone think you have accomplished more? What is the value of Teaching? To develop someone's talent, to make them as good as you are, or to make them better? Ask yourselves these questions when you criticize.*

All the mind would love to say is that you are rejected, and the only thing I know is that you are never rejected, as if "you" were the Conscious framework! *I beseech you, do not hold to yourself thoughts that you cannot utter to a person's face, because they are not to yourself. If I put this microphone close to you, you might be surprised at what it is recording.*

We have a few more minutes and then we must stop. Yes.

> John D.) Sir, I have been considering the term you use called remembrance, and I was wondering if you could say that the difference between memory and remembrance is the same as the difference between coming to know and knowing as Identity, or Identity as fact?

You call it memory but is it memory? It really isn't. Memory is a misnomer for what really is happening. Memory is the way the mind accounts for being so sloppy! Forgetting is what the mind does when it doesn't want to have to do what it knows and tries to say it forgot it!

You know, people must want to forget terribly how much they are in Love.

> *I tell you now, when you have once loved,*
> *you cannot say you have forgotten, for you*
> *never can. You cannot make these*
> *declarations to anyone and say you didn't*
> *consciously make them.*

Which is true: Consciousness is present, or memory? You see, the mind can never construct a box in which to shield itself from the attack of Light. It can't. There is no such shelter.

It is amazing how you put me and this Work on one level, and you and your work on another. Just unbelievable! I had a very a good example of that. A man asked me the most incredible thing on architecture. It was so exciting. I had all kinds of phone calls; I spoke with several people about the repartee we had together, saying what a blessing it had been to him, and I never had one word from him. Why? He was working so hard on putting a hundred and fifty million dollar blueprint together for Ottawa. It means nothing! I think it is such an important point in teaching. *Do you mean to tell me that you are ever going to put together a hundred and fifty million dollar blueprint if you deny the Source?!*

> *Do you think you are going to dream up*
> *anything that will be living through the ages*
> *if you dream it up because it has got a*
> *hundred and fifty million dollar price tag to*
> *it, when I AM beyond price?*

The I AM of you — I am not speaking of Kenneth Mills here at all. I am not speaking of the I AM as "me," Kenneth Mills — but I am not saying I am not part of IT either, any more than you can say you are not part. You are not part: you are ALL, as I AM. Make heads or tails out of that if you can! Well, you're not supposed to! That is the whole point of your experience, trying to make heads or tails. **This is the game you play in life, trying to make a head or trying to make a tale of Life!**

You have to be very careful what you do and how you do it and how you consider one another. Do not take my words literally, because I do not mean for you to put one another down, and I do not mean for you to raise one another up unless in so doing you are adoring That Which IS, and then you find that **it is impossible to do anything other than exalt one another as I have exalted you.**

> *Jesus said, "Love one another as I have loved you." I say, "Exalt one another as I have exalted One to you."*

It is an Unfoldment of paramount news. *Paramount:*[17] if you don't know what it means, look it up. There are others as beautiful as you, somewhere. Why don't you put on your great Helmet of Light and let it so shine that no matter where you are walking in the minds/mines of time with this great Lamp, you can see even in the darkest places somebody who is waiting to be found! **Don't walk through life with blinkers on!** Just see and watch that there is only the One Act, and others limit it or magnify it and call it too much action, too little action. **Just see it as It IS, the One Act. In This I AM satisfied.**

For in That I AM given to praise!

▼

---

17.   One possible application of "paramount": The root of this word means "above or beyond the hill." The hill could be seen as referring to Golgotha, the "hill of skulls" upon which Jesus was crucified, "skulls" denoting in this sense the head, or the purely intellectual approach to Truth, the cold advocate of the letter of the law which leaves little room for the heart. This attitude often annihilates the possibilities of genuine spiritual realization, portrayed in this context as the crucifixion. When Mr. Mills says, "It is an Unfoldment of paramount news," he is thereby pointing to an experience that is beyond the head or intellect, yet one that nevertheless embraces the intellect, but from a redeemed and elevated Standpoint.

II.

How
the Garden
Grows

The identification with "you"
is the identification of limitation.
The identification with "I"
is the acknowledgment
that I AM All
and therefore unlimited.

How the Garden Grows

This is the first meeting with those who have found a Visitor who has found pilgrims, a meeting to melt the ice so that water could be what it is, and the suggestion that it is other than what it is, is laserized in the Light of That Which IS acknowledged to be All. We will just chat.

I felt that it might be nice for me to meet you, since you all think you know each other and you don't know me, and it would give you the opportunity to be, perhaps, more confused (or less susceptible to the condition!) if we met and if we chatted a bit about what you are doing and what I am doing on my visit here to California. The purpose of my visit has been to see a new part of the country and to see part of the landscape and see how the Garden grows. There is no purpose in being here other than to recognize that all that which grows in the Garden is a miracle and all that which blossoms is the evidence of the promise that a flower holds for those who would grace the face of time.

The remarks that I have just made, of course, include you [a guest who has just arrived], for you are wearing the blossom, and let us hope you fulfill the promise. So, when you walk in the garden, you do not necessarily have to clip the flowers to enjoy them; you just see what they are and let them fulfill their promise. And that is what I am doing, although I do not think many of you have thought so. I do not know what you thought about meeting me, especially in certain regards, but there is no regard that is important save the miracle of a blossom.

Joseph gave me a list of where you are registered,[1] but, of course, you are registered as if you were born, so it is no surprise that you are registered in a university of division when the whole promise is for a *Universe of Unity*. Trying to bring parts together to make a whole is difficult.

---

1. Most of those present at this gathering were students at the Graduate Theological Union or at the University of California, Berkeley. They had been invited to meet Mr. Mills the day before he gave his first formal lecture in California.

In this close range you can see me as I seem to be, and may I see you as you seem to be and know you as you really BE! There is nothing that I will say that, I am sure, the multitude of the people who are in your proximity have not said, and, therefore, do not feel that you will hear anything new. But if it should be Truth, then you will, of course, recognize IT in your garden and wonder why you are not the living evidence of it. Because where your thought is, there are "you;" and where your Knowingness is, there am *I*.

So, the thoughts about being just a Canterbury bell or a snapdragon or a calendula or a marigold or a cleome or a larkspur or a tulip just limit you to your patch, but to the Cosmic Gardener it is all a miracle!

> Robin J.) You said a couple of minutes ago that where my thoughts are, there am I.

No, where your thoughts are, there are "you."

> Robin J.) Where your...

"Where my thoughts" — you say it.

> Robin J.) Where my thoughts are, there are you?

Yes, "you."

> Robin J.) And where your Knowingness is, there am I?

Yes, your own I, not mine. Don't put anything on me! It is your own exalting of your own State (which seems to be yours) that is of importance. We use this language so commonly, and we all say we understand and we really do not. **What I mean by "I" and what you mean by "I" and what I mean by "you" and what you mean by "you" may be very different. The sense in which the "you" is used is a sense of** "you" as ephemeral and limited; "I" points to the Eternal and Infinite. The "you" points to the changing and the "I" points to the Changeless.

> Robin J.) How do you use the word "miracle"?

As a marvel.

> Robin J.) But would you say a miracle is something that is a natural product of the Law of the Infinite, or would you say that it is something that is perhaps not so natural?

It has to do with more than you, and when an experience happens that you seemingly have nothing to do with, that is a marvel, pointing to a miracle. I think it is a marvel that you can entertain the thought, and I would *find the Source of the marveling, not the thoughts about a marvel.* The point of any miracle is to point you to the Source of its happening rather than to give you something to think about! It develops, perhaps, a sense of awe and strengthens your faith (if you are in the faith of becoming) that something could happen that could release you from the limited thoughts you can hold about yourself and about your world and about your universe.

This is the way it is viewed by this one. You do not have to accept anything I say. That is what happens: everyone accepts everything everyone says without applying it to Principle.

It is interesting to see how today everyone is looking to tomorrow, *putting off* instead of Being *Now* That which has no alternative. This is perhaps why a Path that is based upon an Uncontradictable is always rather fearsome to those who like to do their own thing.[2] Of course, "there are many

---

2. One way of stating the Uncontradictable is given in the next paragraph: "If God IS All, what is there besides?" The Premise of the Unfoldments is also stated by Mr. Mills as "I and my Father *is* One, Now . . and not 'shall be.'"

paths to God," just as there are many people who have made God, but God as God is usually just thought about and *idolly* worshiped. *A God of Meaning finds the Universe turned into One, and no separateness. To pursue the attitude of separateness precludes the ability to entertain a Philosophical Embrace of All-inclusiveness.*

If God IS All, what is there besides?

You did not create yourself, and the Source of that which enables you to appear is worthy of respect. A miracle! Find it!

So, I don't know how many will turn up at the hotel tomorrow for the Lecture, but it doesn't make a particle of difference whether it is one or a thousand. There is nothing to do as far as I am concerned but to tell you how I see my garden grow, hoping that yours is doing well also. So often people come to hear someone speak and evaluate it according to what *they* have computered, whereas *the whole purpose of any serious intention to go to the root of the changing condition points to the ability to cease thinking.*

You cannot really hear if you try to evaluate what you are hearing according to what you think you know, because you will be hearing everything I say in your framework of reference, which may be faulty, or it may be perfect. This is why the Zen teachers all tell you the emptiness of the mind is so important if you listen to anyone speak. Attempt just to be receptive and to hear how the tea flows from my cup to yours. The Tea Master's guest said, "Oh, the tea is pouring all over the table! It is spilling." The Zen master replied, "Yes, your cup was so full you could not receive any that I had to offer. And you had come to partake of the tea."

> John Mc.) Is it possible to come with an empty cup without any stains of the last time you had tea?

Well, it is, perhaps, if you use the All for cleaning purposes, and Tide,[3] but you are caught in the tide of current events, eh, Sister? [A nun was present.] You look so serious. You know, it says, Your joy shall be full and the cup shall be running over. That is what it is. I don't know who said it, but a man years ago gave me a piece of white birch bark and on it was written, "Joy is the echo of God's life in us." Really, it is a wonder to see the echo which, of course, is only there if there is a resounding surface or a reflective surface.

But then, of course, you know the sun and the moon:

Brother Sun and Sister Moon,
Must dance together at High Noon.[4]

It is direct experience; it isn't reflective. As you know, a reflector can easily be shattered.

If you come to hear me speak tomorrow it will be no different from today, because you will bring to it whatever you have brought today. If you see a flaw in what I am saying, love me so much that there isn't one!

Ruel W.) What is a flaw?

An intellectual question about a thinker who thinks that That Which IS could be right or wrong.

There would be no value in our meeting if you went away thinking the same thoughts you came with, because the hope of a life experience is that you will leave it consciously, devoid of the thoughts that would have limited it to a three-dimensional episode.

---

3. *All,* a registered trademark of Lever Brothers Company, and *Tide,* a registered trademark of The Proctor & Gamble Company.

4. See the poem "Brother Sun and Sister Moon" in Kenneth G. Mills, *Given to Praise!* (Toronto: Sun-Scape Publications, 1976), pp. 122-124.

You have a beautiful city here. I was taken around quite a bit of it yesterday. I saw some of the highlights, and some of the high points. It was marvelous to be able to look down upon the place where we are situated and to see that what appeared as obstructions in your view — be it a tree or a wall or a barn or a house or a body — just faded from the top of the mountain. They are experimenting there, of course, trying to do away with something that isn't there anyway,[5] but it is a colossal, cemented structure, and costly.

I am very interested in looking at the gardens where they are sponsoring all the different varieties of cacti. I guess the majority of them are nice to look at but not very pleasant if you expect them to hold you! The gardens are well terraced and are all part of the one landscape. But as long as you can think in terraces, you have an excuse for remaining the way you are. If you are happy the way you are, for goodness' sake stay that way, and let your happiness point to That Way, the High Way.

> Joseph S.) Mr. Mills, would you continue to speak on the Work which you appear to sponsor and the premises on which it is based?

This talking started to happen several years ago, in 1968, when I talked to two or three people. Up until 1962 I had been a concert pianist and had worked with the purposeful intent of being a fine pianist so that the music could soar from the realm of symbolism.

I studied for about twenty-three years and was offered a world tour, which was something I had been working for. I told my family and my friends about it, and we were rather excited; the world tour was so exciting for everyone. I went to bed but I didn't sleep, and when five o'clock came around there was something that was unresolved; it was as

---

5. Referring to the Lawrence Radiation Laboratories in Berkeley.

though a chromaticism had come into the experience and I didn't know what it was. But my father had always told me, "If in doubt, don't." So I listened, for what, I didn't know. I was up around four or five o'clock in the morning and came to see that I was not going to sign the contract which would take me around the world and give me the opportunity to play.

So I refused it, and the impresario said, "We'll never be able to offer you this again." I said to him that if it were to be, he couldn't help but offer it to me again, because it had nothing to do with him; he just thought it did. So I thought, "Okay, if it isn't to be music called piano playing, what is it to be?" In a short time things started to happen within myself, and I started to speak with a few people. I agreed to speak if I were asked, and only if I were asked, and this is the way it has always been. It started off with three people; I don't know why they found it particularly valuable, because it was just what it was, being my own experience. But they have found it so.

Many, of course, can't stand it; they can't stand "it" anyway, but they call it me to evade seeing their own "it." But that's all right; it's not for everyone. Even Jesus said this, and that's why He spoke in parables, so they tell us. Nevertheless, there were some crumbs even for those who could not take a whole piece.

This is just what has happened and it has grown. I came out here to see how the sun shines where you think you live and move and have your Being. It's really beautiful.

There is no sense of so-called initiation, or there's *no sense accepted* surrounding the Premise from which this unfolds, which is acknowledged, for the greediness of the mind always wants to be satisfied, so you give it whatever it wants while you are busy about the Father's business. So it is with the words. The words hold the attention one way or another, and it's in between them that the Work is done. As you know, when you work in your garden, you work around the plants; you don't dig them up. The only thing you take out are the weeds, and they always grow quickly. So don't be impressed by a sudden spurt through the crustiness of your experience and say, "Ah! A perennial!"

I was away from my house for quite a while, and I went back and looked at my garden and there was this huge plant growing, and I said to the man who is working for me, "What is this here for?" He said, "It's so hardy and strong." I said, "What do you think it is?" He said, "Well, it will blossom soon." I said, "No. It's dwarfing all the zinnias and the asters. It's a weed but it's holding your attention by its appearance of being so sturdy. Pull it up!" That's what we did, and, you know, it was huge, but the root system was just like that of tumbleweed.

Don't take this literally.
Take it deeper than just
the superficial root system.

Take the words beyond their literal meaning and then you'll start to see why some people giggle!

The Premise that is utilized is the statement that "I and my Father are One . . Now, and not 'shall be,'" that "I of myself can do nothing," and that "Consciousness is fundamental, and what you are conscious of will constitute your experience until *I* come." It says, "I come suddenly," and I think it's a miracle to wonder why the "I" has not been discerned as already present.

It's a challenge to live this way, you might say, because you have to practice. If any of you play instruments (outside of your own thought one!) you know the practice that is necessary. You may be a born musician, but did you ever hear a professional acclaim you if you had no technique? They talk about your talent, which is a miracle, because you can't find it in your chalk, salt and water, protoplasm or slime, but it takes technique to transcend the arrogance of your profession. Without technique, "you" are always in the way of Music.

> Jerry C.) I've been here listening and trying to feel things and wondering how much I should jump in. I guess I've decided that if I am to learn, I have to risk. I've never met anybody like you in my life, and I find that a strange and interesting experience. I think one of the things that I feel strange about is the quality of all of us sitting here waiting for you to say something profound. It creates problems for me.

Yes. Well, don't think about it. Just enjoy it. That is what's causing the problem. "Problem," you know, comes from a word that has a root which means "to stoop." But you view from the top of the mountain. When you view from the top of the mountain, you don't have to dive. All you have to do is look with your eyes closed and see. The only risk involved is the suggestion that you are not fully insured under the policy of All-State. Eh, Pat?

> Sister Patricia C.) I guess I am trying very hard, maybe too hard, to be present here. To be here fully, and to be receptive, is really a source of pain, because I'm very hungry for knowledge and spiritual nourishment. I guess I don't know exactly what you are trying to say, but I do sense, almost like we're all holding our breaths, this stillness. It's both good and uncomfortable.

Yes. That is fine, though. Don't be concerned that you feel uncomfortable, because that may be the pressure of your Divinity. If you were not uncomfortable, perhaps you would be self-satisfied in the image of "it."

If you feel uncomfortable, be grateful.
Turn it into a situation of value.

> Sister Patricia C.) You see, I've searched; I've never known any other way. I've spent my whole life searching in one form or another. When you say to look into not the literal meaning but the deeper meaning, well, I think I do that maybe too much! But you're asking us to do that now, and once again I'm trying, but I'm not so sure that that's the best place for me to be.

It isn't, if you think "you" are doing it. From *your* standpoint, you shouldn't do it; I agree with you. You shouldn't do it from *your* standpoint; you shouldn't look for the interpretive meaning, the Higher Meaning, from *your* standpoint.

> Sister Patricia C.) How can you look at it from any other place?

You know the top of the mountain.

> Sister Patricia C.) Yes.

Claim it! You don't have to be walking the bleeding footsteps. Somebody else did that before. You've done it yourself and what has it gotten you? Just wiping up the blood. The place to go to in interpreting on a different level is from the Standpoint of what you call Principle. You know very well the miracle. It's a good thing I used the word this morning. In spite of all your discomfiture, you still seem to be present and holding to the promise of fulfillment in this form of a search. That is a miracle! *So view it from the Standpoint that it is all done and you have to die to the suggestion of being in process.*[6]

---

6. Try this as a moment-to-moment daily practice.

You are not being processed; the only thing that is being processed is the film industry of your own thought projection room. You're constantly developing, and the reason you are discomforted is because you are what? Taking a double exposure! That's semi-metaphysics, a house divided against itself: pandemonium! Absolute metaphysics is the Standpoint in which matter doesn't enter into the solution of your problem, because it doesn't exist save as a suggestion for you to exercise upon in order to vault the bar of suggestion and reveal the wall as only a suggestion of thought.

> Sister Patricia C.) I think it would do me good either to have a replay or to have your words written down so I can mull them over. It's hard for me to get. You use a lot of imagery!

Yes, because you have done such a thing to yourself!

> Sister Patricia C.) What?

You've created "what" instead of That, due to imagery. So that's the way I'm reaching you, supposedly, through imagery, because you have imaged yourself to be in a situation and think I'm there! If I AM not there, you can't be either, because I know where I AM and you don't.

You see, angel, your thinking will never tell you that you've done anything, because if it did, you would no longer be able to suffer. This has been the reward. Your suffering has made you feel your life has been not ill-spent. Now there's no need to have another moment of it, because it doesn't take time to think right. Time is a thought-projection. Drop it!

[Mr. Mills picks up a box of matches.]

> If this is your book of sorrow all wrapped
>   up in a cardboard box,
> And if it contains the means of solution,
>   why would you hold onto the box?

Why not lift the cover and take the risk of seeing what is separated there before you? You say, "Oh, my thoughts seem to be just like this. All separate, and each one ready to strike when I least expect." Well, you know very well, to strike the match you have to turn the box over. You can't keep looking at the surface. It only takes the match to put an end to the box, if you insist on going through an immolation scene. Why don't you drop it? One is instantaneous and the other is prolonged agony. It's the crucifixion, the mental crucifixion.

> They say that there was a Man of
>   Accomplishment by the name of Jesus
>   of Galilee.
> And the reason He walked upon the cross,
>   and they say upon the sea,
> Was to show you that if you could conceive
>   this fact, the Way was laid bare in the
>   Light of Love.
> Give up your beliefs of being contained, and
>   find in the Arms of the Dove
> That in that resurrected State of Consciousness,
>   which He showed in the sepulcher of
>   doubt,
> He could wrap up His own linen garments,
>   and move the stone about.

When He walked right down the road of Emmaus, they didn't recognize Him at all, and yet they said, "Have you heard the news?"

We should be moving in the State of Consciousness where Jesus left off, if you're at all oriented to the Christian concept. If you aren't, He left off in Self-Realization, which He pointed to as a possibility for all those who would die to the belief of being a skeleton in time. He gave the *Key* to open all the doors.

So you have to accept that Standpoint. Whether you want to or not doesn't make a particle of difference; accept it! If you don't, you're just accepting the belief that you prefer your agony in place of it. You don't need to agonize. You remind me of an angel with tarnished wings. You just don't want to get out the Twinkle Bright and sparkle! That's the beautiful part of it. You watch. Don't you fret, you know. You should not fret at all, because What brought you here looks after you and looks after me.

Sister Patricia C.) I believe that.

Don't believe it. *Live* as IT.

Live as the Knowingness, not as a belief!

A belief is forever changing, as a thought is. So live as the Knowingness, not as a believer. See? You *know* what a rose looks like; you don't have to believe it looks like that.

You just relax today and see how, you might say, God takes care of you. The way God takes care of you isn't the way you think! That's why you can relax and let go, and *let* God. You're trying to usurp a prerogative of Deity and are wondering why your world isn't all right. You don't have to look after yourself; just relax, and see the miracle.

The miracle takes place as a Conscious Experience, and that is what initiation is. You know these people who talk about walking through initiation and having candles put out on the forehead or sitting on a flame and hoping to be marked and found approved to enter into a higher state of awareness? Initiation is *really* having the way prepared so you can walk into a realization that you have never had before about that which you *thought* to be, and found wasn't, and which you *found* to BE, IS.

So this gives you some idea of how I talk; now spread it among all the friends who are planning to come tomorrow and if you don't like it, tell them to stay away, for God's sake!

He looks after them whether they come here or not, but if they find not the joy, then know that God must be still in sackcloth, and yet His linen robes were folded in the form of the man Jesus. Remember, they were folded because the linen robes were the robes of the initiate; they were not the robes of the Accomplished One. The linen symbolized the state of readiness on the part of the neophyte to enter onto the Terrace of the Light.

Don't encourage your friends to come unless they are really interested in rejoicing in the Miracle of the Rose.

A man once phoned me and asked me if I would please take up metaphysical Work over healing his toe, his big toe. It was going to have to be operated upon. I said to him, "Well, I certainly am not going to take up Work over your big toe, but if you wish me to include you in the Joy of Knowing, fine and dandy." Actually, he couldn't be excluded anyway. His toe was healed, and the next day he phoned, telling me about his healed toe. I said, "Get over here mighty fast." Because the healed toe didn't prove that I knew anything. It just proved that God is good, in spite of the suggestion that there was a healed toe. We wanted a healed heel! And it worked! He became an outstanding teacher, all from asking to have a sore toe healed. The strangest thing: it was his big toe; the big toe is supposed to point to understanding, and he's an accomplished teacher today. This happened when he was eighteen.

One phone call did it. But I think there's the tendency to feel that if you see a situation that is needing healing *healed,* you feel something has happened. I think the most aggressive suggestion is that you are in such good health, rejoicing in being so healthy, and wondering, "Where in

God's name is my wealth and my wisdom?" If the three don't go together, you haven't found the root of *wealth*.

Look it up in the dictionary!

Do you know, some jackass in Toronto, a high school teacher, told his students not to use the dictionary; it would brainwash them! Go to the root and trace it, and see how far afield you are from having any substantial support in your realm of beliefs. You'll be appalled at the words you use and know not of the field of experience you build around yourselves to work out of, all because of so-called education.

Oh, you've been so pleasant this morning. People don't know what to expect,

> Because they all conceive a picture of a man
> who's going to talk,
> As they all try to conceive a picture of a man
> who ever walked,
> Who walked into the Garden and he looked
> unto the Sun,
> And he said, "I can't see a thing for the
> brightness of the One.
>
> "So I'll look up in this moment, and I'll look
> up and I'll see
> That where I thought I looked, there is the
> Deed.
> For there is no figure and there is no form
> about,
> But I'll tell you right now, in the mighty
> Now, there is this Point of Love.
>
> "For where I thought a vision, I see no
> visionary stands,

For I look from the top of the Mountain,
  and I see the valley at my hand.
But I know without decision, for the Path
  was laid so green
That I would walk right through the valley,
  and see through the vale of dreams."

And so you catch the Moment, and the
  magnitude of Light.
Don't magnify your pictures in the studio
  out of sight!
Don't magnify the finite, unless you see the
  Infinite at hand,
And wake up and BE, God-Man!

If you think you are a man and you think
  you are a woman, fine and dandy.
But that isn't in the Scheme of the menu of
  God's cookin'!
For you dream up your God, and you see
  what you've done:
You've got yourselves all separated, even in
  the Light of the Sun.

Why don't you be happy, and see the Face!
You don't doubt the sun's body, and so the
  rays are traced.
We've caught the fingers dancing upon your
  face in time,
But you know you see beyond the dreams,
  and it wipes away the tears of time.

It's been mighty nice to see you, and I thank
  the Power That IS,
And may you stand upright and say, "I be
  dressed as I IS."

For if you cannot appear respectful as I AM
     unto That Power,
How will you ever stand to face your Self
     when you shall be dressed in the Light
     of the Power?

May you stand One Day and find no night. I didn't say "in one day"; I said "stand One Day." Don't miss a word! If you do, you will interpret it in your way, and that isn't Mine.

Perhaps I'll see you tomorrow. But at least you'll say we've met. What — is the question. Find the Answer, and be graced by a Miracle!

▼

III.

Principle Points

You are not a man of a nation.
You are a Light Experience,
or a Conscious Experience,
and only secondarily
a person with a nationality.
"You" are Conscious Experience primarily.

Principle Points

Now, I'd like to know what you've done since I last saw you, so the best place to start is to say *hi!* What did you do after I left you last evening?

> I'd like to know what happened between
> nine-thirty and eleven,
> Because all good boys and girls can directly
> go to Heaven,
> Provided they have followed instructions on
> the Course,
> They'll grow up to BE . . a disciplined One,
> of course!

I would wonder how many succeeded. I wonder how many secured the Unfoldment by being quiet. I am the Envoy of a School of Accomplishment that points to a directed Light of Obedience. If you think that you have a choice, you don't. Whoever heard of the Sun deciding whether or not to shine!

> If you are the Sun/Son — and it's obvious
> you must be, since you're here!
> Well then, you can't help but smile and blow
> away all those clouds of doubt and fear.

The end of an Unfoldment is the time when you should be quietest and most secluded and uncommunicative, and in a meditative state. Your speculations about your own disquietude appear and you want to gab in order to dwindle the power of what appeared as the Unfoldment. When you are moving, your partners or your friends have no way of ascertaining your development and your action; only you within your heart know. No one can tell you where you're going; only you can mark the way. So, it is imperative to seal it, and the sealing is done in the silence.

This is the most important time. There is so much going on, and so many move into the Frequency of Love's action by hearing the Unfoldment and yet have not a clue as to what the action of the Frequency is.

I hope I will have the grace to be able to give you a little bit of elementary work. If you want to do anything you can do it! As somebody said today to me before we leapt into the lake: "If you really want to do a thing, you can do it. That is why I have moved so much, because for the first time, I've really wanted to change."

This seems to be true.

I'm going to speak to you from a Standpoint that is Absolute, which enables me to speak to you from the standpoint of a dualist, so it seems, and yet has the power to move you right through the dualistic period into the Absolute Awareness that what has happened is a result of being able to pass from one octave to another in the realm of understanding and be kissed by the Grace of Intuition.

During the dinner hour, basics were served. We had the fruits of the vine, and the casserole, and the flavor of mushrooms. (As you know, the mushroom bears no nutrient value but has a delicious flavor. It's always the important part of a nice dish, but you should also realize that the dish must contain substantial ingredients in order for you to feel satisfied.)

It came to me that I should talk to you as if you didn't know anything; I should talk and appear just to be a teacher. And this is what I've decided to do. I'm not going to think you are my pupils; I'm going to expect you to understand what all those who could walk into a classroom should understand.

Of course, the first word that people use is "God." If they don't like what's happened to them, they say, "Oh, God damn it all." And if they love what's happened to them, they say, "God be praised!" So, it is well to align yourself to an awareness of what is appropriate to the Power of God.

Now "God" is a sound, or a word, which in twenty languages means "good." The word "God" doesn't mean too much to most good people, because one minute people can be good and the next minute people cannot be good. But you see,

God IS Good.

So if God IS Good and has persisted in holding a place of magnitude in the Light Language of emancipation and freedom, then the word "God" must be understood! The best way to understand God is to see how synonyms are present in the *soundingness* of God. Mary Baker Eddy gave the seven synonyms for God: Life, Truth, Mind, Soul, Spirit, Principle, and Love.[1]

Those are to be learned.

This is not being given for you just to go home and go back to your rooms and go to sleep and forget you ever heard this. These are to be learned.

Now, every one of those words, when they are used in your language, every time you use the word "Truth," every time you use the word "Spirit," every time you use the word "Love," "Principle," "Soul," "Mind," it must carry the meaning that "God" must carry either you shouldn't be using them! They must be used in a way that they can become attributable unto the Godhead! In other words, you cannot even use them and not pay the utmost farthing for having used them, even in ignorance!

This is a basic. Whenever you hear these Unfoldments, you'll notice that all seven of these words that I've listed are used in such a way that they can always be attributed to God, and God becomes a Living Reality because of the Power of

---

1. Mary Baker Eddy, *Science and Health with Key to the Scriptures* (Boston: Trustees Under the Will of Mary Baker G. Eddy, 1934), p. 465, ll. 8-15.

the Presence of awareness in the gown of the synonyms commensurate with His Soundingness called!

> Bruce A.) If used wrongly, then, they are their own punishment.

Exactly. That's why you always pray to God that you will not be God-*dammed*, and if the prayer is offered with humility and reverence, punishment is rescinded and man has a chance again to be free.

The next is "Man." "Man" is now a sound, like God. Every word that is a synonym for Man must be one that can be applicable to God. So, if you think God is beautiful and God is good, God is gracious, God is strong, God is secure, God is Love, God is Principle, God is Mind, God is Soul, God is Spirit, God is Love — then Man is, because Man is the image and likeness of God!

> *Here's how you work:*
> *You know what God is;*
> *you know now what Man is.*
> *Now, when you feel moody,*
> *ask if God could feel moody.*

If God can't feel moody, you are living a fictitious existence if you are moody; in other words, you are dying in ignorance that moment. If man is feeling depressed, or if he's feeling happy and joyous and the whole world is his oyster, ask if God could feel joyous and the whole world His oyster, or would He feel the Power that could support the world in the Light of His Awareness? Then you will see that a joyousness that is Self-imposed is acceptable in the Light of God, but one that is triggered by association with the titillating comments which would bring about personal exaltation is to be renounced because God is unaware of person.

"Person" is the name given to an object trying to live on its own.

*When you pretend
that you're not what you truly are,
you certainly can't say you're God
when you've behaved as if
you were God-dammed.*

If you are personally active, you lack the power of inspiration, the power of acknowledgment, the power of humility, the power of translation, the power to be flexible, and the power to grow, because God planted the Idea Man and man awoke to a belief that he was what he isn't and fell in the garden of awareness for his own figure! Person is supported by knowing that God is the Light to the appearance of person and Man is the evidence of God! Man is the living evidence of God when he dies to the suggestion of trying to be a God-reflector! Man is the Power and person is the garment that Man wears in the realm of the dream and the dreamer.

Terry M.) Is the evidence the same as the proof of God?

The evidence lies in Consciousness, and the evidence is the proof experienced. Or you might say, the proof of the evidence, or the evidence of proof is in the experience of Life, Truth, and Love lived involuntarily in the prompting of the Spirit of Principle Invincible commensurate with the Ideal of the All-encompassing Good called God. See?

Next: We've taken care of "person." If somebody says you're a person becoming aware, you can say, "I can appear to be a person becoming aware." You certainly appear to be persons becoming aware, but just because you *seem* to be persons becoming aware doesn't mean that you *are* persons becoming aware! To the One who knows, there's only One Person, and that is the awareness that man calls Realization. That is God-lived, God-blessed, and God-Man now known!

Next: "Mind." Mind is a synonym of God, because God saw, God knew, and God blessed His creation, according to the Book of Genesis, which may be considered a book of esoteric teaching for the initiates of the past. Mind is the name given to that condition which distinguishes an appearance from the animal world by being able to figure with thoughts, come up with a conclusion, and have a conscience to act as a guide until intuition dawns. Mind, in the suggestion of being commensurate with a person, is filled with data programmed according to the scheme of a dimension limited to three, when it is the evidence of greater dimensions which must be opened and reclaimed through the vehicle of conscious thought. The thought that it can be aligned to Principle becomes the main-board in the deck of your Ship.[2]

A thought is the proof that your matter isn't dense. The thought is the proof that matter isn't weighty. A thought is the evidence that there is hope, and you pray. A thought is the evidence for those who would be known. A thought comes into the experience of the person via the mechanism of belief, and the belief arises because somewhere along the line of the teaching, men and women were given *the impression* that they were matter instead of the Divine Compelling Force which would cause them to see they were Consciousness and contained in the Spirit of God!

The Spirit quickeneth and the flesh fadeth, all due to the Grace which can descend upon the thought-field when it aligns itself to the ideas and the thoughts commensurate with God and the synonyms.

Now you can see how the work gets slightly heavy, because every thought that comes to your thought must be asked if it can be attributed to Mind with a capital *M*. This is how you dethrone the devil, because the devil came about

---

2. Mr. Mills has often spoken of the Ship of Soul, which must be constructed. He says, "The Soul is not given unto men and women. It is reclaimed by being reassembled. That is the whole purpose of anyone's life. It is not to better mankind, but it is to reassemble the vehicle by which you can quit the gravitational fields of the planet and find the Point, loosely said to be the State from which you sprang."

because thoughts were thought to be power, instead of *pointing to* the Power.

> Mind-full Man is God Blessed, as God
> supplies,
> Where men deny, that God as Man truly
> lives in the I.

"Soul" is a synonym attributable to God, because the Soul must be found acceptable in the sight of the Omnipotent Power. The Soul has never had much power because it has been a sound that people know and that they hope and pray they've got! Because when the matter fades out and the ones left behind, looking at it, say, "I hope and pray his Soul goes straight to Heaven," it's doubtful, if he hasn't entered the State before he left! How is the Soul going to know where to go? God didn't say He was anything but present: I AM a God at hand, and not afar off.

Soul is the sound of a Tone in the Melody of Significance which points to a structuring need of consciousness. Now God Consciousness knows no need, Soul Consciousness knows no need, but men and women who don't know God and experience the Soul find it has to be constructed through the power of thoughts and words commensurate with the Almighty. Men and women are in the belief of structuring a Soul-Force or vehicle that can remove them and their acknowledged merits from one plane to another and find an accomplishment a Grace of God in the Vehicle of Soul.

The Spirit of the Word is the Power to rescind all beliefs about the Soul.

> Jackolyn M.) What then would be the difference between the Soul and the Body?

The Soul is a vehicle that enables man to experience the Feeling of Being I AM. The Body IS the Light I AM.

Spirit quickeneth, and the flesh profiteth nothing.

So, plant your thoughts in the proper soil
and you will find them planted
in the Ground of Principle.

You plant your seeds, your thoughts, that can sprout and bloom according to the genetic spiritual structure and in the Power of Principle which sustains even the appearance of a person, the appearance of a man, and the Knowingness of God, and sustains every thought that is planted, and that is why they appear to grow and some like bad weeds!

"Principle" is That Power which is undeviating and therefore inflexible yet flexible. It's the beginning, you might say the Ground, of the paradoxical nature of existence as it seems to be and as it truly IS, because the Principle Factor is Life, Love, and Truth, seen on every level according to the merits of the Soul-prompter!

Now Principle, in being inflexible yet flexible, is visible yet invisible, and is invincible! It is Principle that can bend and never break into the demand of action for even a nitwit loose on the face of a planet, call it Earth, Jupiter, Uranus, or Venus. Too many have spent too much time on Saturn. Lead: they've got it in their pants!

"Love" is the cohesive action which brings together all the parts commensurate with the Ideal, holds together That Which IS Ideal, and finds the Body Ideal and called Love's Body Omnipotent Eternally Present as Life-lived, Soul-felt, Mind-full, Spirit-blessed, and God-evidenced as the Power of an Eternal Verity!

Now you put all those letters together, and you put all those synonyms together, and you have a comprehensive vehicle of thought-power to free yourself from the suggestion of a material, corporeal, parochial view of being incarnated!

The Totality brings into the fortifications of your vehicle the Father-Mother as the Creative Power and supports the vehicle as it would gain Heaven now and leave Earth in the form of a gift of Love.

> Clive S.) When you were on the topic of Principle: I came across the "principle of causation" in the *Metaphysical Bible Dictionary*.[3] I was wondering if you could expound on that.

What does it say in the *Metaphysical Bible Dictionary*?

> Clive S.) It says that thought is the mode of expression of the universal principle of causation.

The "principle of causation" is the name given in hopes of experiencing the Creative Principle as Man. "The principle of causation" suggests something happening aside from Deity. God said, I saw, and behold it was done. It was done and in the rest, acknowledged. The principle of causation points to the *Creative Principle*, which is always the sustaining Power to enable man to have ideas commensurate with the Mind of God and *building* ever anew the Body of Light. It is not to be found in matter; it is a conscious embodiment as Divine Idea!

Principle is that Power which supports the seeming achievement of resurrection and the evasion of the crucifixion. The Principle has been equated with the Father-Mother-God.[4] You see, so much of this is in Christian Science, but the fascinating part is, it goes through all Teachings of Truth. This is nothing new! If I told you it was something new, it would be a lie, because Truth can never be anything but new because it's Now! There's no such thing as an old

---

3. The *Metaphysical Bible Dictionary*, Unity Village, MO: Unity School of Christianity, 1931.

4. For example: Mary Baker Eddy, *Science and Health With Key to the Scriptures* (Boston: Trustees Under the Will of Mary Baker G. Eddy, 1934), pp. 331-32, ll. 26-8.

Truth; you only call it an old Truth because you don't want to find what happens when it's used now!

Now, we've talked about Man, and we've talked about Love and Principle and the thoughts and the mind. Then we should go to what we call "wealth."

The interesting thing is that it's being given because *Love IS All*, and every flower that is planted must flourish, because Love has made the planting so. Love has made the planter sow and Love has brought the sown to the planter. Love has brought the Light to the sown, and Love has brought to Light the Power of how it happens that a sower, sowing, sowed and reaped the harvest when the fields were white and the door opening onto the vista of an Age commensurate with the garment of an Eternal Truth and bearing the name of an Age prepared to see a New One of Gold.

> "Wealth" is a sound that is mighty and it's
> like "health," you know; it comes from
> the same root.
> It all comes from the root of *weal,* and this
> is how you must have your health and
> your wealth to boot!
>
> Now when you have it on your boot, you
> know you can walk and never let your
> sole/Soul touch the pavement of time,
> But if you personalize your wealth, you'll
> need a boot and have to pay the price
> for the boot of time.

The wealth points to the Substance, and the Substance must be attributable unto God. Look how you're working! You cannot think of Substance, wealth, and plenty unless you can say it clothes the Garment Storehouse of a Living God. God is not dead! You consciously think the thought and name the idea "Good!" That is wealth. It points to

Substance. Mrs. Eddy says that it's "incapable of discord or decay."[5] Why? Because the wealth arises as an Idea of Consciousness, and Consciousness attributable unto a Living Principle called God finds it Eternal. How could you ever lack in the Conscious Knowing that every idea that is used that is commensurate with the Deity of Veneration is the way of claiming the Substance that is Eternal and always at hand, because God declared, "I AM present even in the field of thought, unknown."

> *That's why you have to move*
> *from the field of thought*
> *into the room of ideas*
> *and then into the Palace of the King.*
> *See?*

Now do you see how it's been moved? It's been moved from a dualistic point every time — whoosh — and it's there!

Now, if you were a dualist, you couldn't bring in the Absolute, but it would be the Absolute *unrecognized* that would have you a dualist! The Absolute unrecognized which has you a dualist has your wealth fluctuating as a dualist. Unless you can draw upon your Inheritance with knowingness, you are always drawing on an account of time. The account of time says that one day man shall be, shall know, a living God, and it's put into a future attainment. But it is *Now* accomplished due to the activation of a Field of Consciousness which will give you a Ship of Light to go either to Heaven or hell in the swiftest possible time.

If the vehicle is a Light Vehicle, it is like the spaceship of *2001*.[6] But remember, the Substance of Creative Might was symbolized by the monolith, and it was buried in a crater on the moon. It was there for centuries. This black

---

5. Mary Baker Eddy, *Science and Health With Key to the Scriptures* (Boston: Trustees Under the Will of Mary Baker G. Eddy, 1934), p. 468, ll. 16-24.

6. A 1968 movie produced and directed by Stanley Kubrick.

object, forty-some feet below the surface of the moon, was approached by men in a reflective garment, who went into the pit, viewed the object, but had forgotten that there would be a sunrise. Gradually in those moments of suspension, the sun crossed the arid slopes of a moon experience and the monolith was sunkissed and screamed! Everyone grabbed his ears! It was exposed and resurrected by the direct Ray of the Light! In other words, in the subconscious state man doesn't realize that the primal Field of Power is waiting to be kissed by the Sun.

Now, you can imagine how many winds on this plane it took to blow away the dust collected on the surface of the moon so that the monolith stood revealed. But when it was struck by the Sun, God help those who were present, because not even their reflective thoughts about Being could sustain them and they were bombarded by a Frequency of Pitch commensurate with the Universe of Light!

Now this is the Wealth that lies waiting to be called upon, because the Wealth is the resource center commensurate with Self-appreciation, Self-awareness, and Self-employment. So when you have the awareness of the Self and are thus employed, it is inevitable that you would be in the service of the Wealth commensurate with the Light Substance of the Ages — no longer a black stone but a transparent One freed of the gravitational fields of belief about it and able to be directed between this world and the other stellar continents on the demand of a thought winged with Love. "Let me see a symbol of the Wealth of the Eternal Light!" And man viewed the Monolith, winging its transparent flight between the planets of personal significance. Understand?

Wealth and health are inseparable. When you know you're healthy, you know you're wealthy, but you just haven't claimed it if you haven't got it. Since it stems from God there's no limit! The credit bears no price provided you acknowledge the Giver of all Good and every perfect Gift which cometh from the God of Light, which enabled you to sail on the sea/C (the Christ Consciousness) and never doubt the Harbor Light.

> Priscilla C.) Mr. Mills, would you speak about Consciousness?

Well, we always say that Consciousness is fundamental, and what does this mean? "Consciousness" is the name given to a state of partiality until the Totality is evidenced and man walks transparent like some Holy Thing.

Consciousness is based on the Principle that no thing — no object, person, place, or thing — is present without a *Light of Identification.* The *Light of Identification* has been called Consciousness. To identify consciously implies focus. When man focuses on the person, the place, or the thing, and excludes the Power which enables this to happen, he limits his conscious experience and finds himself having to sustain the person, the place, or the thing.

When the person, the place, or the thing is seen as Idea, the opening is increased, and the Light brings more into view and into focus so that the picture may be taken with a more detailed appreciation of the surroundings.[7] The ideas which light up the suggestion of person, place, or thing are now viewed on the screen called awareness by the Light of Consciousness being refocused from the objective sense to the subjective. It's moved from the belief of an *outside* picture to an *inside* appreciation of what is pictured.

Now, when the Consciousness can view the suggested consciousness, there is where "I" happen! "You" will never know the place. Only the Father of Light knoweth when I come! That is why all the thoughts have to be virgin and trimmed and ready to bear the Light as you become consciously aware of ideas pointing to your immaterial and God Nature!

---

7. See Event One, "Focus," in Kenneth G. Mills, *The New Land* (Toronto: Sun-Scape Publications, 1978).

This is what you people are dealing with, and I wonder if you know it! You are behaving like nitwits! You are not dealing with any speculatory science; you are dealing with avenues of thoughts commensurate with Divinity, the Self, and the possibility of gaining a Ship of Light which will enable you to appear wherever there is a call and to reappear when it is to be answered.

This is why there has had to be such a stand taken on the superficiality of the attitudes toward the Unfoldment. You are dealing with Life and death! Now, there's no greater joy than to "die" . . and know you live, but *there's no greater curse than to be dead and call it life!* This is the curse on the one who went to sleep in the garden.

The curse of Adam is that in Adam all die, but in Christ shall all be made alive. The curse of Adam is that the death state or the dream state is acknowledged to be what it isn't! That is why in the Teachings of the New Age, so I'm told, the action first and foremost among the great Triads of Power to be reawakened into the Conscious Pattern of Acknowledgment is the Christened Adam!

The first Christened Power to have to be brought under the Rod of Identification is the power of Nathanael or Bartholomew.[8] This points to the great imaging faculty of the mind! Now you are starting to dig beneath that moon surface. It's the great imaging faculty of the mind! This imaging faculty of the mind, unredeemed, enables you to don a space suit and live a vicarious life experience at the expense of doing yourself in until "I come," thus said the Lord's Book![9]

I work with you now because the time will come when I will have to be so busy in other ways. To see everyone like

---

8. "Nathanael" refers to the faculty of imagination. In esoteric teaching, the twelve disciples of Jesus sometimes symbolize the twelve faculties or powers of mind in man. For more on these ideas, see "faculties" in the *Metaphysical Bible Dictionary* and Charles Fillmore, *The Twelve Powers of Man* (Unity Village, MO: Unity School of Christianity).

9. Luke 19:13; Revelation 2:25.

this will be always a pleasure, but unless these Ideas can become part of a living action according to the agenda of man's plea for Self-employment, it will only be possible to see those who know what it is to be Self-employed, claim to be satisfied with only being Self-employed, and who find the fun of Being Conscious and knowing you can walk out of the mental and ring the bell, for the classroom will have come to an end for those "graders" who would see how to scale and balance on the Stairway of the Stars.

Isn't it interesting? It bears such a rate of increase and enhancement of Power that by the end of this Festival,[10] what appears to be those present should be the Presence of What It IS to BE in the Light of the Lord. *The Light of the Lord is in the living awareness of the Law,* because "the Lord" is the sound commensurate with an old garment, and it can't be tattered. It's got to go into the new framework of reference and it is now known as the Law. *The Law being brought up to date has to have the figure of the Will!* When the two come together you have Love as the fulfilling of the figure called the Law of Righteousness! And the Prince of Righteousness was called the Chosen One of God!

> *What do you choose to worship?*
> *Your thoughts of matter*
> *or the Source of your ideas*
> *commensurate with the synonyms*
> *of a Living Consciousness*
> *capable of engaging a God embodiment?*

It's a little different, isn't it, compared to having something like shredded wheat or sugar cereal for breakfast; they have no nutritional value any more than mushrooms! But they would have you eat without discriminating what you were eating.

---

10. This Unfoldment was given during the annual Summer Festival of Light, Sound, and Peace, offering a period of intensive metaphysical study and performance with Mr. Mills.

There is not one here who will ever be able to say he can escape in ignorance. It is amazing how people will run when they have to confront themselves! This is the time of separating the chaff from the wheat, and it must be done, because the doorways are opening onto the Fields.

Now, for a few moments I will engage another stream. I would like to speak to you in a rhythm and bring to a close the gathering at this time of those who can seek, find, and look over the horizons of time and see an *Urn on the Shoulder of Aquarius.*

As men would view in grandeur the opening
    vista of a scene,
As men would view with rapture the
    understanding of a dream,
As men would see the Power to support the
    envisioned sight,
Imagine the Power, the Grandeur, on an
    immaculate night of nights!

If men could see the mountain when the
    night was dark, no moon,
If men could see the valley and how the
    scene is viewed,
If man could see an opening on the
    mountain in his sight,
Would he be following the leadings and
    walk through the mountain height?

Look for an opening in the mountain; it's a
    cloud upon your thought.
Look through a cloud of glory to see what a
    combustible situation brought;
Look through the situation combustible and
    see how the mountain bloomed;
It was clothed in the glowing glory when the
    Sun kissed it upon rising into view.

Look unto the Mountain and see the shining
    sea/C,
Look unto the Glory that pictures the view
    for thee;
Look and see the Vision where it has sprung
    to life,
And stand in benediction, "What a glorious,
    wondrous sight!"

Look unto the mountain and see the
    foothills in your sight;
Do you know a Guide who knows the
    Mountain?
Well, find One who knows how to scale its
    heights;
Find One who can open like a magician and
    declare, "Open sesame in my sight,"
And Aladdin with his lamp a'glowing offers
    you the Mountain of the Light.

Can you view beyond the highways? Can
    you see within-without?
Well, you know, the Sun, it kissed the crater
    and there wasn't a speck of doubt.
And what was hidden stood and sang a song
    of praise to Love,
And Man can read the record as the Scrolls
    are viewed by the Dove.

And in this Age of Power (for those who
    would like a zodiacal chart),
You can say it's in that sector under the
    Power of the Aquarian Heart;
But the Heart of Aquarius is laden with such
    beauteous Power Unseen,
That that is why an Invisible Urn is only
    seen by those who can see.

You can see it being turned; others can see if
    they must
How there is the Balanced Power and in that
    Urn, no dust;
And then when the Waters are flowing over
    the pebbles of time,
The pebbles will tell you a mystery; they're
    the song of the unseen stones of mind.

When man can walk upon the mountain, he
    can walk upon those stones
That enable him to traverse in
    Consciousness All Alone.
And where e'er ye should wander and where
    e'er ye should come to rest,
Know that it is in the Power of having
    followed an intuitive behest.

I came not knowing whence I cometh, and I
    come knowing whence I come.
I came not to the satisfied; they never know
    I come.
I came not to the abundant; they have their
    substance of time;
I only come to those who seek the Substance
    that's truly Divine.

I only come to those who know and never
    doubt a Cause;
The Principle Power is called causation until
    man can find how I AM, I IS, I WAS
Beyond all veils of time and space; My
    Place cannot be seen in time,
But I have proof and so have you of another
    Stage Divine.

So as the camera opens and the vista is seen
as planned,
It's all brought into focus by the Light of a
camera-man.
In the eye of a camera you see what you
would view for time,
But the I that can see beyond the lens finds
the Light to enable the I to eye.

So I come to tell you glad tidings of great
joy!
You never were caught in a body of clay; it
was only for fun for you to be
employed
Until you came to the Solution, and before
you realized you were dust,
You had the chance to be so fine that you
know there must be One to trust.

So Soggy Head said to Slicker,[11] "I'd love to
join your band,"
And the Slickers said to Soggy Head, "You'll
have to meet the Finest in our band."
So Soggy Head agreed to wait until the Sun
should come
And dry out all their locks, you know, and
find the *Golden Key of One.*

Then Slicker said to Soggy, "Be prepared
when Finer comes,
Because you've got to comb your locks;
there's no soggy head in the Sun."
So Finer-Slicker finally appeared, and Soggy
Head now glowed
Because in the Light of the Rising Sun there
was no water log to show.

---

11. Characters in a children's story.

Finer-Slicker and all his kids joined the
    happy throng
Now named, given to the ones who
    worshiped the Soggy-headed throng.
So if you kids like a story, there's promise
    for one and all:
If you would be a Slicker-man, find the Finer
    One. So long!

You see, I can teach piano because I love to play. It's so much fun to be fundamental! And what you are consciously aware of constitutes your experience. That is what "Consciousness is fundamental" means practically and in the Absolute sense, because Consciousness has enabled man to acclaim . . that there appears to be a person, a place, and a thing until *I come and make all things new!*

▼

IV.

Near to the Fire

One may be called into the Service of the Light, but it is only in the Light's Service that one knows what it is to answer!

Near to the Fire

This evening, we are in the Stone Room with the largest audience to this date, which has been made for those who would see destiny unseated from the horse of time (the mind) and find how the date with destiny is met when men and women come to see in the light of a Stone Room given to Sound treatment how the captive is set free. We who have gathered on these premises to witness unto that state of Life and its actions perceive, as never before, the steps which appear before each of us as each of us takes a step into the accomplishment commensurate unto each and every goal or aim.[1]

As we view the week of fulfillment and as we watch with attention the bated breath and its form of words and sounds, we are drawn to consider the salient Facts which may be found surrounding Being if men and women have an inclination to question the errant mind and its gallop over the plains of enticement. There are many who have found their way unto shrines and unto places of worship and unto rooms of accomplishment, and there are many who are seeking. To them be given the place of acknowledgment and encouragement. *But you who have come face to face with the realities of Life, find yourselves no longer seekers after Truth but baptized by IT in the flaming engagement of encounter with irrefutable statements of Fact. The reason any lecture can be on fire and any sermon can lift the top of the mountain and reveal a place to repose is because in the act of coming close to the Truth of Being, one is kindled and set aflame by the Flame already present as a living encounter.*

As we peruse the books of time, we find ourselves constantly meeting statements of significance. *Oh, how it behooves us to carry with us a Standard or a Principle in order to discriminate.* Never has there been more need of

---

This Lecture is available on cassette, Sun-Scape Publications ISBN # 0-919842-04-6

1. "Guidance can appear to each one according to the path or goal he has chosen."
K.G.Mills.

discriminating, because in the act of discriminating one is not saying this is right or this is wrong; one is saying only to oneself, "This will enhance my walk in the garden of accomplishment," or "This will detract from its accomplishment." *Discrimination is the great crown jewel.* Do not let it fall to the lower level of your action, but find it and find its setting one of gold in the crown which you will fashion as each Truth becomes a living experience and each crown is filled with the diadems of glowing significance, symbolic of a Truth claimed and then experienced and known. *Thus knowledge freed from its seduction is given unto the service table of time, and understanding reigns as does reason, and in this way revelation may reveal a new place for you who would find a spot of power, a place of expectancy, and an experience of wonder.*

If one is near to the Flame, one knows one's nearness. One feels it outwardly as the warmth on the skin (physical level); one feels it inwardly as the recognition of the skin being warmed (mental level); and one feels it still more deeply as one views the Flame and its warmth embracing the one who would be near unto IT (One with the Flame; no division).

Jesus made a statement that those who came near to Him came near to the Fire. To come near to a high manifestation of the Divine in the form of a Gautama or a Jesus, one cannot help but feel the Presence that is either challenging his way or opening his way, according to the power one brings to the perceiving sight of one living on the Enraptured Way.

> *One may be called into the service of the Light, but it is only in the Light's Service that one knows what it is to answer!*

You who have found yourselves here have found yourselves confronted as never before by Truths. We say they are Truths for they cannot be dwarfed by the intellect's accomplishment. *You can deny that God exists, but you cannot deny that you said so. (Therefore, inquire who it is who says there is or isn't a God.)* You can say, "The Lord reigneth? Tell us another story!" You have just created part of it. You can consider your destiny and think it is up to chance and up to your organic involvement with trying to make a living, but you will come to see that *the whole purpose is not a destiny that is slated for you to fulfill, but a destiny that is to be redeemed in an accomplishment of an act of transcending the limits that destiny would impinge upon you and yours in the name of humanity.* Humanity is destined to be human, but the Truth of Being has found many garments which state,

> *It is one thing to be human, but there is
> the Divine Element that runs forever within
> the consciousness of all those who accept
> or reject a God of living, of Life and
> its attributes.*

We have seen how, in the unfolding pattern of design, you have attributed unto yourselves whatever knowledge has offered to you. You have seen as never before that all knowledge is not worth its name, for all knowledge does not give you freedom; it only talks about it. Most knowledge can seduce you into believing that freedom can only be for the birds! But did you ever hear tell of a bird having to choose its feathers?! No. *But you are in a position where you do have to choose your feathers.* This is the value and the great gift above the level of the natural kingdom. You are given the ability to choose, and you choose what feathers shall be found on your wings as you don them.[2] For you see, *the wings are donned as the arms are raised and given to praise.*

---

2. "'Feathers' symbolizes transcendent ideas; 'wings' denotes the ability of the consciousness to fly beyond the mundane reality." K.G.Mills.

We are forever considering ideas and we forget this fact: We misunderstand our thoughts and start considering thoughts instead of the Father to them. If we would stop considering our thoughts about subjects (I, me, you), we might be freed from the entanglement of objects. *There is no escape from the objective if you try to do so by using the objective as an escape.* All people who have taken drugs, who smoke, who take shots of this in an attempt to escape from being a part of the nature or natural picture, find that the mind is an instrument capable of realizing its own limits! If it were not so, you would not take in a drug or a bit of smoke in order to induce a situation whereby you could taste illegitimately a foretaste of what it is to get beyond the mind's well-stacked data.

Oh, the lengths that people will go in an attempt to experience freedom on a different level of the mind's involvement! The mind was never meant to be involved in an act of freedom; it was meant to be *ridden,* one with the actor, over the plains of illusion, under the gift of hope and the knowing that hope could never have come to be considered if it were not a gift of the gods, since so much of time, space, and the contained objects are inundated with despair. You who fill this room, fill it with expectancy, for you will come to see that *if you expect to get beyond your limits you will be watchful of what will enhance your possibilities of going beyond.*

> *You cannot go beyond anything if you are not willing to move and willing to be moved. This is why response[3] is inherent within the whole program of Light.*

---

3. From the *American Heritage Dictionary*, New College Edition: "Respond: 1. To make a reply; to answer. 2. To act in return or in answer." "Respond" is derived from the Latin *respondere*, "to promise in return," which in turn is derived from the Indo-European root *spend-*, whose basic meaning is "To make an offering, perform a rite, hence to engage oneself by ritual act." This is why response is "inherent within the whole program of Light."

You are born, so we are told, and your response to birth is an ejection from the womb of tender loving care. However, your encounter with your new experience is often not remembered, but you are told that this is how you came. The stork only held a place for a mystery, for not even your parents knew how it happened that in the seclusion of a place, a miracle happened, and you could be found being formed, and later found formed, hunting for Being!

We so often chase a shadow (the objective appearance) and give it substance by calling it names. *We should more than ever before be alert to what it is that is substantial in our lives and forsake the smoke of fires that are incomplete in their actions.* You will note that when a log is given to the fire, you never expect to hear it bark! And yet when all the intellectual driftwood has been released from the watery womb of the mind and brought to dry in the rays of Sun, when these logs are given to the nearness of the Flame — instead of the sweet aroma accompanying transition, we hear the bark of refusal to die and the unwillingness to be changed (no response). I tell you now, if you have any thoughts about entering the fire and remaining the same, you are in serious need of reorganization of your knowledgeable, questionable data! Even iron is changed by being offered to the flame. It may not appear to be, but try to pick up a piece of it after it has been in the flame. It's too hot to handle, and if you do so without awareness, you are burned.

How daring are people today! They consider not what it is to enter the Flame of inspired declaration. They may not look changed, they may not feel the heat of the Flame, but I tell you now, try to handle them after they have experienced IT, and you will say, "What has made you change, dear? I know you not!" You expect from the material body an answer to a question that you would never think of asking iron. *How do you think a mind can give an answer when it doesn't know that it was in it?* It is only afterwards that it seems changed, because what seemed so important in the original encounter is now seen to be of lesser significance as the new Flame has altered the old ember of waning hope. *Hope only appears to diminish because it is never watered with expectancy coupled with enthusiasm.*

It is so marvelous to consider the salient features of Being as long as they have reference to you. But I'll tell you, the salient features of Being have nothing to do with "you"; they have to do with God, with the Self, with That Which IS, and if you can entertain them you are entertaining the Flames, the heated statements imbued with such Force that you cannot handle them and not be touched.

You must see that "you" cannot see correctly from the standpoint of thinking you can make a choice successfully and accurately if you try to work from the standpoint where matter enters into your conclusions, when metaphysics tells you that you must translate the objects of confrontation to a more spiritual sense in order to be freed from the objective, finite limits.

> *This is the purpose of metaphysics: To see that it is a mind capability to translate what appear as the objects of limits into the ideas that are limitless.*[4]

What is the point of translating objects into ideas that are limitless if there isn't a love of wisdom so that insight and goodness may flow into you and find your body filled

---

4.   In the *American Heritage Dictionary*, metaphysics is defined as: "The branch of philosophy that systematically investigates the nature of first principles and problems of ultimate reality. Metaphysics includes the study of being (ontology) and, often, the study of the structure of the universe (cosmology)." The word is derived from the Greek *Ta meta ta phusika*, "the things after the physics," Aristotle's treatise on transcendental philosophy, so called because it followed his work on physics: *meta*-"after" + *phusida*, "physics." To "translate what appear as the objects of limits into the ideas that are limitless" constitutes one part of the practice and science of metaphysics. For instance, a chair is recognized as an idea of comfort; a car or an elevator are both ideas of immediacy. This practice is essential in breaking the notion that it is primarily an *objective* world in which we live. Indeed, when all objects and experiences are reduced to ideas primarily, the world is seen as a *conscious* experience. "Metaphysics is basically logic based on transcendent, intuitive realizations." K.G.Mills.

with this new ardor[5] of Being? For Being gives you a lift, and you feel buoyant, and in this buoyancy you find you offer it unto those who can find themselves knowing how to use their hulk, their bulk, to ride the rhythm of encounter.

For you to think that you will be this or that and that you can make a decision to be this or that, has always given you the feeling that it is up to you which you will choose. It is up to "you" which you will choose when you have lost innocence. You never consider a child considering, "Well, it is up to me whether I will choose this toy or that toy." He goes directly to the toy he wants, and the one who might also want it screams. But *innocence*[6] doesn't know that it doesn't belong to him, because in his *guilelessness* he has nothing at work but the natural inclination to take what seems to fulfill his immediate need. He has not been taught that this belongs to somebody else or this belongs to somebody else; he sees only what it is that will satisfy him without ever thinking of making a choice. You never saw a child make a choice between bottles of milk. If he were hungry, he would take only the milk that was sweet. But it would not be a choice; he would know intuitively that the spoiled milk was never for the *Child* which was never spoiled.

How we pacify ourselves! What plastic toys we play with mentally in order to keep ourselves seduced into thinking that we can *think* ourselves into something we are not, from the standpoint of working from the limited. *The great horse of the mind was given the ability to ride the plains of illusion, or of the objective world.* It was given this great ability because it was to be and it is the means whereby we have the least material experience of its presence in the name

---

5.   To develop the flame theme: "Ardor," from the *American Heritage Dictionary:* "1.a. Great warmth or intensity, as of emotion, passion, or desire. b. Strong enthusiasm or devotion; zeal. 2. Intense heat, as of fire ... From Latin *ardor,* from *ardere,* to burn."

6.   Innocence: not thinking this is "yours" or this is "mine." See p. 63: "If we would stop considering our thoughts about subjects ('I,' 'me,' 'you'), we might be freed from the entanglement of objects." K.G.Mills.

of thoughts and awareness, sometimes called consciousness. We are aware of our feeling-being, but the reason this is not Soul freed to be found in the great shipyard of one who would build the vessel of Soul[7] is because this feeling-being, subject to partials (fragments of experience: body, mind, emotions), gives us not the correct platform upon which to base our life experience. The feeling that we *be* points to the Soul that says, "Yes, BE!" When you experience what this means, you will find that *the Soul that we think we structure is already satisfied in its own loveliness by embracing us in the feeling of Being freed from the titillations of the three dimensions and their power of seduction.*

We certainly are engaged in having to deal with objects. We don't pass through each other; we have to go around each other. We cannot pass through a table unless we know how to balance the vibratory frequency of the structure of the body to meet the solidness of what appears as a table. And when those two meet, who is to see either pass through?

We have to go around objects that are vibrating at a lower level. And we have to pass through "substances" [referring figuratively to states of consciousness] that are moving at such a level of vibratory frequency that we cannot perceive them; but we know their presence, because they wear the garment that all philosophy is hinged to: the children of *Wisdom*, the children of *Insight*, and the children of *Intuition*. These "bodies" (Wisdom, Insight, and Intuition) are present, but they are not seen unless you know how to engage them as one with the innermost core of your own self-resilience, unless you are able to *respond* to them. For you see, you will move around each other in order to avoid collision, but *when you come into feeling contact with these powers of Wisdom, Intuition, and Insight, you come into*

---

7.   "My perception of Soul is on two levels: The Soul in the highest sense is the Feeling of Being I AM. On a lower level, I have often talked about *building the Ship of Soul,* which consists of the practice of incorporating the beams of Truth into the Voyage of Life. The latter discipline may lead to the former experience." K.G.Mills.

the field of such Power that no longer can you appear to act as if you had not met them.

There is a collision if you refuse to use the Wisdom, the Insight, and the Intuition, for in the refusal you know that what could have been done without unnecessary footsteps is now having to be done with all kinds of footsteps. Only the shoemaker knows how many soles and how many uppers are being worn out as you try to find your way through a self-inflicted path due to the denial of following the promptings of the plane of awareness in which you really were meant to live and move and find Being a viable experience.

The beauty of an object is perceived only because Beauty is beyond the object, but it infiltrates it in the way that the sight is endowed with enthusiastic response to some aspect of its own responsive beauty. When we respond one to another it is not our molecular structure that is responding; it is that center of power — any center of power that is being expressed at the moment, such as devotion, beauty, intelligence — that has been stabilized in such a way that it is like a great magnet that would draw that center to that center and find in that drawing a realignment of the structure so that the magnetic field is changed and altered.[8]

There is no reason to engage a path if you have no reason for engaging it. To be a seeker is to be a searcher, and very few people ever know for what they are searching. Because if you ask, "What are you doing here?" some will say, "I am here to sing"; some, "I am here to hear"; some, "I am here to find"; some, "I am here to BE"; and some, "I am here so that others may see I BE." But you see,

> *The great demand is not to have conditional reference points as a seeker, but to have unconditional surrender as one taken in*

---

8. "It does appear that our molecular structure is altered as a result of contacting a higher magnetic (charismatic) Power, whatever it may be (person, object, etc.). The change is usually first manifested in the countenance." K.G.Mills.

*the act of giving oneself up in order to find
what it is to BE One Self seen.*

One said to me a few weeks ago that he wondered if
people had forgotten the purpose for which they had come.
The Christ Consciousness is the purpose, and the experience
of the Christ Consciousness the reason for being present.
But the actions of those present never did evidence what he
thought was the Christ Consciousness, or an attitude even
approximating what would be necessary to approach that
State. A valid discrimination. *Don't forget why you are
here.* And if you don't know why you are here, you had better find out, because you will never be partial. *You cannot
be partially engaged in Self-Realization; you cannot be partially engaged in any work that is to be successful.* Who ever
heard tell of a singer doing a song and singing every fifth
note? There would be no song and there would be no singer.
I suppose you could blame it on the lack of time. It isn't; it's
on the lack of interest! There can be no interest if actions
are incomplete and spasmodic.

Don't expect to remain as you are and come here. If
you do seemingly remain as you are after having been here,
you shouldn't be coming, because I am never the same.
How can you know me if you don't approach me in the
same newness in which I see my Self? If you approach me
each week, each time we visit, in your sameness, no wonder
you do not know me, because I do not know what the "me"
was one minute ago; the only thing I do know is that what
I AM never did let that which was passing to be held as a
weight. It prepared the now, if the moment that we said has
passed was given to Light.

You are preparing your future, because you are preparing to live life more abundantly. But Jesus said, *"All that I
have is thine." Why do you take such small particles?* I say.
*Why do you have to do so much outside if it isn't because
you are bored?* Just because there is a lot of activity doesn't
mean you aren't bored, and just because there is no activity

does not mean you aren't bored. Most people say they are resting because they know they haven't done anything in the realm of awakefulness!

The realm of a wakeful state is known because it sheds such Light on your dream. If you are asleep, you know you are asleep when you have Light shed upon your dreams. You know you are starting to awaken when you perceive how the Light has freed you from the limits of your dream. And you know how you are in bondage when the Light only enables you to perceive your destiny.

> **We are not destined to be limits;**
> **we are destined to be witnesses**
> **to the experience of the Infinite.**

What is the evidence of the Infinite? It is the shedding of Light in such a way that the old appears to fade out, and yet in the appearing to fade, one finds newness appearing and the old feels, seems, looks transformed!

You do not try to put the new into the old if it can't be renovated. You just give up and say, "So help me, God. I haven't done 'me' in enough to be worthy of the garment of your Son." And God will come to you in an intuitive call and say, "If you had only taken yourself out of the cradle when your line was so busy with talk about something that is not, and you had listened to the Voice which said, *'Wake up! for you are beheld and you are held to BE in the likeness of the Infinite and thus the Son of the Infinite and thus freed.'*" But you see, we are so content to remain on the line of indifference when we should be bound to the grace of compassion.

> **Compassion is not having pity for**
> **the passing, but having the ability**
> **to lovingly sustain one in the passing.**

Compassion doesn't commiserate with your limited condition. Compassion *fires* you — sometimes with resentment, because you have not received the pity you hoped you would get in order to go on living lies. You will know whether or not you have found the right Teaching, because when you find the right Teaching, it will bear little in agreement with "you," for **how could the Truth be in agreement with a lie?** *Unless you are realizing constantly Truths, you are living constantly lies.*[9] So if you find a Teaching in which you are not challenged and in which you feel that you are going to have until doomsday to work out your problems, you can be assured that the Teaching is not far removed from you and your circumstance!

It is important to consider with whom you associate, with what you associate, and what tries to associate with you. It is very important to ask yourself, *"What are these people doing in my life? What are these thoughts doing in my mind? And what is my mind doing, making a damn fool of me, or is it ready to become bridled, saddled, corralled in the pen of fulfilling an intuitive prompting to be free and ride the range of Light?"* When it is found so tethered with such a prompting, you find yourself in the saddle, and the tumbleweed of time is blown as you pass, and is unnoticed by a rider who knows the call of the Wind.

Have you ever considered what certain people are doing in your lives? Have you ever considered what certain associates are doing in your lives? Have you ever considered what doing associates are in your lives? Have you ever considered, "What is the meaning of these people in my life? What is the meaning of this association?"[10] Are they founded on facts

---

9.   "One facet of 'realizing constantly Truths' is to constantly remember I AM not the body; I AM the Light to the body." K.G.Mills.

10. Note the example of practicing discrimination. From Shankara's *Crest Jewel of Discrimination*, Shankara, tr. by Swami Prabhavananda and Christopher Isherwood (Hollywood, California: Vedanta Press, 1947), p. 136: "What brings happiness? The friendship of the holy." p. 137: "What should we prize most dearly? Compassion, and friendship with the holy." p. 138: "What is finished as quickly as lightning? Friendship with bad men or women." p. 139: "Where should one Live? One should live with the holy." p. 135: "What are the duties of a spiritual aspirant? To keep company with the holy, to renounce all thoughts of 'me' and 'mine,' to devote himself to God."

sometimes called Truths, because they are unchangeable? Or are they founded on fiction, and do they go along with the novel limits of time because you haven't enough of the permanent facts that can build you a Story that will bypass the historian's attempt to delineate history; but *His story will be known to have been, for it will have changed the knowledge contained by the mind and given it the opportunity to question itself and its ability to perceive what it means to engage the Infinite and Its way of harmonic significance.*

> *There is not Life without rhythm.*
> *There is not Life without order.*
> *If you have rhythm and order, harmony is*
> *found as the uniting factor in order that*
> *a form may be experienced.*

If you have so much of your life lacking in a tangible form (as accomplishments, abilities, disciplines), consider to what degree is there order, to what degree is there rhythm, and to what degree has harmony a place in your experience. Then you will see. Do consider what thoughts you are entertaining and what thoughts are entertaining you. See which is leading, enhancing your ride to the fulfillment of your goal or your aim. It will be done, for Thine is the kingdom and the power and the glory, when God is known, not as someone worshiped afar off, but as a Light to the oldness and the oldness appearing as newness if it is of viable significance in the demands of the day in which you find yourself. And if not, you will find that you cannot find the old when the New has been donned as a living experience.

Oh, the Robe of Righteousness is immaculate, but so is the peace when Love is the Shepherd. The still waters of the mind run very deep, and *you have to be willing to dive beneath the surface of superficial engagement and observe what it is that is buried beneath the surface of your mind that needs to be examined in the Light.* Oh, for tidings of great joy, and oh, the tidings of great joy! But how few are able to stand the tide that joy brings in its engulfing stream of power! It has been said that one Messiah came that your joy may be full. Who would ever have known that His witnesses had ever experienced it? *Joy does not see the situations of time being made joyful; joy only knows that it is a condition in spite of the situations of time in which you might appear to jubilate in the midst of an unexplained enigma. What an enigma: a coincidence of the human and the Divine!* What a historical controversy, and what a hysterical topic for seduction! Why would you try to console those who would attempt to reconcile from the wrong standpoint what can only be seen from One point of view? If the human appears Divine, you can be assured that it is because the Divine is all there is, and you misname it human!

So it is that during this week in these foothills of these mountains sacred unto the past and to the present, you have found yourselves and perhaps you have witnessed unto an opening into that Realm which has been promised as the Fourth Dimension, which would be found someday. I tell you now, it is not afar off, and the three great dimensions are swallowed up when one comes to see that *one doesn't attempt to see through limits; one only dies to the suggestion that there are limits to see through.* Do not ask of yourselves the impossible, just ask if you are making it possible to BE.

May this association with those you have termed your sisters and brothers be likened unto the Saints and the Sages of the Ages, and may you who have sat for seven days on this desert in the sun witness unto how the desert shall bloom and does bloom as the rose, and how in the magnitude of the Light, the great Work unfolds in its enfolding embrace and we find Life as IS, and living a joy to behold.

Behold I stand at the door and knock, said Jesus, and in the declaration we hear: *I AM there.* It is you who have the latch. Will you lift it and let "me" out as *I* come in? Or will you lift it and say, "I am too busy today to entertain You. What do You want? I must be about the sweat and the toil of trying to be a liver." Oh, to turn away such a knocking on the heart! It might have been the Answer living beyond all question marks and beyond the limits of your incarnation.

I can assure you, if you feel the Presence of Love so moving you to consider, "How come I love all these people? I don't even know them," it is because Love is universal, and unfortunately you adopt only those whom you think you will give it to. It isn't the way. Who ever heard tell of a particle in the form of "you" ever being glued together enough to know whether or not you would bestow love upon the way or withhold it! No wonder there are such meetings with particle boards, and so few with remarkable men! *A remarkable man is one who evidences what it is to be able to bear the Mark and remember the calling, Come out from the world and be ye separate.*

You who are found as members of a family, enjoy the family of Man on this hearth of the Sun. *Carry the radiance wherever you go and permit no lie to make you feel unempowered to be what you are in its presence.* Unfold. BE. **"Unfold" is always newness appearing. The absence of unfolding is certain demise. "Unfold" is the natural demand of even a bud. Why would you not support and why would your associates not support the natural inclination to open and reveal the fragrance of your Body (Consciousness) as it truly IS?** Be aware of those who will not support you in the name of your lifework, for what have they to lose? Perhaps your pity. If only they would realize your friendship and thus their gain.

Your joy is full! May the cup of the skull be so empty that it is filled to overflowing, and may it be symbolically given that your cup is so filled that even the saucer (the intellect) is sweetened from its tartness and its state of just being a saucer. Oh, let it fly, and may you see that all other life and living experiences may be wrapped according to the demands you place upon your objective sense of life until *I* come and you see what it is to behold the Simplicity of Being, wrapped in the garment of a new song or in a rhapsody of freedom in which the rapture is only for those who would be found Sound. In this majesty and in this glory, let there be Light! There is. "To let" only signifies it is possible to have.

Remember your Self. It is natural to take; it is natural to give. How unnatural is it to you? When you can do it easily one to one, the accomplishment comes in the act of group action termed a family, a brotherhood, or a society.

> *In such a concerted effort you find the*
> *necessary struggle to engender enough*
> *energy for you to create enough friction to*
> *light your own fire. In this find your*
> *emulation[11] and the immolation scene one*
> *symbolically awaiting all those who would*
> *be surrounded by the Robe of the Flame*
> *(The Living Word).*

Thus endeth this series of sequential Sound Offerings which may have touched you in these moments of togetherness. And may you find how they are contained in your actions, and may your actions appear as anthems[12] given to praise!

[Mr. Mills strikes at a fly on his leg.] A fly, a bee! If I had said it was a bee, I wonder how contained you would have been, especially if I had said, "It's on you!"

---

11. Through an applied effort to change one's character, to be "found Sound," one emulates the transforming Power of the Fire.

12. From the *American Heritage Dictionary*: "Anthem" 1. A hymn of praise or loyalty. 2. a sacred composition set to words from the Bible. Etymology: "Old English *antefn*, antiphonal song, from Medieval Latin *antiphona*, from late Greek, 'sung responses,' neuter plural of *antiphonos*, 'singing in response': *anti-*, 'opposite' + *phone*, 'voice.'" Thus, one's actions in the world should appear as a contrapuntal line in response to the dictates of the Divine. [See "response," footnote 3.]

John D.) Thank you, Mr. Mills, for a magnificent Unfoldment. We are all graced to hear it.

I decided I would just look, you know, with lids lowered, upon the Silence and see how it thundered in the Unfoldment of its own might.

O you never know what you will say, if you
    give yourself.
You never know what you will find, when
    you give yourself.
You never know what you will be, when you
    find yourself given!
You will never be what you were when you
    find the Self given.

You will be for those to see what it is when
    Self is given;
And Self so given enables you to appear to
    be re-marked.

And in this Mark you are so called,
And finding facts, fiction falls,
And in this knowing, power reigns,
And ledge of knowledge is in vain.

Take the power! See it fly
To the ledge where you abide,
Wrapped in knowledge of what is to be
Thought Self-Realized: captive deeds!

O be free from all such thoughts!
For your mind can never unravel rapture,
    wrought
On the anvil of Golden Light,
Until you know the *I* in sight.

Your minds, engulfed in currents of thought,
Can never reveal what *I* is when brought
Into the form where you come and find . .
"Oh, captive?" only because beliefs of time.

"Away with belief!" the leaves do tell;
They cushion the Soul of those who dwell.
Fermata's Hall offers as planned,
A Pause for those to rest as Man.

So, take the finding of this celestial thought,
And find the wings plumed, as you have
    brought
What thoughts you claim for your arms in
    sight;
When they are raised aloft, will you be
    found, ascending in Light?

How do you know what you will be?
Just die to limits. Take courage. Look. BE. See!

▼

V.

The Essence

Do not take unto yourself
the form of flesh
to be the Real encounter
with Life as IT IS.

The Essence

Isn't it wonderful to know that you're here so that you can confront the suggestion that you are something you're not!

You know, if God IS All, that's That!
And then you say, "Well, if God is All,
what is God?" Well, that's That.

It is an amazing thing to see how we have made out of the sentient objects which confront us a society that has been designated significant and impressive and transitory! It is interesting for what appears as me to witness unto this pageant; and as you witness me day by day, you can perceive that I am here with you, but perhaps in a very different way than you are here with me. I am so aware of the inconsistencies surrounding this projection called the human picture. Without our senses, we don't have it! Yet we bow down to the appearance more than we ever consider bowing down to the Light so that the appearance can appear to be "in the Light."

If you stop and consider what the senses point to — they are never really other than a concept taken out of context, that is, taken out of its environment! When we look at a person sitting before us, we see that person and distinguish that person, even if the person doesn't bear any mark that is distinguishing. We see the person but we fail to see the gestalt. We fail to see what makes it up, and we say, "Ah, the person," but that's what we have brought, by a lack of discrimination, to a situation that is transitory.

It is very important just to glance at this, because if we look at it, we describe the person, the object, but *do we ever consider that we are describing some thing by the senses of the thing?!* Therefore, the description of the thing can't help but be the evidence of the functioning of the senses of the thing! Then comes a voice which, in Hebrew, says, If you hear the Voice, harden not your hearts, for the Word of God is sharper than any two-edged sword and is a discerner of the thoughts and a perceiver of them and can see right through this powerful presentation, which your senses imbue with dignity and a spurious, exalted state which it does not have without the senses testifying to it.

If men and women are taught that they are clay (and they can perceive that they are clay, in that they are passing), and if they are not taught what they are that is *not* passing, they can only worship a God ignorantly. Then the picture says we have a God we ignorantly worship and we wait for someone to come along and say, "But no longer is that necessary." Because in the realization of That, there is no duel taking place between the body and mind and a mind that is imbued with God-like ideas, because *the God-like ideas are only for the catharsis of the intellect, not of the Soul!*

If the intellect cannot be purified of entertaining ideas that are incorrect, there is no possible way that one can adopt an attitude of sacrifice and surrender, because the education of time says, "You are so important. After all, you have a mother and father just like you." Some say, "Yes, and I even have grandparents." And I said, "Well, that must be a unique experience, because I've never had any whom I knew!"

If you can have grandparents and believe you have them, fine and dandy. The only place I know where my grandparents are supposed to be is under a tombstone in the cemetery. It means absolutely nothing to me, because I don't know what it means to have that kind of a legacy. It is strange to say I don't even know it in terms of what remains of my parentage — I don't have that kind of a relationship. I cannot believe the stories about my coming. I guess that is why Mum always says I never slept. No matter when she looked at me at night, I was never asleep, and as a baby I was supposed to, and I never did!

I'll tell you now, the considerations of the world picture always came to me very strongly, even when I was a child, so that the parents of the child of form were still challenged by the questions arising from the state of the child-form and moving to the parent-form, which could not answer the child-form satisfactorily! The child-form requested to know, "How come it happened here and how come I have this form and am in a place like this?" I remember saying, "What am I doing living in the sticks?" I never cared for the town that grew up around me as I became aware of it!

My world was my carriage until I was taken out and made to believe that there was more outside than inside, and thus appeared an overemphasis on being of great worth as a form rather than as a state of awareness. The more I became aware of the object, the more I bumped into it. As I bumped into more objects, I gradually developed a sense of trying to stop bumping into them! So I started greeting every object as if it were in my way — and it was — but not *on* my way. Every object I greeted had to be treated as if it were apart *from* me, and yet it couldn't be apart from me if I could bump into it! But how I bumped into it caused me to consider, What was it doing there, like "me," and yet appearing to be different? Yet we were not different from the standpoint of being the same "in form."

Then what made our forms so different that it was a jarring experience when I met someone who looked just like me? I don't say that the eyes had to be the same color, the hair had to be the same color, or the weight had to be the same, but the same *form* — two legs, two arms, a trunk, and a head and flesh! What made the difference?

> *Why was the difference accentuated*
> *instead of the essential Somethingness,*
> *which was not that we were separate*
> *but that the common link was*
> *awareness.*

The reason we stopped colliding with each other was because we realized that we had the same form and we had awareness, but that's where the difference happened. We were being taught that each was subject unto his own likes and dislikes and his own choices, and he could make a choice if he wanted to and make *any* choice he wanted to, if he were outside of the School where the Choiceless was given under the tutelage of the inspired Mastership of those who have sacrificed themselves to the High Light of the Knowledge of Christ or the Self or the Atman or the Absolute. As soon as the forms were educated outside of the rooms and outside of the Light of an inspired Leader, the Masters of Blessedness and Righteousness ceased to have the ability to impregnate the ideas, and the ideas dropped to the equation given unto a form made up of flesh and bones and protoplasm and slime.

What happens without the Divine Enzymes present? There is no possible way to utilize such an entanglement, and calcification and crystalization take place. We have the modern-day dis-eases, because we have forgotten the Standpoint. We have not been taught the Nature of Being as IT IS; we have been taught to believe the form as it is is all-important and not the *awareness* which is the reflection of an untouchable, nondual State, sometimes called the Void of consciousness and the consciousness of Void.

The Consciousness without a form is the Light to the form, but it is not the form if you think that *through* the form you will have your own way! It is all relevant to how you think. The only demand "God" ever made upon *you* comes to you via thought. It is the only appeal. *As a man thinketh in his head, so is he in need of catharsis!! As a man thinketh in his Heart, he will still need a purifying, because, you see, you can't permit your head to think that your Heart is going to do your thinking!*

As long as you look at another and see differences and take those differences as marks of separateness instead of as marks of interest, you will never, never arrive at a fundamental equation which can let you have what appears and not constantly bump into it and find yourself a generator of the

Wonders surrounding the degenerate ideas of Brotherhood. Why do I say "degenerate"? Because we have made the Brotherhood what it isn't. It's not made up of people trying to get along with one another and trying to stop bumping into each other and knocking the chips off each other's shoulders.

The Brotherhood is not made up; it is a Realized State, and those who realize that One and only State can't help but congregate! This is a Divine gregariousness, because it is under the impulse of the Divine Magnetic Center.

The human attempts at Brotherhood have been encouraging at times, but unfortunately it is in times of limits that the Brotherhoods have existed for a short time. One of the great communities was the Essene Community. The Essene Community, so history tells us, was given unto the worship of the One God in the knowing of the Presence, the inevitable Presence of the Teacher of Righteousness. Of course, the higher occult Teachings, which the Essenes esteemed as for only the few, were held in secret from the multitudes, and one had to be ready to see how the confines that are self-imposed upon the form, as a result of false education, could be rescinded, and then the Hidden Teachings could be given without imbalancing the mind too much. An imbalanced mind is only the result of permitting it the luxury of entertaining any thoughts which come unto it. The mind was never meant for this erroneous purpose.

The mind has been in your carriage; it was never meant to go out of character. It is the child that has to be educated, and not on the fallacious statements of a jeopardized picture due to the bombardment of the three-dimensional picture with erroneous statements about it. It was to be educated in the known Facts that could be likened unto the Source or the Wonder of its presence, which it could acknowledge. It could look upon itself and see its limits, but a missing "factor" was evident. That's when it called out for a Teacher, which was termed Righteousness! Because the missing, interpretive part had presence in being *felt*.

That missing factor, being felt, was right under their noses, but people forgot that the mind had the ability to look upon its own limits. How come?

I AM not mind!!
Therefore, I can look upon
my own limits.

How could you possibly be other than your own grandpa, because you can look upon your own limits, and any belief of progenitors enables you to see how you have fallen for being your own grandparents!

If you have never met them, they only live as a result of what you are generating in the state that is becoming degenerate and is appearing to degenerate into decay, termed death-in-slow-motion, called aging!

Who wants to hear this? Hardly anyone. Why? It demands a turnabout — the maypole. "May I BE." No "perhaps may I BE." It's "May I BE," which says "I'm ready." "Perhaps" says "Not today, but maybe in two or three days." And what do you have? A week, another week, another week and another week, and a month and a month and a month, and a year and a year, and ages roll upon ages, and men and women are still fretting and fuming over their untuned strings of Being! as they were two thousand years ago. But who is there, who is here, to witness to then? Because *no dot on a page is capable of translation with power to bring about a rebirth unless the Source is living that enables the form and the symbol to be given unto meaning!*

You think, "Oh, I can consider this." Fools! You *can't* consider this. *This was never made to be considered; it is given to be lived.* You mistake, mentally, the conceiving. How can it then be immaculate? This is given . . and it must be responded unto, and that response is within you! It is a Heart response as soon as the head has had an intellectual catharsis as a result of dialectics. What are dialectics? The means whereby you can take all statements, consider them in the Light of Principle, and find where they are lacking.

Any form of lack
is a result of lack of act!

How are you seeing one another? In the form and thus limited? Or are you seeing one another in Love, as Love, on Love's Way?! If you do, you will break without effort the crystalizations surrounding the exclusivity of cults and religions and messages.

You will find the ineffable Wonder and the
ineffable Light of Unfoldment the highest
concept possible for men to consider,
because the Unfoldment is the evidence of
the intellectual catharsis having taken place,
as your being becomes more fragrant as the
dew/do is active and yet is still on the
unfolding pattern of design termed the Rose
in the garden.

Under the aegis of the Ray of this morning, we can say that we are offering unto you the possibilities and the glorification of yourselves in the Light of *I*-Love. No one can give you what you are; I can only re-mind! Some say, "Oh, but there must be the regeneration." I say, "*Re-mind,* for today it is possible." But how many have ever thought it is possible to have a new mind without the shedding of blood? A mind transplant has never been known to take place, but it is possible to have this happen under the Light of Love, and it is bloodless surgery, because it is done with the purifying Sword of Truth.

We have considered over the ages how Love, Truth, Spirit, Soul — the many synonyms for God — are utilized. May I take this opportunity to tell you that they are not to be mistaken in their use. They are utilized for the purposes of catharsis, so that the mind which arranges all these ideas in keeping with the Divine becomes the evidence of "a disciple of surrender" to the Self that is cognized in order for the intellect to bear witness to the holiness of the Son of God. How? By the power of the Magnetic Center, which, of course, has its most compelling evidence in a voice set free, given to praise, and heard in a new song.

The voice, like a thought, is so immaterial. The form is utilized and the mouth is evidently moving, only because you say it is through this aperture that the sound must come. Regardless of vocal cords and voice boxes, the magnification takes place in the Light of that receptive state of awareness when the male and female become one; there, in this solitary state, I AM prepared for the Kingdom here and now.

What would you consider Heaven to be if you were told you were in it? . . Hell? Well, you are in Heaven! Now what are you making out of it? You are in the carriage of the mind. Are you going to fall from it and think that you are in the age of carnage, where bodies statistically have no worth? In the Light of Love they are of value because the Substance to a Realized State is indivisible and only appears limited to a form because of your education.

You think you sit there with your own thoughts — you do! This room, you say, is filled with much space, and you're occupying part of it with your form; the rest I'm sure is pushing against the walls, for it is filled with your thoughts, if you are having them about this Sound Experience. *You should not be trying to understand what I am saying as I appear to speak. Perhaps I am speaking what you cannot think but know is True.* That is the root of the group formation, be it of a church or a society or of any organization: Someone is able to speak. If the Voice is with you, "harden not your hearts" to hear IT, for IT is a discerner of the innermost thoughts and patterns of collectivity.

When one speaks, holding for you an opportunity to hear what you only subliminally feel — be it as an

Unfoldment, as a sermon, as a lecture — consider you are present because you have prepared yourself to receive a statement about your Divinity which will not divide but unite in the Light of That. The reason that "That" is such an important word is because it bears no relationship to your form, any more than "Love" does, "Truth" does. Don't build these into God; they are not God. They are only the evidence that God is unassailable by your variable natures. For *God's Love and God's Man and God's Truth are not variables; they are constant and permanent in the Light of Wonder.*

The miracle of today is that you can perceive, in spite of yourselves, the wonder of being united for the Soul purpose, for your mind is subject to the thoughts that can purify it from incorrect selection. Thoughts constantly pass; but when you consider (as some have said) your state of awareness as a pure and untouched screen, just as the pictures pass on it, when the light goes up the screen is as pure and as untouched as before the pictures passed on it. You can have *Gone with the Wind* and Scarlett fleeing from the burning house and her man saying "damn," and it being censored. It is unfortunate that we haven't continued censoring, because the language of time is less and less pointing to the Timeless, and the language of time is such an intrinsic part of our engagement in form.

The form, in a way, is a language. You see, we have come, they say, to the point of studying body language, but what we really have to come to see is that the body language is only different as a result of the thoughts that are being entertained by that obstreperous child called "the mind." When you see someone who looks like a stick, consider the state of the mind in the carriage! You are not *willing* the descent of adaptability and flexibility becoming the All-inclusiveness of That which is termed God!

Look at the adaptability of Love. It permits you to think you express IT! And you in your arrogance say, "I will," or, "I will not." Then what do we do? We immediately put in restrictions, put up fences, and say, "We have something you don't have." Fools! God is no respecter of person. God IS, and may you wear the mask. And may your breath be so holy that you evidence the Visitation of a Holy One in the sanctuary of your stillness as you meditate in the active way of living daily in the Light of Divine Understanding.

Understanding is important because it does let you separate but not destroy in doing so. In the days before *me*chanicality became the way to separate milk, you were easily able to separate the cream from the milk. You didn't destroy the milk; you didn't bastardize it by "pasteurizing" it. What we have today called milk is such a bastardization of that which originally came out of the cow, it bears no resemblance to it! The cow would perhaps die if it were fed it!

What do we do today? How many mothers ever consider what they are eating when they are going to feed their child? Of course, if they feed by the bottle, then they say they don't have to be concerned whether they eat sour pickles or Brussels sprouts or drink alcohol or smoke. Go on! You will!

You should look at milk, on one level, as an offering to nourish the thoughts that are in keeping with growth in the Light. The cream is so rich that we avoid it, because it is so difficult to utilize if you are not keeping to the correct demands of God. Remember, "The demands of God," as Mrs. Eddy said, "appeal to thought only." [1]

The milk was supposed to be for the children; the cream top was always set aside for those who would not just sit with it, because it was very evident if you took the cream and did not exercise your dominion, you would wear the spare tires becoming the vehicle that would get you to the grave! The cream top always has been symbolic of the

---

1. Mary Baker Eddy, *Science and Health with Key to the Scriptures* (Boston: Trustees Under the Will of Mary Baker G. Eddy, 1934), p. 182, l. 5.

Teachings saved for the Saints and the Sages of the Ages. For they, as the Essenes knew, carried in their presence the High Teaching, so that they lived. People who go to the Essene Teachings from the printed word are leaving themselves open to what the mind is interpreting the dots to mean.

When the Essenes say, as I am told they say, "Do not eat meat," I wonder, in the Light of the Cream, if they are not saying,

"Do not take unto yourself
the form of flesh
to be the Real encounter
with Life as IT IS."

What do we do? We have people sacrificing for the possibilities of freedom from the form by saying that something that was given unto men could not be touched and used as food. Surely goodness and mercy shall follow in the understanding that we move beyond the conditions whereby what we eat can affect our Spirit. Our Spirit is not in matter; our Spirit is as the Breath of Life, breathing newness, vitality, and vigor into the frameless.

The life of a religious can be one of trial and tribulation, and yet the mind is taught to consider that it has found a way to achieve God through self-abnegation. But I always consider (and always have considered, from the time I remembered) that if God IS All and I have no evidence of a grandparent, then the only thing that I *know* that must have come before me — if they said Something did, and that I am coming after that Something which they said has gone before me — must have only been the Energy becoming the God-Realization. Therefore, the belief of past lives and re-incarnation is only for this story; it is not any part of His Story. "I" was never born to die, and therefore, if never born to die, "I" was never born to live as a limit but as the Limitless, and that is why God is said to be All.

Jesus said, "Be like the little child and come unto Me, because such as these shall inherit the Kingdom." [2] One man once said to me, "Can I sit in your lap?" I said, "Of course!" What kind of a state must be present if it isn't that of a child, instead of that of an arrogant, self-indulgent nincompoop? One man was tied up in knots, to appearance — and of course it was just because he had kinks in his thoughts — and I said to him, "Get up," and he stood up, and I said, "Come and sit in my lap." I said, "I could pick you up, but I don't think I should. You come and sit in my lap." He did, and he changed on the spot. He thought he had to behave as he looked. I wanted to see where he was: at home in being a child!

A child is not an immature state. A child is the state of naturalness when every thing has no other place than just a part of the experience of Wonder. So, be the child filled with Wonder and never let ice cream satisfy your cry for Food!

How we chase after our own things to grasp them! Wouldn't it be wonderful if we could rejoice in Being and find the Self clasping with such a magnetic force that no one could come into your presence without feeling the drawing power of Infinite Life, Truth, and Love. Oh! What a Power, and yet not complete if you permit the thought to think it in form and forget that I AM only an encounter to form, but I AM All in an embrace.

Thank you for being with me.

Do consider this Unfoldment with more than one superficial hearing. It is pregnant with meaning and it has, as all Unfoldments, many levels according to the depth of your root system and the means at your disposal to tap the rich resources from which "I" have sprung.

---

2.   Mark 10:13-15.

O for that Well of Ever-living Waters, and
    O for that tongue given to praise!
And O for that Voice bearing healing to the
    waters, and to the waters of the mind
    troubled, "Peace, be still," and no rage.
O to be found a wondrous happening, to be
    found as a living freed from being
    object to time.
Find Being timeless and the object an
    ornament to decorate the tree of the
    Forest Divine.

From out of the Forest you have come as if
    in calling, and out of the forest of time
    you dwell,
And know, if you're present, your seeding
    bears fruitage, for in the Light of Love
    you have burst your shell!

In the Rapture of Being in the Wonders all-
    glorious, a Rock has been found and on
    this you stand,
And may it appear as brilliant as a faceted
    diamond and offer its Ray for those
    who wish to hear how "I" tell.

From the Fire, the Flame, within the
    knowing of Wonder, may the facet of
    Light beam unto you the Fact
That Love IS All. What is there to tell?

Love IS All. That's That!

▼

VI.

Fundamental Questions

Remember,
Man is in essence
Energy, idea,
and then form.

Fundamental Questions

We are gathered together, for the purpose of *opportunity,* to glean from the pages indelibly etched on the invisible scrolls of the wisdoms and the accomplishments and the demands which confront an aspirant as he would fling aside the inhibiting formations of thought, and move into the Realization commensurate with the accomplishments of Those who have left examples and ideals for men and women to follow when they have freed themselves from the mind to the degree that *intuitive promptings* are at work in bringing about that purpose for which you come in the name of *opportunity.*

You who walk through the avenues of time and who partake of its enticements have come to see, through desire or through faith or through courage, that men and women must be more than they appear, that they must be more than the witnessing presence of the passing. They must be in essence known, and in Essence known as Love! The years that have been enumerated as the calendar of events have offered, unto those who would seek the untarnishable Truths of the Ages, an opportunity to perceive without doubt that those who would put off the swaddling clothes of a material bondage move into the considerations becoming a server involuntarily appearing to fulfill a voluntary act of surrender to the selfless condition commensurate with man's exploration of the Unknown, and yet known because of Example.

All those who are in this world, seeking, are seeking because they feel within themselves a lack of completeness. *This feeling of incompleteness is an opportunity.* This feeling of abundance is an opportunity. This feeling of lack is an opportunity — a lack which points to the laxness which so many adopt with the hopes that "anything is good enough." Saying that "anything is good enough" is really saying, "I am ready to be disposed of."

Many people fail to take an opportunity because they consider this deck of cards that has been built, that has been stacked, according to their own sleight of hand. They forget that they have stacked the cards according to how they want to play the game of life. And they forget that the Almighty Consciousness Eternal is the ACE up the sleeve of all those who have come and gone and left their wisdom etched upon the calendar of their appearance.

The Ace is always up the sleeve; in other words, it is always hidden under the garment of activity. That is what is meant symbolically by "the Ace up the sleeve." It is not, perhaps, what you as mortals think; the Ace is the symbol stating that *it is a Secret that makes your experience empowered.* The Ace up the sleeve says that you have That Power concealed, under the garment of appearance, for activity in the selfless act of the Power of the Masters of the Ages.

As appearances in the realm of questioning (to whatever degree you ever *do* ask of yourselves the possibility of knowing the unnameable Power), it does not matter how much you question.

What does matter
is that you start to laugh
at the matter of limit,
because your form
is only there to be disposed of.

Remember, if you can dispose of your form, you have claimed a state of what is termed freedom from the sting of the first death. If you can see how you are freed from the form through argument, then you will come to see, through acceptance, the steps to be taken so that the second death hath no sting. The other step to be taken is to perceive how the world can be given back to the Arms of Love and how you make up your creation, including your world and the inhabitants thereof. Ye *are* gods!

It is of considerable consequence that you perceive, without the appendages of emotionalism and personalization, the demands which behoove you to move with great sensitivity into the fulfillment of the requirements for seizing opportunity so that you may stand as a pugilist and move as a dancer through the ensuing riptides of mortal suggestion that come to you to give themselves up and not to be accepted in the name of an argument on the chain of an emotional consequence. You who are bound to form . . a group, who are bound to form associations, and who are bound to form clusters of tonal power, are bound to remember. You must never forget the Pitch or the Keynote or the Signature befitting your considered group formation. *Nothing is of power unless you give it power.*

There is no necessity to try to comb the spaces of our planetary system with the teeth of an unprepared grip upon the Facts of Being. People are probing an outer universe and a planetary system because there is such glory in attempting to probe beyond limits, whether you succeed or you don't succeed. Yet those who do not succeed in even being lifted off the platform of gravity with success do not *stop to consider the explosive situation that is at hand when you attempt to enter another dimension without being prepared to balance it with an inner experience.* You can't help but find your seams slightly weakened by the over-pressurized state of opportunity at hand without the attending considerations of significance which make it a balanced experience. We could liken it to the space probes that this country is doing, but it cannot be said to be dissimilar from what men and women superficially do in pronouncing upon the lips of time, "Oh, I am part of this Esoteric Teaching," or, "I am part of this therapeutic treatment," or, "I am part of this cultural attachment," or "I am part of this group that is formed . . ."

You see, anything that is a group is the way the mind describes a number of forms coming together with the same purpose. People coming together with the same purpose have always to be named, simply, "group." Why are people so concerned about groups? It's the way political powers play the game. One with God is a majority, (that is all there is anyway), but when a thousand people or a hundred people or fifty people or twenty-four people know this, it is that many more (in the realm of appearances) who are able to withstand the suggestion that they may be wrong, because their considerations may be the antithesis of those who are only the weaklings of an industrial situation, a commercial situation, which never does revolt (only at the thought of taxes)!

The United States and Canada are two of the great countries of the world that occupy a great portion of this planet. However, when you get beyond the planet and look down upon it, it's very difficult to imagine how you have multiplied it and populated it, ye gods! Have you forgotten that you are the creators of it? That is why "One with God is a majority." Each one who is upon this planet has imaged the same planet. That is why you are numbered as part of a group called the populace of the planet. You have forgotten this type of "wingdom." You have forgotten that you have the mind to fly, and you have forgotten that what you have objectified you now must see correctly!

There is not a thing wrong with the world. The world as Divine Idea is perfect. But remember, you have said, "I am in the world," and then have proceeded to be educated into how to sustain it, in other words, how to think in a specific way to maintain it as it *seems* to be.

> *Do you realize that your whole life*
> *is made to sustain your*
> *precipitated objective experience?!*

Those who are on the search for more *meaning* to life have to ask themselves fundamental questions; *they have to ask the condition of their truthfulness, of their love, honesty, selflessness, and readiness to give up all for a Cosmic Realization.* Then what appears as the loss becomes the

Real gain. It is the only time that you might say you can have your cake and eat it too! What you appear to lose in *re*identification you gain in identifying as truly IS. You have to stand apart: "Come out from the world, and be ye separate." In other words, accept an argument through intellectual considerations so that the outer situation may give you a cause to question, bring about an argument, and through the dialectics involved come to an intellectual situation whereby you stand and show your colors. *You show your colors of honesty, surrender, and integrity to Principle, and if you are found approved by the Light, you will find yourself freed from the fear of the mortal kingdom and the inhabitants thereof.*

Everyone must face the need of being able to stand apart and witness the dream. *The greatest temptation of your nightmare is that you tend to emotionalize it and thus give it the power to sustain itself.* As soon as you emotionalize your experience of illness, of happiness, of joy, of vitality, you are putting yourself in a vulnerable position for perpetuating the nightmare. The reason that the Masters of Power have always pushed forward the idea of raising the Fire is because man knows, through the sensorial apparatus which he calls his body, that there is a place in an experience where he knows he isn't "it," but he has no doubt that he IS.

If there is a problem, where must it come from? It must come from thought-patterns that form around your form because of your innate nature misunderstood, waiting to be understood: the nature of possessiveness.

> *If you would be free,*
> *start the practice*
> *of only associating in thought*
> *with what is in keeping*
> *with freedom in the Light of the I.*

Thus your intellectual paraphernalia is kept under the scrutiny of a warrior and you start to perceive that you are creating your own bondage through possessiveness. You say, "This is *my* body. This is *my* wine. This is *my* blood. This is *my* joy. These are *my* children. This is *my* husband. This is *my* situation. This is *my* person. This is *my* hand. This is *my* eye. This is *my* head. That's yours. That's *mine.*"

Remember, in French you cannot say, "This is my body. This is my arm." You say, "This is *the* body. This is *the* arm." Thus the French have a very easy way to consider their unattachment to the body because they have never been taught to possess it. We who speak English (to some degree, anyway) possess all the marks of limits because our language makes us possess ourselves as if we know ourselves, and thus we are possessed with "a self" we do not know, and through our language we think it is "this."

> *If you are to cease from this identifying incorrectly, then you must alter your language!*

If you alter your language, you are going to alter what you attract. Remember, *Man is in essence energy, idea, and then form*, but form only as the evidence that the three qualities of the Trinity (Father, Son, and Holy Ghost — energy, idea, and form) are becoming understood.

What does understanding this do? Understanding this triangle enables you to build a pyramid of power in which you can be rejuvenated. You will be able to live in this pyramid of power and cause everyone to ask, "Where do you get your energy? Where do you get your vivacity? Where do you get your unlimited sense of wonder? Where do you get your compassion? Where do you get your patience?" You can say, "Because a Mystery is known and that Mystery is how to live practically under an enlightened pyramid of power, not one that remains a mystery between the paws of the Sphinx! Perhaps the Sphinx was pointing to the demand that you had to question your animal nature and see that you could not do away with the form any more than the

Sphinx has done away with it. You cannot do away with the form and you don't need to do away with the form, but you have to pass through the ensuing intellectual conflict that the paws might represent as the positive and the negative, the male and the female considerations wrapped up in an idea, a body, and formed as the Sphinx.

You do not say you do not have a body; you just cease to emotionalize it and call it *yours*. You say, "I am so grateful this vehicle . . ." (Say this within yourself. You don't go around talking this way in Slippery Ed's or The Greasy Spoon or O'Henry's or the Devil's Patisserie, you know!)

> *You move knowing*
> *that the form is utilized,*
> *and you hold within yourself*
> *that "I have the form for the fun of it."*

It's not serious, as you'll come one day to see, but it's a fascinating thing to be a consciousness without a form. There is a level of consciousness where you know you *are*, but you don't have any form, and it doesn't bother you in the least. You know that, partially, when you sleep at night.

Then, of course, you forget about the fact that you are a conscious state in your nightmare of daytime living. Why? You say, "*I pick up my body and I pick up my emotions and I pick up my battle with the hordes of mediocrity.*" Well, do so. What's it matter? Tell 'em to go to hell. What's the matter?! Why are you so concerned about heaven or hell if it isn't because you have been taught to believe that they are places that you will go to; perhaps they are places in which you are living! To think they're in the future state gives you no possibility of freeing yourself from them in the future, and that was the need of priests of the past, to help pray you through purgatory or through the realm of your own imprisonment in belief. Purgatory is where you haven't made up your mind in favor of Truth.

Heaven is where the mind is known to be
made up. And you watch how it is
responding to the Divine Impetus to be free,
and in this rejoice and be satisfied.
Thus the opportunity is at hand, and Man
walks forth unfettered and free into the
Promised Land.

A Promised Land is not the material objectification of
an emotionally starved situation for possession.   The
Promised Land is that state of Realization in which you
know there are no frontiers, there are no dimensions that
can limit the efficacy of Love or Life omnipotently
embraced in the Truth that is eternal and stands forth sym-
bolically presented as Winged Victory. There never was a
head to that statue, regardless of what people have said; that
statue was the living proof that no victory is ever winged if
you have a head.

That is the first death: to realize that your head is only
used as the means of putting an end to what you consider to
be unbecoming in your Quest for freedom from the limits of
materiality, gained through imbibing the opportunity of Life
Unlimited and bearing its fruit in the realm of Light.

If there ever was a time that is important, it is this very
moment. You know, it is so ridiculous to say that this age is
this way and the last age was that way. *Do you realize*
you've made up every age? You make up every situation,
and every situation that is made up is there for you to gain
what you can from it and then kick it in the behind and
leave it!!

Don't think you have to
work through error.
One of the greatest enmeshing beliefs
is the suggestion that you have
to work through an erroneous situation in
order to gain the victory over it.

The demand of an erroneous situation is to face it without any emotion.

What is more conducive to bondage than having your attention held so fast on happiness, on balancing your books and your accounts, or on having enough to go out to the store and buy beautiful clothes? All fun, provided you perceive how it is all happening. The people who get bogged down with the details of time are the people you feel sorry for, because it prevents them from perceiving when opportunity knocks.

Don't think that opportunity is something that is going to be heard; opportunity is usually present when you are willing to be open to newness. It's unfortunate when you become old crocks (like most of you over twenty), losing the flexibility to move into new areas. People will say, "Oh, I'm forty-five; I'm fifty; I'm twenty-eight; I'm thirty-five; I'm thirty-eight; I'm forty-one," as if you were supposed to say, "Oh hee, oh hum." You know? And you call for the doctor and the doctor says, "Oh, isn't it terrible to have such age upon you?"

If you are going to consider opportunity, then consider how open you are to changing your positions. How open are you to speaking to those you love and saying, "Why are you behaving like such an ass? Why are you behaving like such an idiot? I've been putting up with it for ten or fifteen years!" Why do people put up with each other's despicable moods, their despicable tastes, their despicable attitudes? Why don't you fight, and obliterate your involvement with the situation that's bothering you? You don't have to be bothered with it! To think that you're going to reap a benefit from it is just a way of reaching old age and needing a pension!

If you are so timid that you're afraid you're going to offend somebody, then know that you are an offense unto yourself, and you'll never hear opportunity knocking. If you are sure you are right, then your consideration expressed will bear the result of your attainment. It's very difficult for an impoverished soul to tell another impoverished soul that the other isn't impoverished! By your fruits are you known.

How do I know that you are hearing what I am saying? I don't! That's why I am courageous! You persist in sponsoring a state that you know very well isn't in keeping with what you know to be true.

One of the tools of the devil is to make you happy, selfish, joyous, sick, sad. If you identify with any one of those states — "Oh, that person must be living a gorgeous spiritual life, they're so happy, and they have so much money and they're so abundant." Or, "That person must need a great spiritual rejuvenation because they are so depressed, so sad, so bronchial, so stomach-this or stomach-that, they need, really, more spirituality." The devil's tool is so exposed in this realization.

The devil's tool is to make you think that your happiness is yours, your illness is yours, your body is yours, your Substance is yours. As long as anything is "yours," it will never flow like the Truth of the healing, liberating waters of Truth. You possess it and it's nine-tenths of the law. You're *possessed* and you have one-tenth to hang onto to free you.

The old statement is "Possession is nine-tenths of the law." I tell you now, it is a fatal, terminal malady. You have one-tenth to save you, and that tenth power brings forth always a new experience. As the beginning of another year happens beyond the power of the ten, you have gleaned the fruitage, if you are wise, and that is what the zero points to: the accomplished acts of your past so that they give you the power to take care of the exciting new decade in which you have been associated with the Truth of your Being.

There are all kinds of statements made, all kinds of groups formed, but remember this: that if anyone says that they can lead you into Enlightenment, they are in question. If anyone says they can take your karma, they are in question. If anyone tells you you will *become* Enlightened, they are in question. "*Now* are ye the Sons of the Light." "I and My Father *is* One Now, and not 'shall be.'" That is the meaning of opportunity. Opportunity is the ever-growing awareness of newness ever-available, undefiled in the recognition of the activity of Man in the Light of the Realization of an Idea, an energy formed, and appearing precipitated as you, as me.

It is apparent, however, that you can have an idea, and you can energize it. It doesn't necessarily have to be formed, unless you are willing to take the responsibility for the object after it has been precipitated.

You are here with form. Why do you quest to know the Truth which can set you free? The only Truth that can set you free is found when for a moment you can see that as a man thinketh, so *is* he, and as a man thinketh *in his heart,* so is he free from his head. The world has nothing to be criticized for, but for your criticism you must stand the critique of bias and the critique of envy because you are a Light unto the people, for you have found and in finding know the Light that is lit cannot remain unseen upon the hill of accomplishment.

Opportunity is when you are open to the incredible Wonders of a limitless happening all on the range you choose to ride through the vehicle of wonder and praise. You create your world. Don't blame the world for its situation; you did it! Ye are not gods *in the making.* That would have you in process. Your state is God-precipitated as soon as you perceive the Wonder termed another, bearing the ability to give you the *meaning* to the water, the bread, and the wine: the energy, the idea, the form. Elevate this, and in that elevation find the Transcendent Experience and thus be apparent in your loving ministrations, for you *know*, and in that Knowing, embrace all that appears to be the human kind.

A human kind is a rare privilege to meet, for that human kind must be freed from being a kind of a human! Kindness never comes in its transformatory power from a human trying. A human kind is one who knows what the hue-man is, and the power to that is the ray of kindness.

> Never be kind to error! Never take a second
> place.
> Always know that you stand in glory, for the
> Quest your I did take.
> Your *I* remains a constant in the outer and
> inner world;
> The only difference is this fact: That the
> outer one has to be clothed
> While the inner one remains, simplicity in
> garment, power in glory and might,
> Giving you the courage to drop your outer
> "I" and say,
> "I take the Torch of the Liberty of the
> Golden Light!"

You always know your inner Self is the fact, because it gives what appears as the outer self the courage to enter the Age with a heart.

Thank you.

▼

VII.
The Efficacy of Joy

Men and women realize
as never before
that they cannot circumscribe
the Wonder of Being!

THE EFFICACY OF JOY

We are gathered together with a few in the Rose Room to consider some of the facets surrounding that which men and women have dropped into their pool of expectation and watched through the ripples of remembrance.

This evening, the three evenings before the full moon, and the three evenings after the full moon are considered propitious, not only for you to bathe in the Frequency that is commensurate with the Festival of this season, but it is also that time in which those who dwell on other levels of Beingness are said (according to those who believe in such structures) to be able to find a spiral Way of Power between their position and this Speaker. They are thus enabled to catch, for these few brief moments, a glimpse of what is happening, as the Mystical Teachings have stated it, with the great considerations that men have had and have termed "the Plan." They are of expectation and Wonder, they who sit with folded hands, and in the Musical Chairs of a Harmonic State encounter the vibratory Frequency of these energies which you translate as words and which they translate into a composition that is exuding the possibilities of freedom when *men and women realize as never before that they cannot circumscribe the Wonder of Being.* Yet they can allow, through receptivity, the Uncircumscribed State of Existence to be apprehended as they more and more *glean the harvest of their preparedness* to enter into that State of Wonder which is commensurate with those who love the Truth and in the beginning termed it "God."

When man says he loves That which is termed the Source of his Beingness (termed "God" in his ritualistic attempts to worship), and comes to find, through the proper seeding of his mind, that the harvest tends to be rich and plentiful, he gains not only the richness of the harvest but the Kernels of Power that appear as courage, trust, and obedience to *follow* into the footsteps of the Sower of the Seeds of

Wonder, expectation, and joy. For *out* of these come *what you term your habitation here on this planet that you have lucidly perceived and yet completely misunderstood, for you deem it something aside from what you are.* I tell you now, this is all that you are, appearing externalized for the *joy* that you have in seeing how the objects of sense are translated into energies of an unbridled and unlimited Conscious Universe termed "Beingness."

People speak of their karma and they speak of their wonder and they speak of their needs and of their speculations about the proper investments. They speak about what they shall do and what they will do, and yet, you see, these are only the ejaculations of a restless mind. *The unfortunate part is, Conception Unconfined seldom takes place because most people offer these suggestions of what they will be and would be and could be only to those ears who doubt that they could be, would be, or can be That which is termed "Unlimited."* But you see, as long as you align yourself to *this* form with only the credibility of your senses, and you *ignore* the gnawing question that you have to face because you dislike to *face* the Unknown, you have not the answer, from anyone, to the question:

"Who and what am I?"

Then you have to look *somewhere* to find an answer: *Somewhere* a Voice is calling, and that Voice has said, "Come unto Me, if you would be full of the Wonder and the Glory that is not external to you but internally is found the Wellspring of Ever-living Waters."

Now, what does this "Wellspring of Ever-living Waters" mean to the one who has been struck and moved under the rippling rhythm of the Christ or Self Possibilities? It means that there is forever Newness appearing. You do not find the waters recircling as you might find in your pump system in fountains of today. You find the waters recirculating from the very **depths** of the Spring itself. They flow never to return in the same way they have come forth: they water the ground, they quench your thirst, and they offer clouds for the sun so that the sun may say to those clouds, "Drop your dew upon those portions of the world that are under the arid condition of personality and allow the rain/reign of God and His Love and His Son to be Supreme."

You do doubt the efficacy of your possibilities because you *constantly* tend, as most Earthians do, to totally circumscribe yourself within the limited *framework of personality*. How can you ever glean the possibilities of a Vista beyond your wildest dreams? It is because of this that the Heart, you might say, of the Unknown *is known*, because your quest for "the Fullness of Being" is answered as you offer with sincerity before the altar of your own inner state the desires and the hopes for understanding the great paradox of this "Earthbound situation" as it seems.

This Earthbound situation as it seems is just as it seems! It does not carry within itself *anything* that is substantial. You can make it up, you can hold it up, and you can drop it; you can pick it up, you can wear it, you can hold it up, and you can parade, and yet you can drop it. Yet tell me, all you who remember your lives and who remember your past lives, do you think that they are *dead* and *gone*? People who have life readings are talking about what they *had been* with the hopes of impressing you with that information because of what they are *not* at this time. The accuracy of the information is something that is difficult to comprehend, because the accuracy of the information is only perceived when you realize that what you were is progressing; that which you Are is experiencing Now.

That is why you cannot remember the details of your past, because the details of your past are not on the level of your activity that you can comprehend from this level. All you can do is know that they *are*. This is why you attempt to get life readings so somebody can tell you what you were.

The Soul cannot be fractured! That Totality only appears fractured because you *fracture* this by **refusing** . . the Allness of Being. How can you *locate* or find the Self and *deem* your self to be such a limited creature as you entertain *thoughts* that are *totally in*human, *in*corporeal, *Divine*?! *How* do you throw allegiance to these and *none* to the Omnipresence which **allows** this to happen and this *happening* to appear as a form of rejoicing?

This is why it tells you in the Holy Book that your joy must be full. *Why?!* It is from this Fullness that *this* happens!! Do you realize, *this* happens as a result of Fullness. What am I saying? *You* happen as a result of Joy! When you look like "sourpusses," this is why you are contradicting the whole purpose, the whole realization of how you happen!! You happen as a result of Joy and your faces belie you and you seem to be the victims of circumstances.

You see, this is the whole point of a Festival. A Festival is a time of rejoicing in, you might say, *seeing* how various aspects of the Being perform so that you are not limited by the supposition that this is your only performance. This is a performance in which you are adjudicated because you have put yourself on the *platform* of "competitors." Why do I say this incredible word, "competition"? Because you are competitors in and on the agenda of time for *Earth* to *show* the Race of Superman, not the hundred-yard dash! You are part of a Divine Olympiad! So you perceive that the Wonders of this Festival are unique.

Before you, I AM. Why AM I before you? It is because being before you, you allow yourself to try to penetrate what makes me speak, and how *do* I speak these words to you. This is your Wonder: You call me because you are still imagining the Wonder to be external *to* you. You ignore me at times and then embrace me at times, because you think "at times" I AM here and "at times" I AM not. That is the old-fashioned way of thinking the Spirit comes and goes, in other words, is born and dies.

*There is nothing that is Real
about being born or dying.*

If there were something Real about being born, then being born would be all there would be to Being born. There would be no dying. But being born suggests what? Process. There isn't any such thing! Only in the crafts. That is what the crafts do. They perpetuate karma, they perpetuate Paths, they perpetuate religions, and they perpetuate teachings, when actually the fact is: *witnessing*! How many have a chance to witness?

Very few people have a chance to witness, because when they witness they do what? They sit and gawk! They don't even have the vision of a hawk. At least a hawk knows when to dive and forget about his upward flight. He plunges to get what he needs for himself or for his young, just as the eagle does. But the plunge or the descent into the illusion doesn't persuade him that he is part of the illusion. He swells and soars out of it. This is the efficacy of *Joy*!!

Whoever heard of anything ritualistic that is awe-inspiring if it isn't joyful? The old Teaching says, as some Teachers have put it, it is out of *Joy* that the whole experience has happened. How joyous are you in finding the Happening embracing *you*?!

I believe that Seth, in his lectures, said to his voicebox[1] that he was without the need of vocalization and that's why he had to use somebody else's vocal cords; he does not have any himself because where he is he doesn't need them. But since you are here and believe you are here, you do need them. So the information is given to you in this way. We use words. We are all using *words*!

Well, if That Which IS Real doesn't have any vocal cords, then what is being said in Essence isn't words, it is *Energy*! That is why a thought is energy, and the evidence

---

1.   Jane Roberts, a trance medium.

of it is the spoken word! The reason you aren't shocked is because it is grounded! This is the great understanding that must surround the Christ Festival.

> *What is the Christ Festival? It is those*
> *moments that are set aside to consider the*
> *Force of Reality . . garmented in a Witness.*

This is the succinct statement. It is the **core** of the orchards of tomorrow. This is why you are so important! This is why it is, seemingly, such a shameful thing that so few tuned into the class this evening. Will those who have heard this for twenty years, fifteen years, ten years, five years, one year, ever realize that just to speak to another is not necessarily the way you have, to find yourself ordered, to move to these gatherings?! There is a way of moving that is *intuitive*! This is far more accurate than telephoning, because when you telephone you constantly pick up the receiver and dial! What does this do? It disconnects you from listening within yourself to what you are being told. What you are *Being*-told. That doesn't need a voice. It needs a Force! When it's voiced it's called intuition, and when you have followed it and offer something that no one has ever heard before, it is called *insight!* into the entanglement on this web, in this great paradox. When this intuition and insight work together — the *child* that is born! *There* is an ejaculation with conception! It's termed "wisdom." What is the point of wisdom? It allows the witness to start to realize the *Immaculate Nature of Allness*.

This is why this evening is important. You who view me with shallow sight see me only this way. I close my eyes to "you," because I see in a different way. By closing my eyes to you I blot out the suggestion that there are multiples present. I AM rejoicing in the Allness of the One and *love* the play that the mind has adopted for use, and fracturing all this gives me multiples of the Force of "you."

"The Force of you" is one that contains everything that constitutes your form. But this comes from what? The joy of **realization** of the Cosmic Nature of Consciousness. That is why the "you see"/U.C. on a higher level is the Universal Consciousness, because it says, "Go beyond this. Try to understand how these words happen, because you are witnesses and the Presence is all that is necessary, if there isn't a word spoken, if you know to **witness**." You say, "*No*, without your words I would not know." *That is why I speak, because you believe this.*

It isn't my words that give you Knowingness. It isn't your study that gives you Knowingness. It's your study that allows your intelligence to be utilized so that it doesn't get rusty. Your Knowingness comes when your intelligence says, "Put me in overdrive. Run over me and let me have the dynamic thrill that comes with Being on the Highway of Life with our God and as His Christ-Self." Now, what are you saying? "Allow me to entertain the Radiation commensurate with the Ever-Divine Event of Love."

Why do I say "Love"? Because Love is the Force that allows what isn't to appear to be as it is and yet never is touched by the apparent suggestion, and embraces all in the final triumph of Joy! If it were not for this, your cup could not be filled with the Cup of Rejoicing. In other words,

> *Exaltation is essential!*
> *How can apathy and indolence*
> *ever approach the Wonders*
> *surrounding newness?*

What does newness mean? Newness means that oldness isn't there. Why is oldness not there? Because in the Light of Newness there is only Nowness.

Now, what is Nowness? The Presence . . that only another says "is and was and evermore shall be. Earth without end. Amen." Earth without end, ah men? *Earth has met its end by your Presence. Earth has been given back to the Arms of Love.* Why? Because you now see it as it truly is: a stage that you have made up without knowing how it happened, and by your constant openness to drama you enact what appears as your "threescore years and ten." In actuality, you are doing what? You are here to enact the dream sequence of this shadow dance and allow the Light to be seen as a continuous Ray, either your shadow dance could never be enjoyed.

There is no shadow unless there is something standing in the way. What is that something that is standing in the way? A belief that you are born and you will die. As Nisargadatta said, you must become aware that you are not a person. I could not be saying this if I were really "this," because I would be *denying* "this." I am not denying "this"; what I am saying is *embracing* "this" so that what I AM cannot be denied!

Tell me something: now that I have told you that you are not a person, what are you going to do? *Start disrobing yourself of all the trappings that would limit you!* Moods! Months! Years! Professions! Start disrobing yourselves of these limits! Why? Then you will start peeling off layers of belief.

The reason no one makes any progress is that you listen so much to "me" without questioning,

"How does it happen?"

You study all the transcripts of the Unfoldments and *memorize* them, but you never say, "How does this happen?" You think you know how it happens! You even think you know what Joy is. How do you know what Joy is? Is it the opposite of unhappiness? Most people think it is. Unhappiness usually happens because there is unsureness. In other words, you are not fully certain that you are here! You are not fully certain that you can entertain the consequences of considering the Fact that you are not primarily person.

You can say, "Oh, I am a thinker." There's no proof of that, either. You have to dive deep. What do you mean by "diving deep"? You had better tell me, because I haven't a clue. There's no such thing as diving deep, only when you go scuba diving! That is deep. You go *deep* in relation to being on the surface. But to dive deep with these considerations, I don't know what it means, other than this:

Drop the considerations that limit you!

How many of you will go out from this meeting, go back to your houses and behave as if you'd never been here? Go right to your room, shut the door and go to bed? You don't feel right; you feel tired; you're miserable, moody, not sure if it's the right time of the month, not sure you're satisfied, not sure you're happy with anything. After being here!! If you are like that, don't come!! If you can't be radiant and vibrant after an experience of this nature then you are *denying the Nature that is really so Wonder-full*. Why are you so cast down? I can't say, "my Soul. And why art thou so disquieted within me?" I can't say those things! The Soul is not fractured! It was never cast up or down! It was never disquieted within me or *without* me! Do you think your presence makes me greater? I'm sure you think so.

How many of you are considering movement? No, you're not considering movement! You want to stay right in the rut you're in! Why?! Could it be that you haven't bothered breaking the mesmerism surrounding personal address?

Where is the fallacy in your considerations?

You work with a *fraction* instead of the *Totality*! You can say, "I would like a Rolls Royce, but I don't think I should even entertain that idea. It's just beyond my reach." Whatever told you that the present car is within your reach? It wasn't! What made it within your reach? The money you borrowed or the money you earned by dying as somebody else's slave in an office? A car is *never* within your reach.

What is within your reach? Immediacy, comfort! These are within your reach, and the realization of that is the efficacy of Abundance. If I had entertained the concept of the little house in which I grew up, then there would never have been this grand one! It causes what? Everyone to either appreciate it very much or be envious. See the competition?! Everyone is competing — for what? For more and more, which is really less and less, until All is seen as IT IS.

Someone once said to me, "How can you look after all these objects and all these things?" I said, "I don't!" I suppose they thought that the people working for me look after them. I do work all the time so that the people looking after them leave them alone. *I* didn't bring them into my experience! They are the evidence of the multitudinous Realm of Ideation! And I leave them in that wonderful protective State.

I don't leave the Love of Life in the hands of matter. For it was the Joy that gave me the opportunity to find the Spirit of Truth that seems to compete with the spirit of delusion. *That's the stage you're on: the stage of witnessing, or the stage of appearance in contradiction to the stage of illusion. What is the difference? You are on the stage knowing Truth. Others are on the stage believing it is to be known!*

If Man *is* Truth, what else is to be found? How can you adjudicate *my* actions unless you are adjudicating me from that standpoint of a competitor? Do you realize that you can say, "Oh, Mills doesn't approve of marriage." I've never said that. I have said, "Just be sure that when you *do* marry you know what you're doing so that happiness will be." People don't want to hear *that* any more than that they are not person! I've never said I don't approve of marriage. I have said, *"You had better be sure of who you are before you marry somebody." Because if you don't know who you are and they don't know who they are, how can you expect to be happy?* How could I say otherwise, knowing that two doesn't make happiness?

The only thing that may be happiness is the Realization of Oneness. Then there is no division.

When I was a child, everyone wanted the wishbone, because if you grasped one side of the wishbone and somebody else the other and it broke and you got the larger piece, your wish would come true and the other poor fellow's wouldn't. His wish wouldn't come true. Isn't it crazy the superstitions we believe, and how we're ridiculed when we believe something that is *beyond* superstition?!

Do you think this is the only power we have?! Do you think this is the limit of you? Of course it isn't! But you don't know how much more there is available until you *renounce* your limitation, in other words, your citizenship in limitation! **You have to announce that you are a Cosmic Being, not an Earthbound anything!**

What do you have to do? The basis of your life is understanding the root of "revolt." You *must revolt* against the limitations of the average teaching.

Who knows what Force is utilizing the vocal cords? Certainly, the Words of Truth, if that's what they *are,* are doing it.

> *Any word you utter is the evidence of the*
> *Force that is termed "God."*
> *Any thought you think is the result of the*
> *Force you call "God."*
> *Every movement you make is a result of the*
> *Force that you call "God."*

Agreed?!

Well then, where is God?! Why do you behave as if you weren't That which you really are?! You are not a poor struggling mortal trying to become immortal and find Self-Realization. There's no such fodder!! That's only for the mind! You are *already realized,* but won't accept it because

you want your exits and your entrances and "as you like it"!!
How often are you the merchant, trying to sell something in
order to get something that maybe doesn't belong to you?

Do you know, wealth and the absence of it doesn't
mean there is any criteria of one's accomplishment. You can
say, "Well, so and so is making so much money now. They
are so successful." Great! *But if they are making a lot of
money now, perhaps it's not because they've learned how to
make money, it's because they've learned how to be less of
an obstacle to their own Fullness!*

What do you do? You have too many *layers* of skin.
One of the old exercises we used to do down on Oak Bay (I
gave it one night at dinner; I can see it now), I told people to
take an onion and mentally peel it and tell me what happened
when they finished. I never got an answer. I don't believe
there was one tear shed! Because they did it mentally and
they thought they had done it. You should *weep* for joy!!

What is the great need of your Mission? The great need
is for patience and the demand is Example.

> *Are you an Example?! Have you the
> patience to be misunderstood?*

You've witnessed it; why haven't you got it? *You* have
caused me to be misunderstood! Why haven't you developed
it? You have led people to believe the Unfoldment was different than it is because you were not anything like the
Wonder of It.

Perhaps now you will see the importance of study in its
correct perspective. You study to hone the mind and the
intelligence to bring it under the reign of an Ideal. You go
to the root of some of the words in order to perceive that the
words that have been used are symbolic of a Root that has
many layers of meaning. Then you start to perceive on the
Higher Level where no words are necessary how life changes

before your very *eyes/I's*. And yet not one of those I's is upset about it because they are all in agreement with *working*. How? In agreement with the underlying Principle of Oneness. The I's, the multiple I's, are there as facets of the Light. As the sunlight passes through a crystal, a many-faceted crystal, it shows many different hues. But it's only the *one* Light.

Somebody said to me, "Look at the way the diamond is shining on the ceiling as the sun is shining on the diamond." I said, "Yes, it's the evidence the diamond is somewhere. If you know where it is, it's on my finger. But if you don't know where it is, you say, 'Look at the rainbow.'"

Don't you remember what Mary Baker Eddy said about the finger "tracing aloud a bow of promise upon a cloud"?[2] Another said, "Don't mistake the finger that is pointing to the moon." For what?

The whole purpose of Being is to see how you are in no way circumscribed, only by a thought that you are "this," but you witness "I AM That." What you witness is what you are when you cease to draw a circle around "you" and "me" as if we were separate because of circumstance.

The Point IS; the radius can be extended according to the plea of the mass, and out of the past a Voice is calling: "Have you heard? If so, come unto Me and be joyful and be glad, for you see and in That is the universe perceived." And this Jewel called the Earth is once again faceted and given back to the Crown of the One rejoicing in the multi-faceted Nature of the Light.

This is very simple. This is very pointed and I hope you will sit on it! Consider and realize what it means to see, to BE, and to do! There would be no need of any Teaching if it were not reaching fulfillment as a Witness.

---

2. Mary Baker Eddy, *Miscellaneous Writings* (Boston: Trustees Under the Will of Mary Baker G. Eddy, 1934), p. 388, ll. 5-6.

*What is the Witness? The One who
perceives and never denies the Testimony of
Feeling the Being of Presence I AM.*

Thus finishes this Transmission from this Plane, and as we walk in the byways of the Light and through the Skyway of Gems, may you find These have made a Pave´ of Wonder for you to consider as you *set* your Diadem of Wonder and consider placing it upon your Crown.

> Remember — only if you need to.
>
> BE present — it's so simple!
>
> Postpone — it's impoverishment.
>
> BE — and your cup will be full and your
>   saucer will be overflowing to those on
>   the lower level who are waiting to have
>   their thirst quenched by the Wonders of
>   Ever-living Waters.

May these words be heard and found acceptable in the Sight of the One Altogether Lovely. For those who are present and not present, may they be so moved by the Vibratory Frequency of this Kaleidoscope of color that they will be moved beyond the limitations of their personalities. And may they see themselves dressed as such: personalities, only for this Mardi gras of Light!

> It's a moment of Wonder,
>   It's a moment of Joy,
> It's a Moment that we have spent together,
>   All-One.

▼

VIII.

Be the Star

Every thought imbued with Love
is setting the captive free.

Be the Star

I should ask, first of all, are there any questions that any of you people have before I start to launch into an Unfoldment? Yes.

> Michael H.) Sir, I have three, and the first two are just to make sure that I understand what's being discussed here and what we are to accomplish and become aware of.

Yes.

> Michael H.) Is it proper to say that the seat of this experience lies in the intellect and not in the emotions or the feeling faculty of the Soul? And secondly, if it is only felt or perceived in the Soul, what is the proper manner of elevating it to its rightful place? And my third question: Could you please explain humility and how we are to observe it in our practice. I find this a point of mystery, because how do you practice this if you are constantly in the Presence of the Divine?

Well, those are all very interesting questions. Start again with the first one, please.

> Michael H.) Is it proper to say that the seat of this experience lies in the intellect and not in the emotions or the feeling faculty of the Soul?

It begins with the intellect, but only from the standpoint that in what *appears* as this evolution from sense to Soul, men and women are engaged constantly in attempting, in one way or another, to free themselves from the perceptual as well as perpetual horizons of the intellect's limitations, and therefore the body's limitations, and are trying thus to engage the experience of the mind and separate the mind from the body.

When you are thinking of your freedom with the intellect and you are feeling at home in this corporeal temple, you can't help but feel emotion. Why would you destroy it or deny it? Of course, it takes great humility to realize that the Wonder to conceive of something greater than your intellect's approval is the evidence of That Which IS beyond it! The second question?

> Michael H.) You've answered the second one! The third one: Could you explain humility and how we are to observe it in our practice?

The best way to observe humility in your practice is to observe the readiness with which you agree to spiritual commitment and the commitment to the inevitable upheaval which commitment to any spiritual practice causes. Because spiritual practice confronts everything that has to do with the suggestion of a confinement in matter, with the mind pointing — through the Soul, the Feeling of Being I AM — to that Condition that is totally free of the limited suggestions of the body in the time-space continuum.

Humility is forever the garment you wear when you're facing the destruction of the limits that you have allowed to surround you in the belief of service to the One Altogether Lovely. You need not worry about having humility. It's obvious that you have it either you could never have forsaken your robes. You are dying to being a *personal* worshiper and finding there is no mediumship between the Divine and what appears as you. Yes. *Hum* always, whenever you are wondering about humility!

> Doug P.) You told us we must train our minds to reduce confidence in this realm and

thus gain access to our potential. Could you explain that a bit more, please, how we can do this?

The food of the mind is thoughts.

*The way to train the mind in the beginning
is to see that you accept
only those thoughts that are
in keeping with your Divine purpose.*

Then the mind will cease to interfere with those thoughts that you are entertaining that are Divine. You see, the mind doesn't know whether it is entertaining Divine thoughts, hellish thoughts, good thoughts, or bad thoughts!

The whole thing that has constricted all of mankind is the encounter with the environment in which he lives. So many have come into a social encounter with all forms of time that they are constrained by the social encounter and its demands for achieving success on the broad scale of social acceptance. The only acceptance you must find is yourself accepted in the Light of That which is termed the Divine Principle or the Divine Ideal. You can't expect to find yourself accepted in the sight of those who are still trying to create an impression and dominate others in your social environs. You don't have access then to the higher potentialities at all, because *those are closed to egotistical involvement.*

As long as you are egotistically involved with one-upmanship, then you are closed to those higher promptings which would exculpate you from the situation.

Doug P.) Then you've just got to think right.

Think right until rightness appears as your thinking.

Irene S.) Do the *false* beliefs cause disease

throughout our sojourns, which we continually bring back with us?

A diseased condition is really an imbalanced condition. Various people have various ways of describing it; some call it a karmic condition of the body, some call it a karmic condition of the mind. *A diseased condition, when it presents itself, whether it appears of the body or of the mind or of the spirit, is a suggestion that there could be a creation apart from That Which IS, in other words, that there could be two creations! There is only One Creation.* That is how you act as practitioner to the suggestion of *otherness* and the realm of duality where one-upmanship is in vogue today. (It hasn't made the magazine in fashion, because it's what binds the pages in a book!)

Success today is an outward manifestation instead of inner Presence which allows another to perceive his Unlimited Possibilities. You don't make any attempt to be other than what you Are: humility personified in the garment of always intoning or humming a note of praise. You know, there were all the Ten Commandments, and we have added the eleventh:

Make an altar of Earth.

And the twelfth is:

Exalt one another
as I have exalted One to you.

As long as you do that, you are involuntarily blessing everyone upon whom your thought rests.

So many people consider themselves spiritually well as long as they are physically well, and people look upon a physically well person and think he must be leading a fine life. This is not necessarily true. *Whether or not one is ill or healthy, the Truth is the Truth, Love is Love!* You have to find a Love that doesn't die or change.

> *The greatest form of Love is That which will not leave you where it finds you and will not allow you to be other than what you really Are.*

Emerson M.) Is that to say that Love Unconditional is the Ultimate Love?

Unconditional Love could be said to be the Ultimate. An *Unconditional Love* isn't something that starts and stops and is oblivious of error when it appears manifested. *It is what takes care of error by realizing it's nothing and allowing it to return to the source from which it sprung.* Just as five never has an existence as the result of two plus two, knowing as you know that four is considered the correct summation of two plus two, the five *never did* have an existence. It was *thought* to; that's what made it five.

David W.) You mentioned one-upmanship earlier. If we could overcome the ego, one-upmanship would not be a factor?

If you would overcome the ego, you would realize how the ego is the suggestion that there is something to overcome. The ego is the greatest coverup of despair. *The root of all your dis-ease may be the overidentification with ego.*

Emerson M.) Sometimes it's difficult to recognize the ego.

You will recognize the ego when it starts to react to otherness and when it tries to put you in a place of feeling insecure. As soon as you start to feel insecure, that is the ego warning you of its presence. When God is working through you (not really "through" you; that's what people say) then your Presence is contained with the Force that bestows, involuntarily, a Grace that lifts the veil of suggestion with much greater ease.

Perhaps one of the reasons that most people try to engage a spiritual path (as it is termed) is to free themselves from being framed in time, because *the time framework is so corrosive.* It is wonderful to be freed from time! An idea can never be timed; it's only when it's precipitated and thought to be objective that it becomes subject to the variable conditions surrounding the precipitated, manifested state.

All your thinking should move out from the Standpoint of an Ideal, because it allows you to train yourself to perceive that the mind is errant and it will not discriminate in what thoughts it takes. It appears as a discipline at first, to attribute all your thoughts to the Divine Principle or Ideal. Some teachers say you don't need either, but of course you do, otherwise you will start putting "you," "yourself," up as the ideal. There is nothing more fallacious, because *thinking that "you," "yourself" is Real is not an Ideal. You are constantly changing and the Ideal or Principle never does change.* It's untouchable and it has nothing to do with the series!

> *Make sure every thought you think*
> *can be applied to the Divine Principle*
> *or to the Ideal.*

You will start to perceive how little control or how much control you have over your thoughts. Then, as those thoughts are more in keeping with the Brotherhood of Man and the Father-Motherhood of God and the wonders of the mind's ability to manufacture this whole experience, you start to realize what a creative activity the mind is capable of perpetuating. If we do not perceive that the mind is creating this experience, we think we are involved in it with no other alternative than to be currently involved in its time, its signature, and its limitations.

It's wonderful to pretend to be doing what you are doing. Who would ever know what you are doing in Actuality? Who would ever know that you, in your simplicity, are on the verge of recognizing the Sublime? In your simplicity?! My goodness! *Who would ever realize by looking at you that you are the actual Presence of the Living Unconditional Love?*

This is a tremendous threat, because *when Love is Unconditional, it can't allow the acceptance of anything that is unreal, whether it appears in the newspaper, on television, or in statements.* So when you read statements in the newspaper, hear them on the television, see them in books, you have to correct them.

> Breck S.) This Teaching creates such profound movement and disturbance in one's life. It's becoming more clear to me that if I attribute Reality to any of "this," then I begin to get stuck in it and in the whole process of being a mortal searching for excellence. To take that leap of faith into the Divine, adhering to Principle, is sometimes scary. Do we just jump?

Oh, of course you just jump! It's always scary. To suddenly divest your thought of its jurisdiction over your everyday experience and say, "To hell with 'you,' I'm leaping into the Lap of the Infinite!" is quite an experience, because the mind doesn't have a clue what the Infinite is! But you know IT's there, either you wouldn't be prompted to leap.

It was like that when I first started to dive. It was one thing to go in eight feet of water and learn how to use all the equipment, but to go out into the sea and put on all the gear, and sit on the railing of the yacht and then fall off over backwards was quite another thing. I didn't leap; I fell! It is quite an experience because suddenly the whole environment, everything, is different. Everything! The farther you descend, the more you perceive the density of the water and its oil-like nature. At a hundred feet it's as though you are looking through oil and yet it's perfectly clear. Where I dive is very, very clear. You can see for a hundred feet in every direction. The pressures are totally different, but I still live and have my Conscious Identity.

The pressures are tremendous at a hundred feet, at three pressures that I am not accustomed to at all. The pain of entering the various pressures: thirty-three feet, sixty-six, and ninety-nine — whew! — until you learn what to expect and how to take care of it and go on. Then you realize that you are a guest with an incredible number of hosts: hundreds and thousands of fish who are very curious, who say, "Brother, what are you doing down here?!" You can't tease them; you have to respect them.

So when you take a leap, you have to be prepared to assume a new posture, a new pressure. In that upheaval you feel when you commit yourself to a mind excursion through the framework of a spiritual journey into the Unknown, you are really saying, "I am going to take on the upheavals and the chaos and the constant changes which undoubtedly will prevail." If they exist below the surface that can be recognized as water, they can also be experienced in the unrecognized dimensions in the Rarity of Being. Those pressures are termed *the pressures of your Divinity* or the pressures that you meet as you ascend to that Holy Place beyond the need of the mind's approval.

When I descend to perceive the wonders, I never ask for my mind's approval. I tell it nothing. I just Wonder! And that's what I do in order to *ascend*. That's how you come and go at will, so you can appear to be what anyone wants you to be while you remain what you Are. It is so simple; it's not processive.

Order never comes out of chaos.

It is so wonderful to note
that when chaos is present,
you are perceiving it because
Order is the Law of your Being.

That is the trick that very few people ever realize. So when chaos seems to surround you, know that if you perceive it *as* chaos, you have nothing to be concerned about, because God lives as your very Presence in the perception of the lack of rhythm, the lack of harmony, and whatever the lack is that confronts you. It's all a suggestion that there is a creation apart from That Which IS.

So wherever you're working, wherever you BE, you can imagine the Wonders of knowing This, because you're in a world in which the social environment is such that most people are just wrapped up in being the vendors of their success, whereas you are not "vending" anything. You are only *venting* the great Zephyr of Knowingness that comes with the Magnification of what you know to be Real. This is a viable experience because it has meaning.

You see, you are among a very rare minority because you are among those people who are scaling the heights and leaving suggestion. You are looking down, like a bird, upon suggestion.

If you approach your experience from your work position and look *up to* the Star, it's a wise man who doesn't lose Wonder! If you assume the position of being one who looks *up to* the Star, that's all a thought.

Take the other thought:
BE the Star,
and look down upon this!

It's a very different experience! Being the Star at a hundred feet under water and three atmospheric pressures and looking up, you're not fooled by what's up there! Being up there, you certainly can be fooled by what's down there if you haven't been willing to undergo the fall into the Unknown.

So just look out from the Star and then you have a very meaningful experience, because as you look out from the Star, you realize that all that you see is embraced in your one pattern of awareness. Where is your horizon?! It only exists for those who walk on the horizontalized plane with a body and mind and seldom aware of a Soul (other than the one they wear out on their shoes!) Can you imagine the secret ingredient you will add to all your courses! What a seasoning! They will wonder what your herb is!

You know, with all the work that you do, in the prominent positions you hold, *if your ego is involved, you cannot perceive correctly what has to be corrected.*

Lucille F.) That's right.

You have to go right to the facts of the situation and not to what you think or anything else. You would go to the facts as a result of analysis. [To Lucille F.] You can tell them what they must do in the future, whether it's to do with a province or a country, either they would never have you in an advisory capacity to the whole government, in this country or in any other country. She is so capable *not* because she got a wonderful mark in school but because she doesn't limit the capabilities that naturally happen to one who looks out from the Star. That's the true cap and gown ceremony! *What you view is always with Wonder, and what you see may appear to others, who are looking up, to be wise.*

It's a great paradox. Remember, in the dock of time, if you are ever called to witness, you will have to witness according to your Realization. Your Realization, now known even with this one meeting, has to come from *the Standpoint of Principle, not from the standpoint of person.* Because coming via person is coming via the mask: your coverup! Coming from the Standpoint of Principle allows you to stand naked. Your person always involves a medium. It's a mask.

How would you recognize Me if My Voice didn't bear this form for you? Yes. I'm not the least bit concerned about manifesting it for the moment. I'm *using* it. It doesn't bother me in the least, because I AM not in it. "Me" may be and "you" may be.

So don't be surprised if you have any upheavals. Just know that you can never regurgitate Truth, because Truth is never ingested. *Truth is the Power to the system that suggests process but is never in it.*

> David W.) Sir, if we consider and live from the Standpoint of the Star, that should enable us, then, to start to perceive the falsities or the processes that we have built up and accepted.

Yes, it does.

> David W.) An interesting thing happened to me. About a week ago, I was walking from my customer's office to the car and suddenly I just stopped. It was amazing to be able to perceive that I was sort of living in a dream: everyone rushing around doing his job and supporting this dream and not aware.

That's why I call you the minority. You are the living example of what I mean. The living minority. *Very few people realize they are in a dream and very few really want to be awakened, save only to get up in the mornings, to go to work because they have to have the paycheck.* It's not because they really want to wake up. It's because they have to; otherwise, they are not paid for continuing their dream state.

It's wonderful to be in the service of the Action of What IS termed the Light because then you are the priest unto every situation. This is why I have had so many encounters with the priests, of the past as well as the present, because they have always asked. One priest came to me, a practicing priest, and to my utter amazement said that he had lost the ability to empower the Mass and would I show him how to empower the Mass. It was one of the most powerful experiences for him.

I knew nothing about the Mass other than that you can't have an object or a symbol without it bearing meaning. Unless that symbol or object bears meaning for you, there is no empowerment ceremony present, not even with the ability to extend the imagination enough to believe that what is observed in the Mass could possibly be what it is supposed to represent. Of course you can extend it very easily, but it doesn't have any meaning until it becomes an experience. Then the wafer of belief can contain the whole ingredient of the Transcendental and the wafer just held there for you as an offering until "I come." *I come suddenly! I don't know where it says you've got to spend the next twenty-five years becoming Realized, do you?*

> *You have to be very aware.*
> *It would seem difficult to be very aware,*
> *but it isn't when That is the Essence of Life.*

>> Dale R.) As one becomes more aware and living more so in Principle and in Truth, then everything else in comparison becomes more and more an obvious lie?

It seems to be, until you realize that in the lie, in many cases, lies the wonders of the talents and abilities totally unfulfilled, because from the standpoint of a lie they never can be fulfilled. This results in what is called social frustration. That's why you will never be frustrated in Essence, because, moving from the Standpoint of That Which IS and being That and accepting That as your Being, your creativity will naturally burst forth! Most people cannot be fully expressive in their creativity because they are socially conditioned to the restrictions of every culture in which they find themselves. And the cultures are far from being free of infection. Do you wonder why all these strange viruses appear? The virus is the result of duality and the *belief* in it.

As long as there is a belief, there is a believer, and as long as you have a belief and a believer, the time framework is evolving in order to sustain the dream.

> *Man is a Conscious State of Being and has nothing to do with being men and women.*
>
> *Man is a Conscious State of Being, and then you may appear to love. "You" can't help it. It's the Ultimate Condition.*

You can be the great lover of the world while you only love your Self as you truly Are.

> Helen M.) Mr. Mills, as men and women adopt that Standpoint, they are moving in the realm of the new culture where there is no race consciousness, no right or wrong.

That is right. There can appear to be a race consciousness, but it isn't going to be the factor which will influence the intuitive Wisdom as it flows forth for the beneficence of those who have asked for Grace.

No call goes out from the mass that is unheard in the Father's Heart of Love. I'm positive it is heard. I wouldn't be here otherwise, and neither would you.

You know that little old story where they say you have to realize "you're your own grandma and your own grandpa" and "your own this" and "your own that." That's what you realize, too.

> *When I and my Father are One, who is*
> *there to go between the I That IS?*
> *If I is All, where is the "between"?*
> *Only "thought" to be, when realized.*

One of the benedictions in the church is "God be with you, betwixt me and thee while we are absent one from another." God is the only Presence that allows another to recognize another, but the mind diversifies it and classifies it according to its limited education.

I always said as a child, "I have come to do Thy Will, oh God; the Law is written in my heart." I had a terrible time all the time I was growing up, because I was never understood. I questioned priests and I questioned nuns and I questioned ministers. I questioned everyone! They all had answers that bred questions. My answers never breed questions. That's why most people don't enjoy being with me too long, because you start to feel the various pressures, the deeper you dive. The first ten or eleven feet are the most difficult on your hearing.

> Irene S.) Mr. Mills, you have spoken of the mansions of the mind. In the Bible it says, In my Father's house, there are many mansions. Could you clarify that for me, please?

It's the same consideration. In my Father's house there are many mansions; if it were not so, I would have told you.[1] In other words, there is no limitation to the possible extensions of Being found acceptable. The only limitation is put by a man himself who considers, through the framework of the mind, how he can remain to be this counterfeit of time and the Authentic at the same time.

---

1. John 14:2.

The Father's house of many mansions comes to you in whatever form is needed to quell the tempest of suggestion. The Father's house is a contained State of Ideation, exuding the Fragrance of Being and ministering the perfume that will be acceptable to your garment at the moment you need the Scent of Being and its Reality.

Don't allow the framework of your former references to index you in the time sheet of this event. You have changed a tremendous amount in one week. This week I notice it, and it's marked.

Irene S.) I have felt it also.

It's wonderful to be at this point in life and realize you're just starting it!

Angelo A.) Mr. Mills, Jesus said to love your enemy. If Love is the Ultimate Answer for all of us, how can I prove this myself?

Oh, that is easy. It's no hard work at all. You know how much you love, and when you realize that what you perceive is your creation, then what appears, even as the enemy, comes to you for the Love that you bear, to give itself up. *This is how you love your enemy, by perceiving him and gracing him with the Love that is Infinite and not confined to the temporal considerations of a mind endowed with verbology, but with a heart that is overflowing with Love.*

Your concerns for the world and its plight come to you because you have enough of the present Wonder of Newness to allow it to appear new. Remember, what you appear to be going through in war and in conflict is all due to the environment which has prevented the natural creative expression that is cooperating with the Divine Impulse to co-create and be at One with God.

*Every thought imbued with Love
is setting the captive free.*

So, when you love your Self enough — as you do, because your Self is the evidence that God lives in an act of worship, in an act of acknowledgment, and as an act of Grace — then you bear a Scepter of Power that no one sees you carrying. If they did, they would come running to you and personalize it, because they wouldn't realize it was the evidence of the Impersonal appearing personal and garmented as "you." Only those who *have* the Light will see what is walking in your clothes. That's the same with all of us. We wear wonderful disguises!

Many of the "Greats" in the world wear many disguises of ordinariness. Many are in high places but don't dare to reveal themselves, because if they did they might find themselves questioned. They'll meet you privately, though, or they'll meet you secretively. What is of value is usually secretly held and not talked about. *The mass is usually in such a mess that they have no idea of the sacred or the holy.*

*Remember, it's Principle, never person.
Never allow your mind
to define your opportunities!*

The mind defines your limits, your imagination puts them into question, and your *redeemed* imagination allows those that are in keeping with That Which IS to manifest.

It used to be said that in the New Order, in the New Dispensation, the first thing that would have to happen would be the Christened Adam. I've always said, "No, no, no, no, no. Leave poor Adam and his rib out of it!" It is more than that. It has to be the Christened Nathanael, because it is the imagination that has caused all the problems. We have imagined vain things. Vain things! *The redeemed imagination allows the thing to be seen as it really is. You exchange the object for an idea.*

Every time I see the world arise, I know *I* is present. Even when my world doesn't arise, and I seem to go to bed and lie down, I know *I* is present, whether I sleep or don't sleep.

So, that's how you take care of your world. Isn't it incredible to be such a co-creator?! Oh, it's the most exciting thing. It's wonderful when you have the knowledge because it becomes a footstool upon which others can rest until they perceive the Wonder of their own ability to create everything that appears around them.

> *We agreed to be this,*
> *and we agreed to be here, you know.*

> Lucille F.) Is one with the knowledge more of a co-creator than one who's not yet aware of it?

Yes. But knowledge doesn't give you freedom unless freedom has been gowned as knowledge. *Knowledge* then would become the *known* and the *ledge* from which you would leap. You might say you use your faith as your alternative chute to liberation!

I don't take it terribly seriously. I only appear to because you seem to. I'm just being what I AM. I'm afraid the days of being liked or disliked have passed! Otherwise, how could we ever BE? How could we ever have a bird's eye view of more than a maple?

> Joe D.) Mr. Mills, is the redeemed imagination the true union with the Self, the Communion?

The redeemed imagination allows you to see that you are inseparable from IT. The unredeemed imagination would have you trying to analyze how you are *part* of IT. At this very moment, in hearing that, you are altogether One with IT. It's only your mind that will separate you from IT.

Don't assume the responsibility of personally being a support system. *BE* as *I AM* and that will appear as the support.

> Daphne P.) Since we are One, is there any need for prayer?

Prayer only comes for consideration when you are in the state of becoming. Your Presence is a prayer in the Realized State, because the Realized State is a balanced state. Prayer is nothing but the attempt to readjust and be adjusted. That means to be equalized and regain your equilibrium to BE the Father-Mother God, the Creative Principle of all that exists, seen and Unseen, world without end. Amen.

You can see how you'll bless so many.

That is the great Pentecostal Fire, because that is felt by everyone. Even if they don't understand your language, they are changed by hearing your voice. When you are set free, the voice is set free, and the voice carries a frequency that can alter that one listening because you are hearing through a vibratory frequency. Thus the vibratory frequency appears *to attune your nature to the Harmonics of Being.* Remember that the Words used that are attributable to the Divine are of the Frequency that will attune the strings of your so-called "symbolic heart" to the sounding board of your Beingness so that you will start to evidence the volume and the magnitude of Being to those who would *wonder* what Sound Being IS.

In other words, you are a Song! That's why I always sign my letters, "Man is a Song." You are an instrument being pitched by tightening the strings. Then you can use the Bow of Promise upon your strings and evidence aloud the Wonders of God Being Love manifested. *Confidence rests in Being untimed.*

> Daphne P.) Sir, there was something I wanted to share with you. On Sunday you mentioned

that Love is like a sunbeam. I've never seen a sunbeam, but this morning, driving to work, a sunbeam came into my car. I could actually see the dancing of the beam in the car. I can't even explain the feeling that came about and I heard a voice saying, "You are in the Light. Stay in the Light and act in a manner that others will see that you're in the Light." The voice was sort of in my heart. I just wanted to share it.

Well, the sunbeam is always that portion which reaches you through the pane/pain of suggestion, of divisibility, and Man is not divided. It's his mind and his thoughts that separate him from the Creative Source, the Creative Principle.

So,

> As the sunbeam dances upon your
>   windowsill and you grace it with
>   attention in time,
> It appears to caress you gently as it erases
>   the cobwebs of your mind.
> It causes every beat of the heart beating with
>   expectancy to dare
> To leap within the Chest of Promise, and
>   close all suggestions of despair.
>
> You move with a sense of Wonder as you
>   traverse the realm of time,
> Bearing the dancing beam of Glory as the
>   sunbeam casts your mind
> Into a state of receiving — the Wonder to
>   behold
> The dancing of a sunbeam upon your
>   threshold!

There in the Foyer of Being, you were
    ushered to that place
Where you could see in the smiling sunbeam
    that a Bow of Promise had thus been
    traced.
For *I* will not leave you comfortless! You
    will always have a sign,
And the Bow of Sunbeam can be a Bow of
    Promise, as a rainbow beyond the pain
    of mind.

       Daphne P.) Thank you!

Did you like that?

       Cordell W.) I'm trying to understand most
       of it.

Don't try. You just love.

*Don't try too hard. You'll have a trying time if you do.
When you try too hard you always have a trying time.* All
we want is a trysting time! Do you know what that means?

       Cordell W.) No, Sir.

A trysting time is when you are making up with Love
so that you can be joined forever and nothing on Earth can
ever break the bond of that Holy Wedded State.

Look it up! It's a wonderful time. It seldom exists
today, for it could be called the wrestling state of spasmodic
interests, periodically endeavored according to the waxing
and waning of a planetary influence!

       Cordell W.) I always grew up thinking that
       there are right things and there are wrong
       things. But hearing you talk tonight, I got the

idea that "you are what you are" and there is no right or wrong about that.

You are what you are! That is right, and that is neither right nor wrong. Where your "right or wrong" enters is when you are what you are and you are faced with a choice.

As soon as you have a choice,
which will you choose?
That which is passing or
That Which IS Eternal?

When you choose That Which IS Eternal, then the right or wrong is seen to be concerned only with the passing. Your Rightness will alleviate the suggestion that rightness or wrongness has a place in your validation of Life and ITs living.

Even if you don't understand it, I've told you and you've heard it. It's so good when you don't understand, in a way, because one of the greatest myths of our education is that you have to understand before you can accept anything.

Understanding is the result of experiencing
what you have accepted. When you have
experienced what you have accepted, then
you can offer your experience and that is
termed your understanding.

So, any child who says, "I don't understand," it doesn't make a particle of difference. Accept it! You'll know whether it's right. All you have to do is *live* it and find out! After all, I can only say what I have experienced; I never prepare a speech. I never prepare a Dictation because I always feel that the words of my mouth and the meditations of my heart shall be acceptable in the Light of all who are Altogether Lovely as I AM.

You hear the Unfoldment and you feel that I speak, and yet I have never broken the Silence.

You know, the Creative Force could never have made a mistake in the creation. The only mistake could have been in how *we* conceive it, so perhaps *we should have a different type of conception: one that is unconfined by hypotheses and further bastardization by suggestions.* This is why it is said that in the New Dispensation the Masters of the Age will be born from a different type of womb: It's termed the larynx or voice box.

> *The Great Creative Sound allows you to perceive how you can be reborn instantaneously with the acceptance of your Right Identity.*
>
> *You know you didn't create yourself.*

You know, your mother and your father had to tell you:

> "Cordell, I cordially greet you and call you
>   my son,
> To raise you on this planet and hope you
>   will never be an errant one,
> But hoping the days will come and go
> As you gain your wings and fly."
> So, here you land in my nest and we take
>   a peek
> Into what you shall see and what you
>   shall BE.

When you are to be born again into a Higher Realization, there is no time for you to go through the womb of belief and be educated for eighteen or nineteen years and then come out still wondering who you are! *What we have to do now is be birthed through the voice box or the Voice that can sound the Pitch that is in agreement with the Essence of Being so that man will recognize the Pitch as being unalterable in his Soul.*

Now, *Soul* doesn't mean a thing to most people. It's a synonym of God, and when it does mean something to you, it will be defined in a way that will undoubtedly be fragranced in Feeling. That Feeling that you start to feel when you identify yourself correctly as "I and my Father are One Now, and not 'shall be,'" gives you the moment to be born freed from the cacophony of the mind and its faulty thought-patterns.

I and my Father are One Now and not "shall be." That's the great value of having had a Jesus. It was one of His greatest Teachings, and who believes it? Everyone thinks he *will be* (in the future.) I and my Father are One **Now**!

Totally new Standpoint! You see what I'm saying?

Cordell W.) Yes.

That's why all these people are defying the sense of age, because the New Age is when they shall be born again. *You are born again the moment you realize the Divine is All there IS to you.* That is the moment that you minister unto the people involuntarily, not from the standpoint of the social restrictions of one-upmanship that you know something that they don't know. In your Light, they only appear as a part of your own expression. The ones that would shoot you are just those thoughts that would originally have put you down and left you a non-accomplisher, a frustrated expressionist, a frustrated creative artist. As long as you remain in that social structure, it is so structured that you are bound in the realm of belief, but a belief and a believer can easily be unbound because you can't bind an Idea other than to its Source. *Man is Divine Idea. Men and women are the perverted or counterfeit because they change and the Divine Idea is Changeless.*

So hitch your wagon to That which never changes and allow your wheels to go around and burn like those of Ezekiel. Then you will have the meaning of the Wonder of the Invisible present as Fire!

The Fire is that purifying agent which
redeems the garment of suggestion
and allows it to remain a vehicle
prophesied and fulfilled.

Isn't it exciting to be new?
Do your clothes still fit you?
You'll undoubtedly change!

▼

IX.

The Seal of Approval

At this point in your incarnation
you are to choose whom ye will serve:
the passing or the Eternal.

THE SEAL OF APPROVAL

This afternoon we find ourselves in this green room in the Light of the Rose and the Ray[1] that has such promise for the Age, which has deemed to be named, deemed to be acclaimed "the Promise fulfilling the prophecies of the past." Into the books of time has It come, through the mind has It streamed, ever waiting to be accepted in the folds of the heart. For you who are present are witnessing as never before to the birth of a New Age. *You are witnessing the birth pains of being born as a worldling through the mentality.* You are witnessing through the Consciousness the mentality and world being reborn; and through the Light, the consciousness (mentality) is being freed from the shadow,[2] which dances in front of itself[3] and precludes the great Sun of Glory from being witnessed as a living experience. *For you are found, and you are known, and you are called out of the forests of time and once again are empowered to walk this plane, offering unto those whom you meet, unto those whom you seek, and unto those who suddenly come into the temple of your presence, what it means to be in the Presence of a living God Power.*

We are moving through the rip tides of the suggestion that you are mortal and that you must put off your mortality and gain immortality. *You are witnessing, as never before, to the attempts of bringing incompatibles together and creating a union and expecting it to be lasting.[4] It is an impossible situation! It is impossible to join together what God never intended to be joined together, because He in Himself is Altogether Lovely.* And as the Son, the evidence of the Creative Might, how could you be other

---

This Lecture is available on cassette, Sun-Scape Publications ISBN # 0-919842-03-8

1. The Uranian power.

2. Objectification.

3. The shadow, or objective level of consciousness, mesmerizes itself by its own "dance" (activity).

4. Incompatibles: Spirit and matter, matter and mind, subjectivity and objectivity, all trying to be united from an incorrect standpoint.

than altogether lovely, altogether satisfied, in the image and likeness of That Glory which has been offered through the pages of time by those who have testified to His living Presence in the name of all those who have leaped beyond a saint or a sage; and into the Lap of Deity they have walked, garmented in the garments of unpretentiousness, and have carried unto the threshold of the minds of the manger *the possibilities of a life freed from the encrustations of belief and given once again back to the wave of the great Stream of Everlasting to Everlasting, where Love is only known and only appears as the Crest of a wave upon the shore of time, and never buffeted by the riptides of suggestion and circumstance. What is a log to a wave on the Sea of Light?*

We are being treated this afternoon to an Experience which comes, as we say, occasionally, because so seldom are those in the Presence ever attuned to witness unto and to partake of an Experience which can be of no meaning whatsoever to the rationale of the mind or to the reasonings of the mind, but which when found and heard is forever bombarding and knocking at the door of the great power, of the great storehouse, and the great treasure-trove of your accomplishment as you have walked over the byways of time and through the picture books of the mind.

> *You who have come together are here*
> *for a Soul Purpose, and that Soul is to*
> *once again be attuned to the Pitch*
> *of universal significance.*

That Pitch of universal significance is the one in which all men may once again find themselves according to their wish to partake of a Symphony so that those who may be accompanied in their elocution and in their dissertations may once again give a *gain*, and in that gain, find the possibilities of what it is to never take a chance, but find that there is no lottery where a ball shall be rolled, a card shall be tossed, or a cube thrown into the air with the hopes of winning. You will never win the race of life by being in a relay race; only in the race that is in rhythm with the Footsteps of the Almighty as they leave no footsteps upon the sand shall you be given the Torch which shall bear the Light from generation unto generation, as long as there is a horizontalization of the Plan.

To be stranded on this plane where there is no change[5] is what is termed the dire experience of living as a human. The human has been so programmed as to feel that every moment has to be outlined. And as you know, it is impossible to outline your moments; the outline is only in your appearance as an action is fulfilled in the restful state of the tranquility surrounding the Center of Life, Light, Consciousness. You who have partaken of this experience know that as the bell rings and men and women are finding that they are attuned to the frequency of its pitch, *you are finding as never before that the time is ripe and the tree has blossomed, and now is the time to change!*

The reason we are talking about change is because it goes with being what you are not. *It is impossible to change what you really Are!* That is why there are rip tides, because you are trying to be what you aren't in an effort to be what you are! And that is how a new year is born, because if you will notice, symbolically the "year" begins with the "roads."[6]

Men and women have come from the Root (the hidden resources of Being), the tree and the branches (the "Y" in the road).[7] *And at this point in your incarnation you are to choose whom ye will serve: the passing or the Eternal.* That is how a new year is born, because in the new year, unless

---

5. From the dualistic standpoint of the Earth plane, there seems to be no change from, or alternative to, being human.

6. Reference is made to the letter "Y", which appears as a fork in the road and which represents duality.

7. Men and women really have their source in the Divine, but to all appearances have come from the stock of time — the tree and its branches, which appears like the "Y" in the road, the year (time), choice, etc. The "Y" also suggests man's most basic existential question: *"Why?"*

you have heard beyond the hearing of the ear and the seeing of the eyes, *you know not of what God has in store for those that love Him and find Him a living, pulsating Reality as the very Consciousness that is the Light to the mental state which enables one to indite a good message.*

A new year is the belief that an old one has passed, and it is only a suffering for those who are believers to believe so. You are not trapped unwillingly in the groove of being a "hep cat" in a rough time; you are capable of leaping beyond the high cuttings and the low cuttings you have utilized in time;[8] you can leap because *you can think beyond the limits of your own contriving.* Every limit that you have contrived is because you contrived it; every year that you have found a limit is because you have taken the wrong turn when you made the choice.[9] *Every time that you have a choice to make it is because you have not surrendered to the power and the Love of the Self. There is no wrong choice known in the Light of Sonship.*

The suggestions that you suffer or that you enjoy or that you accomplish or that you do not accomplish are not to be considered right or wrong, good or bad, provided you made the choice with no choice, provided you did what you had to do because of the almighty endeavor to stabilize on the Foundation upon which you wish to build a Life and a Temple of the living God for those who would worship through mediumship.[10]

You appear an Earthian, and this is right and good; it is so much fun to have it![11] But it was never meant to be thought something it is not, any more than your body was meant to be an obstruction to the Light by having a false identity in the name of a "you" and a "year." You will note

---

8. That is, whatever level of accomplishment one attains or settles for in life.

9. The seeming choice between being human or divine.

10. Provided your actions and endeavors are not purely personal and selfish, but aimed toward the benefit and emancipation of those who are caught in a mediumistic worship of God.

11. That is, Earth.

that the line traced has the same condition with you and a year — each begins with "Y" and this is the reason it is imperative to adopt *without*,[12] thinking beyond your nose! If you stay at the periphery of your embodiment,[13] you cannot go too far afield in finding excuses for being what you aren't. If you are going to practice being God, you will have to alter not only your breathing (which you have to alter in yoga if you are doing a meditation exercise), but you will have to alter the "Whole" concepts if you will be mindful of your lineage and heritage.[14] *And your heritage is this, that the God within is not without identity.*

You have all escaped the years allotted to your expression because you have not surrendered to the God within, which must have identity. You have created a counterfeit eternality of the God within by taking the O of the Omnipotent and giving it to the mind to structure in the likes of "you"! *And that which has seemed so real to all of us is now seen in the clarity of the Light to be nothing but an attempt to deceive the Elect in the name of an ego in the face of the Light.* The reason the ego has so much a semblance of reality is because what is standing in the way of the Light creates a shadow which seems to go in and out with "you."

> No matter just where you trace it,
>   you will find
> That it is always around you, too,
>   and you will find
> That you are forever searching to find
>   a place to get rid of this constant
>   shadow in your time.
> And the only way you can ever get rid of it
>   is when the Sun seems not to shine!

---

12. "Without" refers to one's outer, worldly activities.

13. "Periphery of your embodiment" refers to the practice of watching your body objectively.

14. One has to alter or drop what one thinks Unity or the "Whole" is before it can be experienced.

The only time people really feel disquieted with "you" or with "me" is when the Sun shines; then they are aware of their shadowlike nature. And that shadowlike nature tries to get you to dance, as if you could dance your way out of limits! You can't. You can only *sing* people out of limits when "you" cease to be a singer and find Song experience.

The Authentic Nature is such that it permits you to have what you need to have, but it also is the way to be rid of what isn't rightfully yours. As long as you persist in claiming "you" and "yours," you will have "you" and "yours" to sustain. As long as you feel the burden of having to sustain, you know that God has been forgotten and you have attempted to take the throne, you have tried to take the place of the Creative Might. You find life then a burden — scheduled, regimented, and boring. But when you find that the Little Books[15] which have been closed (which were the housing of prophecies and promises) have been opened, *these Little Books suddenly take on meaning when they are freed from "you" trying to interpret the Word through a mind that has refused to be one with the Authentic Nature, which is likened unto one having, as a gift, the Mind of God.*

Since this is the season of gift giving and gift receiving (and it is so much fun), it might be well to consider what the Authentic Nature, garmented sometimes as Santa Claus, has given you, not wrapped up in your stocking, but given you so that you could fill a suit for those who do not know the Fire! If Santa Claus is a counterfeit, you know very well the reason he is a counterfeit is because he may laugh and shake like a bowl full of jelly, but when he is really warm he can take off his clothes, take out his pillows, and take off his beard, and all you have is the great image of generosity and tenderness and a hearing ability unwrapped, and in the appearance, just like you! It is so sad when you realize that Santa Claus has been made up, for you have cried out over

---

15. The Books of the Bible, or other Esoteric Literature.

your years for some presence, anything that can appear to come from someone other than your own.

Now, if you are so the recipients of fine gifts, do you not stop to consider what must be the Gift from God to His Son? Now, I know you can say, "Well, I have been taught through the open books of school that I am the Son of God," if your schools have permitted religious teaching. If they haven't, you belong to Mr. and Mrs. Arbuckle or No-buckle or Yes-buckle or Would-buckle-if-could-buckle, or Mr. and Mrs. Why-buckle. "Why-knuckle . . down, if we are agnostic and atheists? Why bother to knuckle down or kneel down to the Wonder of the Unknown?" *You can never approach the great Gift that is yours if you do not approach it by realizing you don't know the answer to your presence.* You do not know the answer to your presence, because anyone who tells you the answer to your presence has been told the answer, which is usually incomplete and inaccurate, because no dreamer can ever testify to the Truth of a dream, for the dream has no Truth to it; it is dreamed and dreamt, supported by a dreamer. So, don't think any nice Dr. Question or Dr. Fiddlesticks-in-answer can ever tell you how you came, because when he slept, he did not know you were around,[16] and when you came he only knew a bill could be found, with the hopes of dollars!

> *You can only approach the great*
> *Gift of God, or the Creative Principle,*
> *or the Creative Urge, from the standpoint*
> *of attuning yourself to the demands*
> *of this mighty Creative Principle.*

You say, "Oh, how can I attune myself to the likes of a Creative Principle?" So simple: *Write down on a piece of paper everything about you that is not fixed, everything about you that is mortal. Everything that is on the paper is*

---

16. The sleeping-waking consciousness cannot perceive beyond itself.

"you" and everything that isn't is the Creative Principle!
And you think you have an alternative?! You do not know
the great Seal of Approval — or have you forgotten it?
"This is my beloved Son in whom I am well pleased." How
convenient to say, "I don't bother with that taffy, because
Jesus was supposed to have said it and I'm a Jew," or "I'm
a Hindu," or "I'm a Buddhist, " or "I'm a Moslem," or
"I'm a hypocrite," or "I'm a Judas," or "I'm a Peter," or
all the other names you have given to things in order to have
company.

You were never meant to be "this" but That (what is
left over when you can no longer outline what you think
about yourself, your world, your universe, and your creation). It is so simple: Have you ever looked at the wonder
of pushing a pencil on a piece of paper and seeing salt,
water, chalk, protoplasm, or slime trace something intelli-
gible? What a miracle! But it is nothing to blow about,
because monkeys can now use computers, and they know
which buttons to push to get a banana! I do not know why
you have rejoiced so much!

In the beginning of this Age which is dawning (which
has dawned but is just securing itself), I do not understand
why you get so bloated up over so little. If God said (and if
you don't like the word "God," say X said, or Y said),

> *I AM All, but as long as you look* up *to Me*
> *you have two paths; but if you look down*
> *from Me, My Roots go into the ground*
> *and I walk with no question as to*
> *My Royalty of Being.*

What equipoise of thought force is demanded! *What*
graciousness of bearing is claimed and called forth if you are
the living emissary of a living God and claimed His Son.
This *XY* force equals *"you"* minus the limits of mentality.
You have to square all your dealings, because why? Because

you have failed to muster your resources; you have only taken your accomplishments, personalized them, and this is not enough to energize your actions in such a way that they carry a transforming and transfiguring power. The C *squared*[17] is the Christ Power beyond and in the appearance, and the matter is only the result of belief when truth tries to mingle with error. *Error in premise is error in conclusion.*

This is my beloved Self in whom I am well pleased is the Seal of Approval, and it is your gift to walk forth not as missionaries trying to bring to others some good ideas about hopeless situations. You are an *advocate* because you speak of the kingdom of your own accomplishment, regardless of the size or the acreage you have cultivated. You speak from your own God's little green acre! *This will help stabilize and bring forth, into the cognition of those you meet, the possibilities of finding the world given back to the Arms of Love and the embrace such an accomplishment when the All-Christ-Eternal is found embellishing the banner-like thoughts of men who know the power I AM.*

The God that has been worshiped as the God of Isaac, of Jacob, and Abraham is fine and dandy if you want to keep the books open to the past in an endeavor to prevent the future Man.

> *But I tell you now that the God worshiped as something beyond men, even of those ancient days, was offered up in the name of men, because they could not conceive of what it would be like to be the Son of God walking, clad in the human garment, and yet carrying the Power to translate before your very eyes all the limits and the sore distresses of the sole/Soul that is calloused from walking in the asphalt jungles of belief and yet attempting to pave the Highway of our God as if all men and*

---

17. "C *squared*" represents the Christ embracing body, mind, Soul, and act.

> *women could walk it as an avenue of*
> *freedom, when you do not know what it is*
> *to be a material master of limits and thus*
> *succeed in leaping beyond them and*
> *finding yourself the custodian of Power*
> *that can rescind all limits when those who*
> *carry them are willing to surrender to the*
> *power of Love as God.*

The reason God has been worshiped is because you have worshiped "you" so much. Love you cannot find, because you can write about IT. The *I* you cannot find, because you can only write about IT. But as soon as you have come to the end of your script, you will realize that there was more God behind the last dot of the last paragraph than there was at the moment when you looked at a piece of paper and wondered what to put down on it to fill it up. The last dot on the page said, "This is what happens to a sentence if you don't know 'I AM the Light to it.'"

The dot on a piece of paper as a part of your history is like you on the picture book of the mind, or, let us say, is like you walking on tape through the projection booths of time and letting other people see your image and you going to see other people's image so that you may identify and revel in the identification! But you forget that what you have reveled in, what you have empathized with, has passed upon a *screen* which is completely unaffected by it. And this is how you must be as Conscious Being.

> Let the pictures of the world, of you and
>   they that dwell therein,
> Pass on your screen of awareness.
> Do as you would have done;
> Be as you would be; do as you would bow;
> Do as you would bend; do as you can when
>   you meet a "could";
> Do as you will as *I* will when you meet a
>   "would";

> And Be the Power when you would meet an
> answer,
> And Be the Answer to one in power who
> would question, *why?*

You are present, for you have walked knowing not "why" or "how" or "why should I be there with this man"; you know that it is not "why" or "how" or "can" or "could" or "would." You know very well, if you are not here after having been here that you are never quite as at ease with your "bag."[18] Because why? Because *the mind, being so much like a garbage collector, will take anything it is given, but it never expects to take anything too big for it!* And when you get *this* Message, you have got such a big thing in it that it cannot do anything but blow the top right off your censorship!

> Oh, you think you are wonderful; I know
> you are.
> You think you are grand? It's the Plan;
> You think you know what a year comes to
> mean
> In the Light of the Love of the Plan?
> I tell you now, in the twinkling of an eye,
> That all shall be made to stand still,
> For when God knows what you should wear
> as His Son, why,
> It's all dressed up as Will!

The Age of Aquarius is such a gigantic might, and when it is well stabilized in the years that lie ahead, some of you will be able to have those coming after you to say, *"Well, somewhere it is written that someone said that we were to help stabilize the great power of this Age of Love and Freedom and unheard-of accomplishments."* It is true, as I have told you so many times, but there are so few of you

---

18. The body-mind.

who have been with me from the beginning. The great Ray of Aquarius, one of the great Rays of the Awakener, is the Ray that is likened unto the Uranian power (for those who are trapped in astrology).

The great Uranian power is a living force of change; and that living force of change is such that it does away with anything that obstructs your opportunities or your growth or your accomplishment when you have once surrendered to the Awakener. **You cannot go back to positions outgrown;** *you cannot live in peace with what you know is only part of the story.*

The great promise of Christmas, we are told, is hope. I feel the great promise of Christmas rests in its ability to be present beyond time and thus appear every moment! We should always be giving gifts to one another; we should always be sharing gifts with one another. And the healing that takes place would affect the nations objectively, for the Subjective State is One Altogether Lovely, wrapped in God's Promise if you are a custodian of a Little Book; in Light's Benediction if you are mystically inclined; clad in the Eucharist if you are a mystic and a saint hoping for mystical experiences.

But as all who know the Wonder of Promise as act, you will see as never before that the Seal of Approval marked you as "Realized," and gave you, as the result, a world once again back to the Arms of Love.

You have a great gift; you have a great promise! And the future planning has you the builders of a nation, has you the custodians of its wealth and you the great advocates of a Missal of such Light that the only Sound that is heard is that of a Song, when the head and the heart are wrapped in the rhythm given to praise!

My wishes to you are for a future not postponed but for the Nowness accepted; and in this rejoice, for I AM the same yesterday, today, and tomorrow. The Gift of the Ages lives in the humility of the mind that can accept the Totality of Being without concern about the ribbons attached as acts in the sustaining of the kingdoms of this world in the name of the Self or the Christ or God's Beloved Offering. In this be satisfied (to all appearances), in this be glorified (to those who can see), and *in this be prepared, for God knoweth a willing servant and is the Power to the nib of a pen and the Light to a tongue that can appear to give forth a soliloquy of Self rejoicing in Self, just for the sheer delight!*

The Divine Light is so sheer. Walk through it and find how IT rests on your brow as a Child!

▼

X.

The Need of Change

Unless you are surrounded by the True Identity, there is no identification of where the opening is to the next dimension.

THE NEED OF CHANGE

I am sitting in a chair overlooking the sea and its incredible turquoise color, and the wind is softly caressing the palms. I wish you could hear the waves as they gently touch the shore. The wind has died considerably so that the reef is not outlined today; it is hidden, as all reefs are, and it is only when there is turbulence that it reveals itself.

So it is that as we journey in this Expedition in the Considerations that far transcend the confines of this form and its formations, we take what is obvious and translate it into that which can be of significance when a symbol bears a meaning, a symptom releases its might, and a sign has pointed to man's fulfillment and the completion of his task when the sign is perceived as it is and the symbol is known to be at the root of a symptom. When one would solve a problem, look at your symbol, look at your symptom, and then see how you are led from the externalized concept of "this" to the unlimited solution as That.

As we penetrate the sphere of many considerations, each one always points to the great need to free oneself from the suggested might of material bondage and its appendages. We know that that which is created and is before us (in every sense of the word) is there on all levels of *meaning*. No meaning can have a Life Meaning if it is thought that God, the Great Mystery, took Himself and put Himself into matter and thus *clogged* the very vessel of His evidence! As long as God remains a Mystery, we have hope. When we think through the framework of an unenlightened, educated premise that God is dead, then we start to enter that realm where matter cares for matter and the possibilities of man's freedom are relevant to his *instinctual* nature.

As we penetrate these considerations, we should realize that every time you have a perception, the perceiver is changed; every time you have a realization, the realizer is more authentic. It is in this area that work is demanded, because it is in this area that each and every day and each and every moment you are a *changed perceiver* and a *changed realizer*, because you have perception and revelation moving into the unfettered Realm that is beyond your limitations.

You cannot think unlimitedly and be a limited thinker!

This is why it is so important *to move radically* from the Standpoint of what is engaged as your life experience and try not to remain bounded by the effects of your activity but to look at the activities as the bounded effects to be opened and read, pointing to your Unlimited Nature only seeming to be bound, as the pages of old have told you that you could be *un*bound.

There would be no point of a Star to take your attention in the Celestial Kingdom, any more than a star to take your attention in the terrestrial realm, on the terrestrial stage, if it were not for a purpose of *prompting*. The Divine Prompter is ever at hand, and the need to listen is evident! You listen when you perceive that *instinctively* you have an urge to do something. That is listening to your instinct, hearing your instinct. Remember, your instinct is there, repressed frequently, and it is **pointing** to a non-discovered area of significance, that of the symbol.

The symbol will often impose its unrecognized self upon the instinct and can often appear as confusion, confinement, and resentment, and bound by you know not what. This is the need self-evident to *solution*.

> *No problem can be solved from within*
> *the problem.*

This is why when men and women are open to perceiving the need of solution, they are willing to be open to perceive a new perception of the situation.

When the experience of this world gives you a moment in the Presence of an Archetype, then you are in the presence of a Pattern or a Mold or a Stamp that has existed for so long that you *find the Living Presence of the Archetype the very Force that demands the solution of a suggested problem.* It is the Living Archetype that causes the ego to question whether or not it is living life abundantly. Usually the identification with ego is so strong that it appears as the incarceration of the individual or the personality to such a degree that the person cannot see the forest for the trees.

We become so involved in our activity that we forget how the activity is expressing the Creative Might of Source. Now, this Creative Might of Source has the direct route and has the direct linkage to the *Soul Factor.* The *Soul Factor,* as has often been said, is a *constructed* consideration for men and women. It is so because the Soul Factor is one that goes hand in hand with the *Intuitive* Might. The Intuition is the evidence of the Soul, and the Soul is the evidence that Intuition has the fortifications of an unlimited Range of Force.

If men and women would see that **Soul is not only the** ***Feeling of Being I AM*** **but is the Creative Might which allows Being to have an identity as I AM,** the Might of Omnipotence is not only **felt** as the Force to change, It is also *experienced* as the *Creativity* that is unlimited. It has not been constrained by the force of the sentient nature when it has been willing to be open to a New Concept so that the *perception* may be once again experienced and thus the perceiver **elevated** to another level of experience.

If you move from one level to another level, you cannot carry the old level with you without it being touched by the new experience. The tendency of today is to make the new experience less than it really is, because to change much would cause others, and even yourself, to be surprised at *you!* And to have to live with the changed "you" would give you, perhaps, a considerable consideration of *Moment.*

If you would *consider the need of change,* then do so from the standpoint that you are being guided by instinct to understand your symptom of, say, displeasure, unhappiness, confusion, resentment, frustration; these are all pointing to the archetypal symbols that are waiting to be translated.

The need of the Light Walker of today is to be able to move *with confidence* onto the band of rhythmical intent *with dynamic force.*

You who have had so much Teaching, be panoplied in the achieved Knowing. Cease aligning yourselves to thought patterns that are malignant. Cease from using words that you know cannot be found acceptable in the Light of your Mystery, God, or — more tangible — Principle, Truth, Love, Mind, Soul, Spirit!

Realize that an idea, however radical, has no way of being severed from its Essence unless you do the cutting, deliberately. Because no idea can spring into cognition and not have Essence present as its force.

If you would entertain what it is to be devoted to the Divine Self in the garment of Unfoldment, then you must realize that Unfoldment **seems** to express process, and this is only the name given to a continuing experience. But remember, the seed in the palm of the hand, if held and photographed with a radionic camera, can reveal **not** the seed but the full-grown flower. So it is that Unfoldment allows each petal to unfold, but you have to move *from* the Seed Pattern that is Light and Light indelibly expressed within the escutcheons of your sense of Beingness and Individuality.

There is, of course, such a play on the stage today to hold your attention: low positions, high positions; low taxes, high taxes; no money, lots of money. All of these are conditions that are there to be seen as a *sign,* a *symptom,* of the age in which you live. It doesn't mean that it is *your* symptom of disease, of disquiet, of dissatisfaction; it **may** mean it is the Archetype trying to have you recognize Its Pattern for *you,* in the Light of That, to be transformed and transfigured.

If there were no Archetype, there would be no pattern for this design. And if the Archetype were not acknowledged, the pattern would have no basis for having any sense of value.

> *What is the point of a world in which no Mystery exists? What is the point of living in a form which has no hope of other than the grave?*

If God is dead, your Mystery is dead and so are *you*. Mrs. Eddy said, "The divine attraction is Love,"[1] and this Love is the very Force that can be felt *instinctively*, but it doesn't need to seduce you into thinking that your instinct, when satisfied, is the evidence of a symbol experienced. A symbol doesn't bear relevance to just a "you"; a symbol is usually from an archetypal situation, such as Daedalus and Icarus,[2] which are of the same vintage.

All the symbols that have come down through the ages are pointing to all of us to *cease being concerned* about our frustration and our attempt to solve our problems on our own. You never can do it, because all problems that are seemingly deep ones are *due* to the unknowing or the unwillingness or the lack of opportunity to *know* Someone who can allow the distressed one to understand what the symbol may be trying to express, and it appears as the activity. That is how you know a symbol exists, because of the way you are driven to *experience* it, in an **unconscious** way. When you *know* the symbol, it becomes conscious and you are relieved of your distress. When it is unconscious, it is because you haven't looked at the *pattern* that is behind the symbol, which is way, way back in the beginning when men formulated this form and said it could be so. It wasn't into a clod

---

1. Mary Baker Eddy, *Science and Health With Key to the Scriptures* (Boston: Trustees Under the Will of Mary Baker G. Eddy, 1934), p. 293, l. 15.

2. In Greek mythology, Daedalus was an Athenian architect and inventor who devised the Cretan Labyrinth in which he was later imprisoned with his son, Icarus, and from which they escaped by using artificial wings. Funk & Wagnall's *Standard College Dictionary* (Toronto: Fitzhenry & Whiteside, 1980).

of earth that God breathed Spirit; it was the *excuse* that men used who were not Enlightened and revealed it so.

The mesmerism of the suggestion is frequently so great that we are inclined to try to solve a problem by using our instinct and our intellect instead of perceiving the need of going *beyond.* Seeing the instinct and its distress as the *symptom,* there is the need of understanding in a greater context the symbology, or *part* of the symbology, you are experiencing due to your activities, due to your allegiance (or lack of allegiance) to the issues that are commensurate with Being.

Unfortunately, *you* have so little leeway!

The work of this Happening is such that it demands *surrender* and *obedience,* which have always been sadly lacking.

The Unfettered State of Being is nonrational! If IT were rational, IT would only *ration* you a certain portion of Divine Food! That's why you were comforted in the Old Testament by the idea that you'd get your portion daily from the King. But that was the *process* again, manifested in so many ways, in prophecy and many experiences.

Now you see that we are *beyond* the situation of prophecy; it is fulfilled in the Now, because *Prophecy is only a garment that hope wears.* When your hope has been fulfilled, so has the prophecy.

When you have found the Diamond, then you know your hope has been fulfilled! In other words, you don't have to *have* the Hope diamond, but you can certainly realize that the Diamond evidences the fulfillment of hope, the end of prophecy, and the *Nowness* and the *Immediacy* of the Divine Self in realized action, activity, and creative might!

> *If you are going to do your Work,*
> *do it from the Standpoint*
> *of using only those words*

> *that are in agreement with your Ideal.*
> *Do not use words*
> *that can become malignant.*

Do not think that agreeing with error is not serious! It is most serious! Words that are in agreement with error become words that support error.

When metaphysical work is done to be rid of error, you are really working the wrong way; you are *working over something that in Reality **doesn't exist**! You don't work to get rid of the five as the result of two plus two; it **doesn't exist!***

Your tendency is to work over the error, instead of looking to the error as a *means only* of doing the Work that is natural.

> *The Natural Work is to see error as nothing.*
> *Why do work over it?*
> *BE the Somethingness that eradicates*
> *the suggestion that error has an existence,*
> *and the Work is done!*

It doesn't take a minute; it doesn't take a second! That's why instantaneous healing is a *must* because it's done in the Realm of *Mind*, whether or not it appears physically! So many people consider Truth to be effective when it can be proved physically. But remember this: **There are Truths that are not capable of being substantiated by material thinking and its description!**

That is what is called "a Psychic Truth," "a Psychic Event." All of Real Living is *beyond* the events that can be described, and that's why They are termed "irrational," because you *cannot* describe what is happening. It sounds as though it's been ordered, but it hasn't been ordered; these words are streaming forth without the ordering, other than the Knowing of the Intent and Purpose of the Soul of This

One appearing to manifest it, to give unto those who would ask to hear what would be the necessary Food for the Satisfaction that is commensurate with Eternality!

You should also know that

*Every thought you think
and every activity you have
and are experiencing now,
should be resolved now!*

It should not just be resolved for anyone else's sake! It should be resolved **because** *the energy that you give to a difficult situation, if it isn't solved and if it isn't given up to the Light, so to speak, becomes an unconscious force that you will inherit as you quit this form!* Life goes on; it may not give you the form that you have to deal with, but you may know that you are not devoid of the form if your thought is malignant at this time.

The form will be commensurate with your highest expectations. This is why **you must hold Divinely oriented thoughts,** because those are the evidence of the interiorization or the state of the interior of yourself, and are the force that you will take with you, whether you think, "I dropped them yesterday (and picked them up), and I'll never have them again." That is not true. You *will* have them.

You take with you the structures that you have achieved by solving, and you take the structures that you have **not** achieved. If there is a problem, it cannot be solved from the standpoint of *you* having a problem, because "you" basically is the problem!

As long as you think *you* have a problem, that *you* are confused and frustrated and exasperated and jealous and envious, then you are doing what? You are saying *you equal* these states! Just as "two plus two equals five," you are saying *you* equal frustration, confusion, exasperation, jealousy, enviousness, et cetera. Is this **true?!** *You* does *not* equal that! *You*/U put upright (inverted) is the great Arch under which you can pass. *You* is only the name given to Infinite Possibilities for others who are lost on this plane to witness, due to the mesmerism, the magnetic quality of matter to matter, dust to dust.

What a great hope has been fulfilled for some! What a Grace is present for all. Yet, you cannot consider solving your problems from under cloudy skies and the temperatures of such *coldness*. You see, the coldness, the frigidity, usually happens when one is confronted. *The coldness of intellect supersedes the warmth of Love.* This is why one is beyond (in belief) the Healing Radiation of Love's Ministrations. This is why,

> *It is imperative for any of you who are meeting anything serious to resort to Principle and not person.*

That Principle, of course, will never have you without person. After all, it couldn't be *named* Principle if it weren't for the Creative Power and Might of Soul!

You cannot disengage the very basis of these Divine Ideals and Concepts. It's impossible to; only in thought can you do it. This, as Edinger points out, is the great tragedy of modern day psychology, because people *do* sever this connection with the mystery of God and become "anti-spiritual," "anti-cultural," anti-everything — and yet look at your world as a result of such a severance *in belief.*

The Wonder of the Divine, the Wonder of the Transpersonal, the Wonder of *unconceptualized* Consciousness, the Wonder of the Might of Omnipotence, howls as does the wind as IT moves through the screens of the mind and as IT moves through the fronds of the palms. If you hear a rushing, it is the wind that has come up to support *in symbolic measure* the Force that has been garmented as the Breath of the Word.

May these few words be of some assistance and a staff unto those who would follow the Calling of the Self within and be prepared to relinquish the din of the mind and its tendency to cloud man's way in his movement from sense to Soul. The Way is marked, and as it says, broad is the way but narrow is the Gate that leads to the Allness of Being Divine.

If you are of a contrite heart, are filled with expectancy, and engage those patterns of consideration commensurate with your Ideal, then do not feel discomforted but rejoice in the Knowing that all these unearthly considerations are so, because Earth is nothing but a footstool for those who know the Rhythmic Walk with the Divine in the Celestial Kingdom of the Eternal Light Way of those who would know the Ascended State.

> *How can you take advantage*
> *of All that you Are*
> *from the standpoint of all that you aren't?!*

God bless. I hope you have received this well and have found yourself engaging those thoughts that are in keeping with the Heavenly State, because this is what you will inherit, according to your thinking. Will it be paradisiacal or shall it be hellish — all due to the thought that you had the right to think any way you *felt* instinctively? **You don't!**

▼

XI.

Seeding

You were never meant
to worship person;
you were to follow Principle.

SEEDING

We greet you on this warm, sunny, Sunday, Thanksgiving morning, with the best wishes and the remembrances of the past and the wonders of the present. It seems as if I am talking into a great funnel of preparedness with no end of possibilities and no beginning of the seeding. From generation unto generation, men and women have gathered together to count the Lord's blessings and have called it the means of attuning oneself to the seed procedure of opportunities and of a new formation. We bring special import to a day by having a proclamation declared that all peoples shall worship in the Wonder of Holiness and in the attitude becoming the Celebration.

In order for any celebration to be of significance, all those partaking in it and of it should be in that state of acceptance in which there are no thoughts other than those which are in keeping with the purposeful intent of a highly motivated endeavor. To bear witness to a harvest means that we have watched the growth of the seed. To seed a field necessitates much work: It demands plowing, it demands hoeing, and it demands a need to secure the proper season in which to allow the seeds to fall from the hand and enter the furrow of promise.

We cast our seeds into that fertile condition and cover them, waiting for the essence of them to bear witness to their growth. When the witness is evidenced, we call it the harvest, and when the harvest is garnered, we call it the season fulfilled, for we have the substance that is essential for sustaining our experience according to the promise of the seed ceremony.

The seed ceremony on the objective realm is very similar to the seed ceremony that is given to the mental realm. The demand is:

What thought will you allow to be buried
in the furrows of your Earth encounter?

*What thought will you allow
to bear witness of a new harvest?*

Are your thoughts in keeping with the hollow caste of this present time?[1] Or are they in keeping with the *hallowed cast* that is the promise of those who have fecundated their fields of expectancies with the hope of a new age and a new world and a new race? What thought-clusters, what seed formations!

Yet what is the characteristic of all seeds? They grow if the conditions are right. What are the conditions that must be present? The soil, the nurturing, and the light. The seed doesn't care what type of hand has dropped it, for it bears within itself its own generic essence.

*What is your demand
in your planting for the seasons to come?*

Are you planning to have your acreage covered and seeded with lack, with procrastination, with infidelity, with cunning, with conniving, with politics, to name but a few?

The Source of the seed rests in the innate, generic Wonder that is commensurate with Allness and Creativity. Without the seed, a wasteland presents itself.

You can't expect to have a harvest unless you have *planted the seeds. You can't expect to have a new world and plant the seeds of the old one.* You can't expect to have fulfillment and plant the seeds of procrastination and expectation for a future event.

Do you know the moment a thought is born and dropped into the great funnel of time, it is always geared for more programming? Do you know the birth of a thought? Do you recognize it? *Or does it come to you, as soon as you focus your attention on it, fully clothed in its creative possibilities?*

---

1.   See "The Holocaust or The Hollow Caste," in Kenneth G. Mills, *Embellishments* (Toronto: Sun-Scape Publications, 1986), p. 108.

How do you expect to have a new world and have the same population populating only the indiscriminate seeds of a Baseless existence? It is difficult to say that society is lacking in a fundamental basis, but it is, for you do not have to look very far to see the results of your seeding.

What have you seeded this past year that has made your harvest this year new and varied according to the unlimited Nature of Allness? What newness have you brought into your experience but the planting, perhaps, of the seeds in the same old pot and expecting a new crop to fulfill a Promise held by the Ages?

If you are to be the custodians of the New World, then remember, you have to have a New World seeding plan — Not *seating* plan; *you can't be reserved about Newness*! You cannot be reserved about placement. You cannot be reserved unless you allow yourself to be *preserved* in the syrup of expectation and the sweetness of oldness and the promise of something upon your bread to make it more palatable in the dreary times of the nonfruitage period.

Why do you jam your situations by congesting yourself with indiscriminate thought-breeding?

If you are to expect a New World, then cease expecting it from the standpoint of a spectator. Even the *potato* had the eyes concealed from yours in order to bear a tube of promise!

Why would you expect to birth a new generation and generate from the same stock, which has generated nothing but limitations for centuries?

*That's why history appeals only to the "me," because it does not reveal anything but the unsuccessful attempts made by people to achieve an evolutionary scale of achievement. The New World cannot happen unless we **emerge** from this gross state of false attunement to the ego-inflated realm of endeavor.*

If you are the vanguard of the future, then you can't be

the laggards of the past! If you are "this," then this is what you are. But if you know you are not "this" but the seed of That, then your Possibilities are infinite, because *the evidence of Allness is Creativity.* What are you creating?! Situations that conform to your limited cultural parameters?

Are you creating a cultural environment of dressed-up limitations to seduce others to follow in your dressed-up promises that are vacant of vitality, virility, and the dynamism of Newness?

How can you expect a New World from an old-world point of view? *You old-timers are suffering from the disease of fluctuation, the fluctuation between "this" and That, because you have never agreed to die to "this" and pass over the inflated road of your own making.*

The future depends upon your ability of a transpersonal happening! How can you be wrapped up in your egotistic world-front and expect to have a transpersonal, viable experience?

You cannot expect anything new without plowing up the old, and when you plow up your old fields, you don't stop and look at the remnants of your past seeding. You bury them out of your sight as fast as possible! In other words, you get what has sprung from your effort *out of your sight* and allow it to grow into its own magnificence. Remember, what you have spewed forth upon the planet has bound you to it in the realm of speculation. This whole great dream of this planet and its inhabitants is of your making because of your seeding, and your present condition is the result of your *faulty seeding*!

The All is creative! Whether IT appears in a happy, prosperous society or in a war-torn society, *IT is creative!* Do you realize *war* is creative?! It's destroying in order for something to fulfill the *urge of creativity* — in other words, the urge of newness, of change.

Why did the great Master of the past say that you can't put new wine into old bottles? For the same reason that you can't put new thoughts into old fields. If you do, you will have an old field bearing new thoughts and you won't know how to utilize your harvest.

. *How do you expect to have a Christened Society from the standpoint of an unchanged society?* A Christened Society, or a Self-Enlightened Society, depends upon the Light Seeds that are planted. The Light has nothing whatsoever to do with a bulb. It IS; the bulb only allows it to be utilized at the level of your acceptability.

The Light Body allows itself to evidence itself by the resurgence of the Creativity and the Light Force of Newness right through this situation of birth, growth, maturity, and decay.

What if you now die to such a seasonal happening and be the constant Newness to what appears as the oldness as you *peer* through the situation of time and others recognize your peerage?

Who cares about having an appearance to be cognized?! Each appearance bears little worthwhileness unless that appearance *shocks* you into considering how *you* look in the mirror of reflectedness.

Someone once asked me, "What is the cause of all this upset in the world? What is the cause of all this turbulence in the world?" It is said to be the work of the anti-Christ, the Satanic, that which is opposed to Newness, dressed up as if it *weren't* opposed to Newness.

One man suggested that if you look in the mirror and that which looks back is orientated in ego, therefore in selfish identification, *there* is the cause of your trouble!

How much can you bear to look at yourself in the mirror? Can you see yourself freed of adjudicating another's uniqueness as he harvests the uniqueness of new seeds planted? How many of you stand and look in the mirror of your mind and say, "Oh, my God, what are they doing? What is he doing? *What am I doing?*" Frequently nothing but adjudicating others so you don't have the perception that you haven't budged an inch, let alone *wormed* your way through the soil of time! At least that would help to aerate the land for another's seeds to flourish! Most of you worm your way through time, hoping not to be eyed. If you are, you *have* to change! That is the Law of Creativity.

Do you mean to tell me you aren't expecting your death to bring about a new form, a new person?

Who *wants* that but you, the "mirror you"?

Why is the "mirror you" so important? Because only by looking in it can you have a face-on view of what others see when they look at you. Without the mirror you have no idea of what your face and your body look like. But then you *really* don't, because you face yourself clad in all the reservations that have preserved you for all these years, with the hope of three-score and ten at least.

Why try to preserve the old, when the Newness demands a bypassing of the mind constructs of the old? *Do you realize you cannot find the New if you look in the closed shops of despair?! You can't go shopping for Newness and expect it to be packaged in the windows of belief.*

> *Newness is the name given to what you can't perceive from your personal point of view.*

Newness is the condition of *a transpersonal state*, and Newness is that which is ascribed to the condition called *metanoia*, which is "to go beyond the mind"! That is the whole new consideration of the new evolution, which is to bring about a Divine Emergence!

I tell you now, it is not new; it has been said to you from the day I met you. It was such a confrontation to some rocks that one man said, "Mr. Mills has dreamed up a new gimmick to hold his students. They must go beyond their minds." What a deluded piece of oldness said it! *It is the only possibility left to any of you, to go beyond the mind!*

> *How is it possible*
> *to go beyond the mind?*
> *By associating with everything*
> *that is not thought*
> *and is known in essence as a feeling pulse.*
> *You know how you feel;*
> *it's how your head garments your feeling*
> *that limits it to a fragrant-less state.*

Why is it that people have had these Tonal Bombardments and Baptisms for so many years when the fields have been plowed, and yet you have *so limited* what you shall harvest?!

Why is it that, as you have received the floodtides of Love and the sunshine of Truth and the open warmth of possibilities, you have permitted yourselves to be more and more engrossed with the grossness of your limited experiences? How many of "you" have *given up* in order for the Work of your Christ-Self to be cognized? It is the hope of a Cosmic Baptism!

That is what the whole new Emergence is about. This is the whole topic of conversation at symposiums. It is the whole topic of consideration by hundreds of people the world over.

> *How many of you give one-tenth*
> *of your day to managing your business*
> *and the other nine-tenths to sponsoring*
> *Light Business?*

Oh, the availability of *Man* Power is not to be found under the auspices of a labor union. *Man Power* is the raw footage commensurate with the Wonder of a Cosmic Baptism due to the Self living as an Effulgence and a Newness unto the timed suggestions of a seasonal sprint upon this stage called Earth.

I'll tell you now, it's a sad state to see all these Seeds, having been planted, bearing no harvest whatsoever for the One who would re-seed the clouds of doubt and bring about a rain/reign of Unconditional Love upon this planet that is supposedly geared for a new harvest and a fulfillment of a new Promise.

Thanksgiving for what? For seeing the inane and conditioned response to the limited creativity of sedated humanity ended!

Why are you people considered Chosen? Because you were and are in a position to nullify the thought-claims of your tragedy. You have the Divine Assurance: Love's unconditional adaptations and bestowals.

Why is yours such a tragedy? Because you know so much and you plant so little and you wonder why there are not others sharing your Thanksgiving Meal.

One of the finest packagers of seeds is called the Steele Company. Why are so many clad like steel? It's unyielding and it will support any load up to the point of having to be buried beneath the soil of unachievement.

How many of you, in the last twenty years, have literally changed *one habit*?!

I remember asking a psychologist once to understand psychologically the effect of doing something as a psychologist might ask a patient to do. I said, "Will you try for one day to walk, every time you start walking, by putting the unaccustomed foot first?" By evening there was a migraine!

What a simple thing to do! That is obvious, putting one foot ahead of the other. I wonder what kind of a head you would have if you had to put certain thoughts *out* of the leadership in your step into time. If I ask you to put your left foot forward instead of your right, and you end up with a migraine at the end of a few hours, I wonder what type of *migration* would happen if you could put out those thoughts that have led you by the nose through time: "I must be secure." "I must have this. I must have that." "I've got to think of a way to be this way. I've got to think of a way to be that way so no one will know that I am not fertile, so someone won't know that I bear no potency, so that I can blame my infertility on somebody else." "I must get myself covered with associates so no one will see that I have no inner assurance that Love is All." "I must preserve my seeming credibility by surrounding myself with those who are not considered creditable."

Most people who are great surround themselves by those who are "a little less great" or "a little more great." Doesn't it all *grate* upon the Divine Sense so that you want to throw the thunderbolt of God into their midst and silence the emptiness of their protestations?! *Why would you expect to penalize the world in the poverty of a spiritual attainment?*

Why would you expect the moment of Pentecost to come when your own tongue is only pitched to fork your own selfishness? The Fire of Pentecost only comes when the tares are allowed to be burned and the wheat to be utilized with the husk of Wonder. (It carries all the B vitamins.)

Why do we have a tendency to be prone? Because the more we sleep the less we have to face our lack. *Why do young people love to sleep by getting so involved with their work of achieving nothing?* Because then they don't have to face the fact that they are maturing and are *the leaders of tomorrow.*

When I hear about the great plans for global achievement, I stand in that stream, a testament (to myself at least) of the waters that are flowing by me into the great unknown Abyss. The whole purpose of receiving the Inspired is so that others may *alter* their courses and perceive the leaks that are happening in their very vehicles of receptivity. The leaks are due to having alternatives to being Authentic.

You can't have an instant meal nutritionally sound. The only thing that is an instantaneous happening is the Allness I AM. When that is realized, it doesn't come in a package, it doesn't come in a deal; it hits you at the moment when you least expect! Yet, that is the moment when the expectancy bears with it the fruitage of a New Wonder.

What is that New Wonder? The New World not made with hands but eternal in the rhythmic, harmonic State of *conceptional freshness.* Do you expect your New World to have to be fumigated for pestilence, deodorized for acceptance, and bastardized by your industry for selfish gains?

> O the sleepy state of Sleepy Hollow,
> Where people cry for the tomorrows.
> But O my God, where is the Grace
> That will strike your heart and thereby face
> The limits of head, the unsure feet
> Upon the path that is called retreat?
>
> If you are in the Vanguard of Light,
> Your only step is the Dance of Light.
> And there is no retreat, for you have found
> Where you walk is hallowed ground.
>
> If the ground is hallowed where you stand,
> If it's hallowed ground, the Earthian man
> Must be hallowed at heart — that is the Plan.
>
> For God is hallowed in His Name so called;
> You call Him that until you wake up and see
>   that Creativity is All.
> You're hallowed. You're spaceless. You're
>   timeless! 'Tis planned.

Why do you persist in being a human and
  not being Man?

What is Man but that State sublime
That is subtle beyond your errant mind?
The transpersonal, we say, is a place to find
The Promise of the World Divine.

Do you think it's going to emerge? Of *course* it will
emerge, but not the way you *think*. Because you plant and
expect it to take *time,* and the New World is not in it.

I AM the New World, but you are expecting it tomorrow.
I AM in it, and you're expecting it in the next generation. *I*
AM in it, either I could not be telling you *of* it.

I cannot tell you *of* it other than by appearing to limit it
by saying "I am in it." Everything that I have said is a limit
is not of it, and everything that I have said of it is no limit!

What is the joy of being a seed?
It's to appear to be unnoticed until the
  flowering deed!

Do you mean to tell me the flower bears any resemblance to that hardly discernible speck? Will you please
tell me how come you think in such an impoverished way?
You are the result of a seed. Why do you expect to bear an
annual blossom resembling a family root system instead of
the blossoms of perennial *Love* and *Wisdom* that entwine
and support every branch of doubt, until it yields to the
apparent weight of demand for change? When you have
acquiesced, *the challenge goes*! And you haven't a vine
choking the life out of you:

You have a Promise filling you that you
  don't live this way at all;

You only appear to live this way for those
    who are part of the fall.
And in that season you shall find
That the harvest is ready beyond the mind.

The cornucopia is filled with thanks and
    praise
For the cards that have come this way,
For those who have addressed what they call
    another,
All dressed up in Love for a brother.
Know without doubt that the season's plan
    is all dressed up for a timed man.

When you can stand at the Center and BE,
Then the Joy of Eternality
Gives you the amplitude of Grace
By Being I AM. Let others appear traced.

You are seeded. Believe it or not, you're in
    full bloom,
So you'd better get on; it's more than high
    noon!
If you are squeezed into space-time and
    believe it so,
Then get on with being Real and your space-
    time will go.

Then you will see a Wonder at hand:
You appear space-timed, *appearing* a man.
But that's for the appearance of the Peerage
    Divine
That says there's this part of "me" appearing
    to shine.
(The rest is effulgent and impossible to
    decree.)

What are you doing that is different in your
    life?
Have you changed being obstinate, willful,
    selfish — "perfectly all right"?

It *isn't* "perfectly all right." *Don't allow yourselves to
psychologically prepare yourselves for being what you
aren't. So many of you psych yourselves into conditions so
you won't have to allow your* **conscience** *to* **live** *and be a
guide unto your state.*

How many of you are sitting there thinking
    about the dinner that is to come?
How many of you who are sitting there have
    never considered the harvest of One?
How many of you are offering words of
    thanksgiving and praise
And thanking God for this day in which you
    parade?
Why would you give praise and thanks to a
    God unknown
When the God lives as "you" enthroned?

*You were never meant to worship person;
you were to follow Principle.*

What is the point? Imitation. What is your lack? You
lack the willingness to imitate.

You dress your lack of imitation up in words so that no
change happens at all. All the Star-Scape Singers know.

When they imitated my Voice, they thought
    it mine
Until they adopted it, and then how the face
    did shine!
Because I kept my mouth shut, and out of
    theirs would come

A tone that was redolent as the Son/Sun of
   this One.

The world calls it their voices; only they
   know 'tis Mine.
Each voice they utter is all due to the Sun
   and how it shines.

Who has ever imitated this life? You wouldn't dare.
You're all *afraid* of altering your *course* unless conditions
make you. When I gave up concertizing after twenty-five
years of preparing for it, what do you think I did it for?
Don't think of a reason; *I* didn't have any!

Do you always have to think of a reason for feeling the
need of change? If one of you who might be writing music
wants now to go out and plant tulips for the rest of your life,
great! Perhaps there will be a *new* tune that will bring you
in residuals other than seasons.

How come you never consider an alteration in **your**
life? It's happened in mine, and I have lived. It's very interesting to look over all of you and see how you have never
even considered giving up what you've spent twenty-five
years doing to do something you don't know anything
about!

Ohhh! What about your old age security? *You wouldn't
worry about it if you knew how old you were.*

What is old age security? The soporific offering to your
gradual seedy state. What's a *seedy* state? **The one that is
before your deliverance or your change.**

I seed your clouds. How do you seed yours?
I seed your clouds and they offer
   refreshment as planned.
Do you seed your clouds? Or do you just
   create more, saying,

"Hide me please. I don't want to be seen
as I AM."

Why don't you want to be seen as the Beauty you are? Because you will *stand in the stream* and no one will like it because you will cause ripples around everyone, little eddies. What does an eddy do? It gives a little whirlpool, a little funnel that allows you to disappear, and after the ceremony no one gives a hoot about it.

Do you expect to have something emerge if you don't make room for it?

How are you going to see a New World emerge when you've got your old one filled up with your antiques all wrapped up in your family, so limited to trees that are dying as a result of your ignorance of balance and of respect to the wonders of a Light Creativity?

What is the root of all your problems?
What is the root of the world problems?
What is the root of the lack of Emergence?

Your *sub*mergence in material beliefs, and dressing them up in spiritual terminology.

As the Dalai Lama said: "Unless your religions are lived, they're worthless."

What is the point of all the different ministers of all the different faiths coming in to have a meeting together? In other words, having a fraction of their gods all together and no one believing or *living* any part of the God that they worship. What a sandwich! No wonder he said he was the last Dalai Lama. He realizes that most people just want to sandwich everything. The new deli sandwich; all corned, all conditioned, when the Truth of Being bears no lineage.

Lineage, as you will soon see, is the limit to the Liberty of Man.

I read recently about the word "repent." The word that Jesus used, "to repent," was an Aramaic word called *tob*. It meant "to return," "to flow back into God." In the act of Love you perceive the actions and you **know** there *has* to be a return; otherwise, there is no proper repentance.

Repentance is always for a sin. A sin is not necessarily missing the mark; *it's a breaking of the Divine Law.* That is the higher sense of sin. That's what's so serious. It's the breaking of the higher Divine Law. The only way to repent is to return and to *flow* once again, not *into* God but *as* God. Even the terminology is wrong, you know?

Jesus never was born (any more than Buddha) to be followed. What have people said to me, "Oh, Mr. Mills, *replicate! Replicate the Singers!*" What do you *think* the High Teaching is demanding? *That the Christ is replicated. Replicate yourselves!* Every one of you sitting there, *replicate yourselves.* Turn around and look at your neighbor and you're *facing* a Christ! The New Order! Then what type of an Emergence will come from this Seed?

Thanksgiving for what? The perception that:

> Creativity must have its day,
> Whether it's war or pestilence, famine, and
>   dismay.
> Will it be this, or the Joy profound
> Giving the old world in a new gown
> Back to the Arms of Love and ITs way,
> And the rhythm and the Eternality of the
>   Heavenly Day?!

What are you doing but being a shadow on the way, walking under a cloud of doubt, giving you, "Well, do you suppose he's right? Or isn't he right? What will I do if I change? I'll lose all my friends. And what if they know I'm associated with *him?*" Are you still living two thousand years ago when you thought you were going to be fed to the lions? *You will be today, too.* They'll be the lions who you **believe** will stop you from being accepted.

Don't fret. (They allow you to move into different octaves — every fret you have. No pain, no gain! No fret, no achievement.)

What is an octave? The achievement of utilizing what you've got without thumbing your way and having it marked by calling it heavy.[2]

Don't expect to hitchhike spiritually and remain hidebound. If you're going to hitchhike, hitch your state to a Star and see what will open.

> In the dance of a sunbeam upon your
> windowledge of time,
> Are you going to open the door or
> defenestrate through your mind?
> Are you going to BE One or are you going
> to continue to be two or three?
> Or will you just give up and BE, a Light
> Deed!

Oh, you know, it's not very challenging to you old ones, but my gosh, to the young ones! What way will you find tomorrow will be when it's all wrapped up in a New World and a mirror that doesn't bear any image of limitation? *"On this face are written the Possibilities of Infinite Being utilized for the exaltation of Wonder and the reemergence of the Light to an Ageless Wonder!"*

This is the Seed Wealth you have inherited. Don't expect to count it as money and call it your assurance.

> Don't be reserved in being new!
> You weren't when you came through the
> birthing tube.

---

2. Reference to piano playing: the fault of a heavy or "thudding" thumb.

You came out and you screamed and they
  didn't know how to deliver you, and
  you found
You were making a mess wherever you were
  around.

But then you grew up and you weren't anything like you were. Do you realize that you can't wear any of the shoes that you once wore when you just became a little Earthian girl or boy? You can't wear them! How come you can't get into your shoes of twenty years ago, ten years ago? Why do you expect to get into a New World with the old shoe concept? It just doesn't fit. You can't put your new body in your old shoes. You can't put your New World into your old world of historical data and content.

You are well preserved. Continue to be sweet, but certainly untopped so that it may be found. So many people keep their tops on so tight that no one has an *inkling* of how sweet they are in Essence. You know? They are so screwed. They don't understand they haven't struck the Core of their Being at all. They are so *screwed up* and bolted by conventions that what's in that container can never be found. Belief has you screwed up, and I tell you now, the Truth breaks it totally.

"Know you the Truth and IT shall set you free." Can you imagine it being said to you? Then you can't be. Why don't you claim your freedom and find how the New World really IS and how the old one becomes your footstool in the seedtime of a Light Harvest.

I AM with you always, even to the end of the seasons. If I were to think of *you*, I would cry. When I rejoice in the Substance that IS, my limit is not found.

Think of me when you have your dinner, for I have never forgotten you. Happy Thanksgiving to all of you.

Thank you for being here and holding this fort while I engaged the enemy of oldness in the Bombardment of the

Baptism of new considerations. For the Emergence of the Light is essential and the Emergence of the Light People is a must. Evolution is for those who feel they will *evolve* into a New Race. There can be no evolving into a New Race. A New Race is a precipitated State of conscious awareness in which an Ideal *lives* as the fecundating Power to the entire perception of what *you* call "your world."

It will never be *thought* into existence, *lived* into existence, *evolved* into existence. It is a **precipitated State** due to the willingness to *accept*. **Now** is all there is. Is there a Second Coming? NO!!! That is the carrot held before those who wish to worship.

> Follow; allow the Work to be
> Fulfilled beyond your thought-filled seed.
> See in the growing, the day is at hand,
> The Irradiance of Being, Radiant Man.
> The Quickening Radiance is found at hand
> In Being Real, I AM That I AM.

Thank you. Thus endeth this reel for the moment that a magnetic field has caught this impelling Force just so you can say it happened.

▼

XII.

Correct Words

It isn't in matter that Identity is found;
it's in the Reality which allows us to be free
from the fettered state of conceiving
within the framework of "this."

Correct Words

Correct words are used to prepare the mind, to diminish its force so that it cannot degrade the information that has to deal with That Which IS beyond it. This is why words are important.

We say "words are important" because that was one of the embellishing statements I received years ago when I had no thought of fulfilling any Commission such as "You must learn to speak the Word again."

This gave me a great deal to consider, because I was a concert pianist and a teacher. My wife and I had divorced after many years of marriage, and I decided to live in a little house by the side of the road and be a friend to man. I decided just to teach, to stop working with concert pianists and advanced students, and to work with children so that they could be prepared so well that they would not meet any blockage later in life. If the foundation is correct, then they can fly.

So I did this. After about two years of living in this house by myself, I met a woman who had met an older woman she felt I should meet. This older lady was brought to my house and said how nice it was to see me again. I thought, "My goodness, I've never met you before." (Being very naive at that time, I had not thought in terms of reincarnation.) "Well," she said, "don't you feel you know me?" I said, "Well, perhaps. I don't feel you particularly a stranger." She said, "Good." Then, after I had a couple of tea times with her at her home, she said, "I don't know what you're doing in my life. I'm going to have a life reading and I'm going to ask what you're doing in my life." I said, "You're going to have a what?" She said, "A life reading." I had never heard of such a thing. She said, "There are a certain number of questions I may ask, and one of them is, 'What is Kenneth Mills doing in my life?'"

She did have the reading, and to give you the jelled statement it was simply: "You must give him the message that he must learn to speak the Word again." She said, "How may I help him?" Apparently it was said to her, "Leave him alone." I've never seen her since.

Then I went to hear a Buddhist monk speak three times. He was visiting in Toronto for three weeks on his way to Thailand. He did not speak the English language well, and as I sat in the audience he looked right down at me, and every time he had difficulty with a word in English I'd close my eyes and tell him silently what the word was and he'd say it. This was a fascinating experience for me.

At the end of the third lecture the girl I was with said, "Aren't you going to thank him?" I said, "No, I have thanked him with my eyes." So, in the usual way in those days, we tried to sneak out at the side of the room to draw no attention and be inconspicuous and get out without causing any disturbance. The monk, having completed his lecture, said in a booming voice, *"Words are important! You must learn to speak the Word again."* I died! I sheepishly got myself together with all my wool and went up to the stage and spoke to him and thanked him. I said, "I thought I had thanked you." He nodded his head and he said, *"Yes, but words are important. You must learn to speak the Word again."* I started to say something else, and then, as if to say, "That's enough, brother," he just closed his eyes and entered a meditative state.

So, I went back to my little house by the side of the road and decided I didn't know what it meant, but whatever it did mean, I would speak if I were asked and I would remain like everyone else if I were not asked. Within a matter of a few weeks I received a phone call from a man who said, "Mr. Mills, may I come and talk to you?" I said, "I don't know you." He said, "Well, I'm the artist of the paintings you saw at the gallery." I said, "I know nothing about art." He said,

"Oh, but I must talk to you." Then I remembered what I was told and I said, "Oh, oh. Yes, come." That was the beginning.

What about you? Tell me, what have you been considering?

Doug P.) I'd like to know where you learned the Word.

I don't think I learned it. I must have *earned* it, because I have always accepted the basic understanding of my childhood that *I of myself can do nothing; 'tis the Father that doeth the Work.* I was brought up in this teaching, and so I always consider when I speak to anyone: *May the words of my mouth and the meditations of my heart be acceptable in the Sight of the One Altogether Lovely.*

The Word, to me, may appear to be the corresponding identity to the Realm of the unknown and yet experienceable Silence. You cannot have a Divine Idea without a corresponding identity. That is why the Absolute Teaching is not a void lacking in anything. It is the fulfillment; it is not the nullification of anything.

It allows that to appear which isn't and allows That to appear Which IS. That which appears That IS is never in the form of a limit, and that form of a limit couldn't possibly be if That Which IS were not the Light and Power to it. It's a great paradox.

Breck S.) Your Word is the life-link to that Reality we don't know. It would be nice to have more of an experience of that in our lives, as a living experience rather than just something we hear about. I think that the Word is alive, because it is a living experience. It's not just sounds or something on a page that we read or think about.

Yes, sir! That's right.

> Breck S.) Could you tell us more about that experience, Sir, that you had when you had to unlearn so much to speak the Word again?

Well! I didn't unlearn so much as I dropped the associating of thought-patterns and thought-forms with that which did not conform to the Ward of my Being, which I have always claimed as the Divine Principle, the I AM.

I felt it must be a Wonder to be the Voice of the Intangible, yet so tangible, in the experience of dropping the suggestion that "this" was Real and that what "this" learned gave me the ability to scale the heights beyond learning's comprehension.

When One is asked to speak, the underlying *leit motif* is that of Unity. It is that of the Undivided Garment of Wholeness and Allness which seems to permeate the structure appearing as words woven upon the loom of the mind.

We have not been cast adrift on this planet for this incredible drama staged here on Earth without a Prompter of Infinite Significance.

When one achieves a sense of wonder of the Unknown, the wonder is magnified in recognizing that the Unknown is accompanied by Wonder. The aroma of Wonder allows one to drop the feeling of being "this" and allows one to consider:

> *What is it beyond "this"*
> *that allows "this"*
> *to seem to be Real?*

Most of the Teaching that we have received in time has been that which allows one to be led onto the Path of Righteousness, wholeness, and completeness, but men and women have a historical past and an unknown present and, of course, a festered future, because the virus of false education based on the premise of duality has infected the entire system of considerations for exculpation from this plane of contrived mental conveniences.

It has been the prompting of the present experience to put the brakes on this very controlled evolutionary scale of accomplishment, and to offer to those such as you who are ready to consider the extremities of time and the inevitable suggestion of age which accompanies it, and allow a halt to be made by saying,

> *Stop!*
> *Consider:*
> *Are you going to continually look up*
> *to a Star in order to foster*
> *the astral imagination,*
> *or are you going to adopt a Point*
> *from which you can view?*

That Point is the one of Attainment. That Which IS attained and considered the Highest is That which embraces you but does not allow "you" to speculate about its Vestment.

It seems that few today are ready to allow an unusual concept to be present in their considerations. That concept is wrapped in this garment: I and my Father *is* One NOW and not "shall be." That dresses the present in an unexpected force, and reduces the past to the story of "his-ness" and "her-ness" and the future to the picture book of the mind, which others will color because you have allowed the palette beyond the rainbow to brush your period in time with an exclamation becoming Wonder!

It is hoped that people such as you have the fortification becoming the urge for newness and freedom, all wrapped in Unity and Wonder, to be held aloft in your considerations, because you are hearing This, which wrests from the grasp of time that which feeds the insatiable appetite of "timers" — the old-timers, the present-timers, and the future-timers. The old-timers were filled with the wonder of searching for a new land, and the future-timers are dressing it up in the speculative process of the unknown achievement from the standpoint of "tinsel-ized" propaganda.

You have the ability to say now, to yourself, that you will be That Which IS Real, and by so doing you open the entire vehicle to receiving the descent of the Forces that are termed Cosmic in proportions, because they come, not from this realm of three dimensions, but from the Realm (you might say) similar unto death. Death is the realm where you do not have to face the idea of question but revel in the experience of what you have done when question-and-answer were answered. The question-and-answer were never meant to be static; they were meant to fecundate and seed your presence with the present Seed of an exodus from this land of objective confinement.

Everything about you that is Real is not verified by your presence, but your presence testifies that there is something that is Real, either it couldn't appear to be.

> *We say That Which IS Real*
> *is known because it is a constant*
> *and is untarnished*
> *by any timed considerations.*
> *It is fixed and it is permanent.*

That one feature that lives in a pulsating rhythm within you is the sense of an Identity which you really are hoping to know, but in the go-between time, called the Earth-time, you call it "Doug," "Irene." You are wondering where and how does this incredible thing happen that you could consider yourself without doubt, without having to say "I AM." You are here answering to a name all because the call to you is made because of the unannounced

I AM, which is Omnipresent for all those considering themselves named for time.

> "I am Richard," "I am David,"
> "I am John," "I am Christopher,"
> there is no doubt.
> I AM, I AM THAT! That's all it's about.

So you see, in the name-calling you have the ability to play your parts on the stage called the world, but in your realization of that Divine State that is termed "I AM" (it's only termed "Divine" because it is not open to your considerations), you never have to consider that you are present, but it's a wonder to consider that you are present without ever giving gratitude to That which allows you to be present and capable of being cognized: the Power I AM!

That's why it is said that "I AM THAT I AM." If that is the case, God (you might say, until you know what God is) did a great job of hiding Himself. He didn't hide Himself within you at all, and He didn't hide Himself without you. You did it! God is Omnipresent and Omniactive, but your fall into matter caused you to consider He was a manufacturer of duality. He didn't manufacture anything! The Power of God fractures the picture of duality so that all those who perceive the I AM State return immediately to the Star.

You are like an "E.T." You don't have to look up and ask for the ship to come and get you, and wonder if it's ever going to come and get you! You are the immediate custodian of That Presence, which is the at-easement surrounding Home.

Man is at home; he is perfectly at ease at home as I AM. You are very at ease at home, because I AM is the presence there. The fireplace is the hearth, the center of your home, and the Fire that is termed equated with I AM as Love is the Fire that attracts all unto you.

This is why, if you can adopt this Baptism of consideration within yourselves, you can walk the streets bearing an

Individuality which is very easily discerned, because there are countless thousands walking the streets who look just like a variegated form of clonage, as you could appear to be unless you carry this awareness.

It's marvelous the way we have *cloned* ourselves, and now we have to *clothe* ourselves in the becoming Garment of That Which IS termed the "Immaculate" and "Wondrous."

It's a Conscious experience; that's why Consciousness is fundamental. Your awareness can change, but your Consciousness cannot. *Consciousness is the Light; the awareness is that which allows it to have its way as you move within the framework of a timed experience.*

> Christopher M.) Is it not true that to try to imagine what it would be like if we lost our memories, forgot who we are, fell into a state of amnesia, is the exercise that we and the Godhead entertained when we stepped through the doorway from our forever Home into this life?

That's why we are here, because we are here bearing the I-Identity for your *re-cognition*. That's what you are about, because it has been a pattern of forgettery. We have questions about our identity, which really is the whole root problem of our culture. We don't have a correct identity, but we do have the ability to remember it. That remembering first comes about as a question: "Who am I?" and then, "What am I?" "Who" can give you "this." "What" *allows* "this" to be. "What am I?" comes as a question even when "Who?" is the question.

So you are in a wonderful, wonderful place, because it doesn't take time to think right. *It doesn't take time to be Real unless you want an excuse to perpetuate this veil of tears.*

John D.) So we are all part of the One?

Exactly! That is right! There is only the Oneness and it has appeared fractured because of all the minds that have been set to look at it in the many-faceted aspects of Being. *In Reality there is only One,* and the suggested races, colors, and creeds are just the way the paint-book of time dresses it up to keep us entertained.

It isn't in matter that Identity is found; it's in the Reality which allows us to be free from the fettered state of conceiving within the framework of "this."

Every time you try to reason from the standpoint of "this," you are reasoning from the standpoint that isn't accurate because *it* changes. So every time you perceive the Unity that IS, then you will say, "'This' is all fractured and appears as a multitudinous number of people because my mind is incapable of bringing together, in the objective sense, the enormous, gigantic concept of Oneness." You can conceive Oneness beyond the fractured state of the mind. That's why you don't fall for "this," and for being separate.

Always remember this:
keep your thoughts
always attuned to Principle.

Mary Baker Eddy said it beautifully, "The Divine Principle of the Universe must interpret the Universe." [1] It's wonderful because it's true. If you interpret from the Standpoint of the Divine Principle, then everything you realize is yours, and no person can give it to you. Anything that appears to come from me to you is only appearing to do so. That is the reason I came: to allow "this" to offer, to you, what you ARE. I appear to be what I am not by offering to you what you ARE; it's only *because of* what I AM that I offer to you what you ARE.

---

1. Mary Baker Eddy, *Science and Health with Key to the Scriptures* (Boston: Trustees Under the Will of Mary Baker G. Eddy, 1934), p. 272, l. 28.

To consider just being a diver into this play, into this sea of mediocrity, allows us to go on following, touching this path, touching that path, and saying, "There are a million paths to God." Well, guess where those paths are made up? I am sure God didn't say, *"I'm making up a million paths to follow Myself."*

Today I think the people who are searching are really people who are on spiritual relief. They are people who feel that something owes them a living, instead of questioning the Wonder of Being appearing to live.

I have always just been what I AM, and that is how I have lived. I have always tried to be just as I AM, and appear to be what you want me to be while I remain what I AM.

People will be very surprised to find you bearing this empowerment, even if you don't understand one word.

This doesn't have anything to do with your understanding. That's why your heart had better be right. This doesn't matter whether you understand or not. *Love is Love. Love is such a Force that it breaks asunder all that you think.* Even if you think you could go on blundering, you can't. It's a powerful Force, and that is why the Word is marked. *When the Word is with God and the Word was God,* what is left? There is no right!

This is how the Word, in itself, is its own environment. You live in the Environment of the Word.[2] This is why you will be so enhanced in your force and your power, without even opening your mouth! But you will be asked to! They will say, "What has happened to you?" You know, you're gorgeous to look at, you're beautiful, but that isn't by chance. Nothing is by chance.

The beauty that we see is but skin deep; the Beauty that IS is what allows the skin to appear. You are skinned and

---

2. See "The Environs of the Word" in Kenneth G. Mills, *The Golden Nail* (Stamford and Toronto: Sun-Scape Publications, 1993), pp. 33-45.

alive! So many Teachers, you know, are plagued with students who come for their scalps so they can just attach another one to their belts, and the number of Teachers seems to imply the number of scalps, how many Teachers you have scalped. That is very, very serious, as anyone who has studied will tell you, and anyone who has been endowed will tell you. **There are not really many paths to God. In fact, man makes them up according to his number, but there is only One.**

Isn't it a terrible thing? It puts an end to all your searching!! *It puts an end to all your excuses for not being Real.* It's terrible! There are no particular exercises that you think are present — but you have to exercise as never before. Why? It's not to lift the weight over your head, but to allow it to fall and still be. *It's the weight of your beliefs that has impressed everyone. Can you imagine the buoyancy of your state without them?* That's the buoyancy that comes with Being! It never goes with weight. Did you ever see buoyant weight? Why do you think everyone is trying to lose it!

> Linda P.) I don't know where you're taking me, but it's wonderful.

Where I AM taking you is beyond your
    thought,
And when you drop it, consider not
Where you left it; leave it to chance.
For you leap beyond that when you see the *I*
    and dance!

Allow others to say you took a chance,
But having done so, now you may dance
In the Rhythm of Being, found complete,
For in your heart you claimed, "I now
    will seek."

All the exercises that we do in listening and the exercise of ascribing only those thoughts that are considered in keeping with Principle are all the exercises that allow you to bypass the jurisdiction of the mind and its limits. You know, to say that you can think any way (other than when you are with Mr. Mills) and expect to achieve anything, is perfectly ridiculous. *You have got to be Real wherever you are, whether I'm there or not!* The most important thing is for you to realize that your very Presence is the mightiness of That which allowed the world this seeming appearance! You are the world you wander through and can leave it there as a dream, but you *see,* and then lo and behold, it only exists within your dream.

You're not lost without your world. It's only when you awake to the second degree of sleep that you have it to keep yourself entertained until *"I come."* Then it's not entertainment, it's *entrainment.* Yes. Just look how you've been entrained.

>Kevin N.) It was stated that the mind was limited?

Yes.

>Kevin N.) Is it not limited by our perception, or the limitations that we place upon it?

I have the mind but I don't consider it limited, because it stands aside as I am allowed to revel in what is beyond it and utilize it and verify what is beyond it by a seeming cataract of Sound called words.

That's the incredible part about the mind. It goes with your clonage but it is imbued also with what you might call a Light sensor, which allows it to respond to a Radiation that is cosmically grand, infinitely hopeful, and galactically engaging!

>John H.) Sir, last week you also said that the mind is the decoding machine for the five-sense world.

That's right. It is, and it's also the coding machine. It codes and decodes; that's how it keeps itself going. I break it. That's why we put an end to time. The Eschaton[3] is at hand because as soon as you realize What IS, time fades out as a limiter. The voiceprint is identifiable, the craft is ready for takeoff, and the landing is well geared for performance.

When you come to see a Star-Scape rehearsal, you will see that the demands are always unbelievable, and the considerations are always so fantastic! We dance, we hear a Music that is not heard, we offer considerations that haven't been considered, and we give new considerations for experiences and leap right beyond them. We had that experience last night at the rehearsal.

John D.) Just listening to what you are saying this evening, I think that the things that are cloaking our eyes will disappear when we are that Real, because the mind isn't taken up by trying to control the "cloaking things" in front of us. We can concentrate on the things that are Real.

That is right! *Do that. Now you have some idea what is Real: That which never changes.* That which never changes is That which is always with you and always will be with you.

John D.) And it's the One Path.

That is how the One Path is labeled "the One Path" and why it is so attractive and yet so terrifying, because so many people feel that when they walk the One Path, they haven't got a chance to be what they are. Of course that is a fear until they realize that what they Are is beyond any fear and it is not at all a viable excuse for fearing being Real.

---

3.   The "end of the world" or "last days," from the Greek root *eschatos*, "last, farthest."

So many people say that life is making a material success, and your wealth and your health are the results of how well you are living your life. Well, perhaps it is the most mesmeric state you are in, to think that health and wealth and success are the evidence that you are really a blessed spiritual being. Perhaps it is the tool of the diabolical to have you so sedated with such wealth and success and happiness? and peace? and stillness? Whoever heard tell of these ridiculous things?! They are all passing.

You will never achieve anything if you aren't coiled. How are you going to spring out of "this"? You can't, if you are just peaceful, sitting there twiddling your thumbs. How will you achieve anything?

Life is creative, it's doing! You say "I AM THAT I AM." That's great, but it doesn't do a thing. *The "AM" was never meant to be a catatonic state.* That's why it's in the Book as a catatonic state, because the Book is a catatonic state.

"AM" is always the AM-ing of the I, which means the Father-Mother-God is active as your very Life. When you can declare I AM THAT I AM, then you have the opportunity to BE if you wish it. When you stop wishing, then you are That. I always remember a metaphysician pointing that out to me. *Just to declare "I AM" doesn't mean that it's going to be anything other than just a dead statement. It's true, but nothing happens; it's not creative.* You have to take the AM and put it into the activity: the AM-ing, the creative.

> Emerson M.) It's kind of like saying, "Man is a Song" or "I am Song" and never singing.

That's right!

> John D.) It's also the same thing with "There is a path," but you must walk upon it.

Exactly. Or "Love is All" and you're not loving, you're critical. You know, people talk about love and being in love, but *Being IS Love and Love IS Being and it is critical when you think it's personal; it can come and go! When you are embraced in That Which IS a living experience, it's a constant. "This" has only a passing fancy, while That Which IS is Truth eternally dancing.*

> Irene S.) I have spoken to a few people behind the Iron Curtain where there has been a repression of religion for a number of years. I have asked some of them, "Well, how do you feel about not attending a service or a Mass or anything like that?" They say, "Well, it just leaves me absolutely cold; I don't find anything there." How do these people eventually find a way? They just can't seem to touch that God within, like a lot of people out there. So, going to a service and not going to a service is not doing anything. They are in limbo.

That is quite right; they are on spiritual welfare. I was in the Baltic states — Estonia, Lithuania, and Latvia — a couple of years ago, and also in Moscow and in Leningrad, Czechoslovakia, Poland, and Yugoslavia, doing many concerts. I did radio broadcasts and was interviewed. It was amazing, the things that happened in these communist countries. In 1988 in Russia, and in 1986, in Poland, Czechoslovakia, and in Yugoslavia, we did *The Fire Mass.*[4] The people were stunned that we were doing the Ordinary of the Mass.

We were given permission and were asked to come to

---

4. *The Fire Mass*, original Latin Ordinary of the Mass with additional text by Kenneth G. Mills, music by Kenneth G. Mills and Christopher Dedrick, recorded by The Star-Scape Singers, conducted by Kenneth G. Mills (Toronto: Sun-Scape Records, 1989).

these countries to sing, and we did it. The places were mobbed! In Vilnius we gave our performance in a huge Roman Catholic Cathedral that had become an art gallery! It was in the center of a beautiful park. The night we arrived for our concert, there were uprisings and the entire park was surrounded by soldiers with machine guns, all on the periphery of the park. They parted when our cars stopped, and we went in to do the concert and everyone who came, they allowed through. The place was packed. We knew it was a propitious moment to be there.

So, lo and behold, we sang. A few weeks later, in the papers there as well as, I believe, in the *Globe and Mail* in Toronto (we found this out when we got home), there was the picture of the huge cathedral! No one knew how it happened but it had been given back to the people, and for the first time in fifty years, a High Mass was celebrated with the church filled.

I could go on for hours about our experiences of singing, but they're all concomitant to the experience of Being.

When Man is Authentic and One Divine,
He's wrapped in the attention of what it is
    to be entwined
Within the framework of a vibrant scale
That allows each one to be heard to satisfy
    whatever might prevail.

Wherever he finds himself and is equated
    with Light,
He must be there to give the Pitch and the
    Sight
To all those who would be sprung out of the
    past and into the Now,
For it is a day that is garnered for the
    present somehow.

For the fields are white and the harvest
    prepared;
Are you a gleaner, without despair?
This is the moment that the Day hath made
When the Light dawned upon you, and you
    said, "'That I AM' is my Glory and my
    dismay.

"For in this conjecture that I am not this,
My heart takes a leap, and O the tryst
That must be awakened with the Divine
    Accord
That I am at One and thus employed,
For I see in the Rapture of Being Divine
The glory of Being, in time, Sunshine."

This is your lot, this is where you're cast;
You're part of the Stage, and may you last
To fulfill your roles and to find in the
    applause
That others have recognized themselves all
    because you live and never "was."[5]

Thank you.

▼

---

5.   "I AM always and never was." K.G.Mills.

XIII.

Freedom Is Found

What is going to undo the bondage to your perpetual false creation? Agreement to adopt principles and postulates commensurate with a newborn claim to freedom beyond the thought structures of limitations sponsored by believers.

Freedom Is Found

We are having a conference with those who have landed from the perch of preparation unto the birth of a Nation that is expected to be perceived in the newness of Spirit, in the unfolding pattern of design which will be according to the innate promptings of those who have conceived, within the framework of their spiritual gestation, those principles and postulates that will once again be anchored unto the plane for consideration and gowned in the panoply of newness, demanding fidelity to Principle, fidelity as Love would have Itself be manifest, and thus parade before the wavering solidarity movements of the mind and find in the Benediction of that said Presence that those waverings shall be the rhythmic wave in an action of rhythmic might, as all nations bow to the Wonder of the possibility of being born free in the realization of Individuality.

To conceive of the great Plan for the world, to conceive of the great concept of the world, and to *conceive* shows without doubt our ability to create. But certainly with doubt much of the world looks upon what it has created and the monsters it has let loose as a result of its thought-forces manifested after the personalization of possession and finding thus, in such an act, the reverse happening: the possession *by* personalization. This in itself reduces the possibilities of those who remain a kind of human, not realizing what it is to be a *kind* human! In this realm we leave open the doors to the speculatory process where men and women are concerned about the exigencies of today from the standpoint of today and where, hopefully, in the very near future, they will be precipitated into a new consideration which may irk the success problem and reveal the new Standpoint, that to try to solve a problem from within the problem is as ridiculous as trying to have a car go by putting a liquid in the tank that isn't gasoline! You cannot find the proper ignition; you cannot find the key.

This Lecture is available on cassette, Sun-Scape Publications ISBN # 0-919842-12-7

Remember, there is not a thing happening on this plane that was not planned to happen. But what kind of planning did you do? Was it Home planning, world planning, or selfish planning? And what kind of refuse have you to deal with, not only in the everyday world of unconsumed resources and waste products, but in the realm where the mind is given over unto the odds and ends of bits and pieces of a puzzle about which men and women fantasize the missing parts from the cauldron of their own unsatisfied conditions?

To talk about creating balance from the standpoint of person is the most ridiculous thing going . . going . . gone! Men and women will never achieve balance through the mechanical means of outer objects or inner objects. *The whole object of balance is to free the object from being an object and find it as it IS. The whole inclination of today is to achieve a balance without change,* hoping that a miracle will do it: the laying on of hands, the wringing of a scarf around your neck — oh! the wrapping of a scarf around your neck[1] — or in bygone days, the use of crystals to waft and wave through the various bodies of your emanation, expecting to bring about a balance. I mean, we are balancing *beliefs!* And that is not what you are here to do!

You are not here to balance beliefs; you are here to find out if there *is* one! *And how can you have a belief without a believer?* If you are what you are now said to be, the Divine Emanation, where is a belief but in hell?! And what is the damnation of hell? To get out of it *without changing* your beliefs! That is why hell is damnation, because you think that money can buy your way out, that a practitioner can *buy* your way out. In other words, you *think* so much that you forget what you ARE! You think so much, you are occupied always with what you aren't, and what you ARE is not thought! That is why what you aren't seems so impressive, because all your machinery does is think. It was born to think! But there was an *aspect* of your "ass-dom"

---

1. Considered by some to be a healing method.

that was beyond all this limitation: It was the ability to question *what* you think. *This is where, you might say, freedom is found.*

Most plans for freedom never happen because *freedom cannot exist on a false premise or a bed of lies.* If you think you're going to bring about peace and satisfaction and unity in a world where there is a divisive approach to the Fundamentals of Being, you are absolutely the maddest of dreamers! You cannot bring about peace and harmony when you are no melody in your own right. In other words, *you have to know the Melody of Individuality and the individual melody that is contrapuntally accepted in the Divine Fugue of Life!*

You cannot be precipitated into the venues of conflicting opinions and expect to bring out a pinion on the wing of an eagle! You cannot expect to fly high above the suggested objectification and remain in the nest of unfulfilled personal wishes. If you wait to have your personal wishes fulfilled, you will wait till the proverbial doomsday. *And what is doomsday? The mirrored image of moods-day!*

Remember, you cannot deal with success, the happenings of time, wrapped in alternating currents of attention and lack of attention, presence and lack of presence. Some have been guided onto the periphery of what you call Divine Considerations, what you might term as wholly acceptable considerations because they are attributable to an Ideal. When you have once started to question everything about you that isn't attributable to a Divine Ideal, how much of "you" exists that is Divine?

> Did you ever find the Divine aging?
> Did you ever find the Divine with a heart
>   condition?
> Did you ever find the Divine with corns on
>   the sole?

Did you ever find the Divine with an
    ingrown nail?
Did you ever find the Divine deaf?
Did you ever find the Divine sightless?
Of course not!
Because what you have claimed as Divine is
    beyond the description of believers!
You are in the realm of believers for the sake
    of those laggards.
A believer is a laggard, degreed for evasion
    of being discerned as such!

Why do you think there is so much learned, doctored erudition?! It is to evade detection of spiritual poverty. What is the value of having doctorates when you are dealing with an incurable situation?! You can't! You can say, "Well, what am I going to do with my life? I'm young and I've got the future ahead of me." Go on! What are you going to do with your life when you're old and have the future ahead of you? What is father going to say to son? "Go on!" But what is your recognition on the periphery? There must be a Center, either you could not have that circumference of activity! So that Center, if it is fixed, cannot have the periphery with the *option* of achievement. What is that achievement? To find the Center of your city four-square within the Circle of Creativity. That is the great mystery of the square within the circle and the circle within the square!

How do you have the ability to be manifested and to live with the Force of the Unmanifested? It is by being so pointed that others call you a "pain" if you are bothering their exterior mental considerations, or a "balm to the Soul" if they are in agreement with your point for encompassing the Structure of Being.

What is the value of considering the future when your "now" or your "present" is in such a hell of a mess?! The only thing it will be is still a future "hell of a mess." Why?

Because you are leaving it clad in one of the great maladies of today.

> *What is that malady of today? Giving to tomorrow what you should have done today. That is called procrastination, and procrastination is the very root of your future.*

If you live now, you would not know of a future. You would call it the continuing, perpetual creativity of Being Present! This is why, in Essence, That Which IS has never incarnated, because IT has never come to go and IT has never gone to come.

So, you can say,

> Gone with the wind are your dreams of
> winning salvation,
> As long as you are a believer trying to be
> saved.
> Gone with the wind is the hope and
> expectation
> If you do not know the
> Might of the Omnipotent One.

> Gone with the wind may be scarlet and
> hairy!
> And you would wonder what happens in
> that realm of doubt.
> Why, Love sets fire to what is not equated
> with the imperishable Power that is
> termed Love Eternal.

> What is gone is ne'er forgotten, when the
> ash of remembrance is fanned in the
> embers of Light;
> For out of the ash shall arise the Phoenix,

and my God, what is man to be given
but an opportunity of a second chance
of living life?
What is living but the evidence of Being!
But how creative when only selfishness
abides?
How extending is your creating activity
when the world is famished from side
to side?

Gone with the wind? No, It *comes* with the
wind, and it's termed the Zephyr
That comes from the zenith of expectation's
might!
And in the moment of the nadir you can
perceive with wonder
The inclination of the Zephyr is to fan the
Fire of Light.

Gone with the wind? It's the moment of
releasement from the breeze that says,
"Your end is nigh."
For this plane that is termed Earth and
equated with all the men and women
who there reside
Gives to those an opportunity for daring to
be the balance to the pendule that
would limit your life.
And you can say with the knowing, "The
Power is present. Where I live and
move and have my Being,
I co-create with my God, the
Fecund Light."

Gone with the wind? You must be coming
and going and cognizing only
spasmodic breeze.

But I AM always present and sowing — the
　　Divine, Perpetual, Eternal Tease —
To tease you into being equated with
　　something you're not, so it seems to
　　time,
And to tease you into seeing the *T* equated
　　with the Truth that sets free when
　　you're just a captive of your made-up
　　mind!

O what a flame is that scarlet! It's
　　wondrous.
O what a flame that burns so bright!
It leaves only the residue, no waste but the
　　ashes,
And they bear the aroma for those laggards
　　who said, "Where is Light?"

*The tendency of today is to equate what cannot be
equated. You cannot equate what is not thought with
thought.*

What are you?
(Horror upon horrors!) Thought!
What is hope?
A gift to thought.
Why does thought need a gift?
It's the one chance of having something
　　offered without turning around and
　　giving a kick to the gift horse.

Remember, whatever you are given and you accept
becomes yours to ride, because every thought builds a
rhythm.

You will never be without thought because you were
born as a result of it. Do you realize you got here because
someone thought?! They expected so much; and you had

the whole world on your side in a dream that said if you would do a certain thing, *you* would be a creator! And the whole world agreed; that's why you all have the same type of inhabitant. It was agreement that did it!

> *What is going to undo the bondage to your perpetual false creation? Agreement to adopt principles and postulates commensurate with a newborn claim to freedom beyond the thought structures of limitations sponsored by believers.*

It's the most unsatisfactory answer that anyone who was striving would want to hear. Anyone striving to create a new world would not want to hear it! But you can't create a new world when you're living in your old one dressed up as if *you* were going to dramatize the old in the garment of something new.

The New World is an adventure beyond an objective discovery! The New World is something you claim as an act of responsibility to inhabit and to experience the vegetation verdant with the wonderful agreement that one adopts in choosing those considerations that are in keeping with the adventure of stepping foot onto a new shore and going inland to find the Homeland of man's dreams.

Man dreams reams of material! It's all been published. What he has never published is the news that all of it was to awaken you from your dreams of the passing, and to awaken you to the Wonders of Being an observer, offering your hand, your smile, and your Love to those who do not know that the smile they perceive, the Love that they say they feel, and the hand which they say is so powerful is their *own* experience appearing to reach out to the outer limits of their frustration and being bound to the Wonders of their *own* possibilities once again fanned into the forefront of their considerations of newness and the claims of all that is commensurate with it.

The ads for today are all offering beer, cola, ginger ale, whiskey and wild, wild women to sponsor your life in a cause of mesmeric sedation from having to face the emptiness of your industry. You must be alert to the use of the boob tube to bomb your minds or your attention spans with such fragmentary formats of deception that you find yourself entertained instead of laughing at the incredible presumption made upon a supposed intelligent populace that they are falling for this filmstrip as if it would tease you into an authentic life experience! Remember, the reason you go to a striptease is because it teases you into considerations that you think are legitimate because you pay the price. But remember, the price you pay may strip you and you find yourself no longer teased but tormented because you have moved onto a level of seduction that would have you give up your Adventure and chase a faulty attraction to a shallow reef.

You will never be able to sedate your yearnings for the Higher Way. No one on this plane was born without a possibility to better himself. If we are wondering whether we have enough jobs to go around, perhaps the reason there is a scarcity is because there is such a withdrawal from doing what you should do unto others as you would have them do unto you. Everything is wrapped up in "me" and "mine" and possession, and what you have are people and worlds in need.

Recently I have been having telephone conversations where there are problems, problems, problems all over the world! Of course there are! What would these people do without them?! What would you do if you didn't have a *problem?!* You'd say, "I wouldn't have any income! I make my income by having a problem!" Do you realize the governments would be bankrupt? How can you make money if you haven't any problem? You'd have to revert to the system of bartering! "I'll give you a loaf of bread if you'll grease my lawnmower." What would the income tax department do? Will they tax your grease or your bread? It would not surprise me that there would be no need for it. Then they would really have to see.

Have you ever stopped to consider what your life would be like if you did not say you were a mother or a father? Or that you could be a mother or you could be a father? Have you ever stopped to consider, if you did not identify as such, you might be That! And being That, what have you to do but expose everyone who does not want to be That, by being That! Now that is what you call your corporation beyond the corporeal status of coming and going. Now, that type of corporation exists as a Light Body because that Light Body empowers only those thoughts that are in keeping with it. That is why it is said in the High Teaching that you have to be obedient and then be in agreement.

It is so interesting. I have listened to questions and I have listened to people talk for years. I said this morning, "It is so interesting to talk to people and to find it's exactly what people talked to me about in 1956, '57, '62, '67, '72, '77, '82, '87, 1990! The words haven't changed one bit; every young person has the same questions that I listened to before they were born!" And they think they have inherited a world that is growing?! I find the same questions coming out of young people that came out of their parents! I'm sure that some of the parents whom I have known had the same questions when *they* were babies! What hope of evolution as a result of belief?

Your satisfaction is not in joining belief systems. Your satisfaction is the condition of an experience that blesses involuntarily because of your place on this great circle or in this great square where the bell may ring and the bout may begin for you to evidence your knockout blows to those who contest your crown of victory.

You are a chosen people. Why? Why is it said? It is said to *everyone*. It just happens to have been thought to be said to a few. If I say, "You are a chosen people," what do you go to? The people you do not even know, a land you do not even know? I am sure people say they are a chosen people and they do not even know why they are chosen because they have never been told why they are chosen.

Because they have money? Because they are selfish? Because they are out to sponsor the chosen people?

> *The chosen people are those who know the Allness of the Divine.*

That's why it was given to the chosen people at that time. It was said in the Bible, *Ye are the chosen people. Why? Because first and foremost they worshiped something beyond themselves and they called it "Divine."* And the Divine is that which you know exists but you don't know how in your hell it does! So, you create a statue and you call it names and if you do not know what to call it, you are forbidden to call it anything! Then what happens? You start calling it something, and that poor something that you have created out of your mind is where you are: out of your mind!

Why must God live? How can God live, if you do not worship? *How many of you worship to attune yourselves to that part of you which is Divine?* Most of the time you read books on the way to work and keep up with what is being published so you won't be nincompoops. You want to understand what is philosophically encroaching upon this subject or that subject, and what is psychologically happening on this subject, and physiologically having an effect on this side of you, and psychologically having an effect on that side of you!

How many sides are there to you anyway?! There are supposed to be all kinds of *facets,* but who ever said there were sides to you? I thought the sides were to be the evidence of your ministrations of Love, Wisdom, Power and Insight! What are you evidencing? Fill in those sides in your life — worry, lack, "No one loves me," "I'm all alone." Or, "Here I am, I've got my own! I've just appeared to belong to something, because I get bored occasionally." But after all, you know sugar isn't good for you! That is one of the juiciest situations to get into: to be so self-content that you become almost crystallized with the most delectable something-or-other. Ask Susan; she had it last night at dinner and it was scrumptious. It was brittle and tasty to the outside, but inside it was soft and creamy.

That is the wonderful part about humans: outside they are crusty, and inside they are so soft and, unfortunately, gooey. *What you need is not a creme brulée; what you need is to have some form of Force that will cause the encrustations to dissipate.* What breaks up a crystal? A mighty blow! Well, why do you think when you have a crystallized condition of thought that it isn't going to take the mighty hammer of Vulcan to blast it to smithereens?! And you mean to tell me you are going to be happy about it? After it you will feel vacant, and you'll wonder what is your lot. What's going to happen? What type of colonic are you going to have: low, high, internal, or mental? What will come out? The only thing that could is refuse.

Are you taking in "this"? If you are, you're going to be awfully heavy. Because most of you will not be able to digest it. You know why? You will think too much about words. You will not have any digestive problem at all if you see that *the words are leading you to the Divine Enzyme: Truth.*

It will take care of all your mental problems, because it has a Divine Chemistry that brings about its own Self-renewal. "Self-renewal" is the name you give for not understanding the perpetuality of Life. A Self-renewing is inevitable, and it has nothing to do with your perpetuating your image and likeness. It has to do with creating that which is beyond the limitations that go with the belief of being a reincarnated human.

Don't worry about all the conditions in the world. Why would you? Just look at them and see what part you have played in bringing them about. As long as you view from a divided standpoint, you have a divided encounter. As soon as you view from a united front, you have a Power upon which you can depend.

> *Take Principle, not person; God, not a myth; and Love, a creating Principle to fecundate your life experience. See in the Wonders commensurate with the concept of Individuality that a nation will never be other than those who make it up.*

Will you be made up in the image and likeness of the Divine, or will you be made up and foster division and attempts at wholeness, attempts at newness?

> *The new world is not tomorrow.*
> *The New World is NOW.*

The moment you think about it, it already needs to be polished with the wax of the Sun. It will wane in the light of a reflective nature, the dust will settle upon it, and once again you will be back into your mesmeric flow of moonlight and sunlight, the mesmeric influence of night and day.

How often in the day do you ever hear anyone say, "You are the one"? It's only in the night, when you don't have to look. Then in the morning you say, "Oh! What did I say?!"

Now is the accepted time! The world's future depends not upon the world, not upon the multitude; it depends upon the individual willing to become that Indivisible Wonder and that universal, involuntary Beneficial Factor appearing to be at that right moment when the currents of a Divine Event cognize your presence and all those, outwardly or inwardly, say,

> "Hallelujah! For we have seen how the
> Pentecost of Light

Has spoken to each one of us in this hour of
the Wind, its Fire, its Might."

All those who have heard may consider what testimony they will write upon the Scrolls of their achievement as they pen their cadence to the composed life experience in the Light of Individuality, Indivisibility, and the Universe given back to the Arms of Love.

Yours is a Mission possible, creditable, and wonderful, as soon as you forget yourselves, forget your petty attractions, and get on with Being new and breaking anything old that would bind you to a system of belief and that of a do-gooder.

Remember, the mesmerism of today
is to personalize so that tomorrow
may be populated with those
who are going on!

Remember when you were born? Somebody told you, "You have to believe us, dear. You *were* born. I saw you come." And then you might say, "But Mum, Dad, who saw *you* come?" And they said, "Our mother and father saw us come." And you can say, "Yes, but where are they, other than a declaration that they saw you? Who sees you now?" *Are you the result of a belief system, or are you here to awake those that sleepeth so that they may gain Eternal Life?*

What is Eternal Life? Only that possibility which can bestow upon all those who are willing to relinquish their hold on a divided approach to life and find themselves blessed, adjusted, in a newness becoming an adventure perceived and manifested all because you agreed to awaken.

To be awake must mean that you had been sleeping. And if you are awake, why sleep any longer in the cradle that has the same questions of two thousand years ago, three thousand years ago, yesterday, still being asked. *What creative evolution is happening? If your creativeness is so great, why are those being born still asking the same question?*

The trumpet gives no uncertain sound unless it is placed to the lips of one who was never schooled to use the breath correctly, and the lips. We dance through the two lips, and we dance through the tulips.

> From above, these tulips/two lips said,
> "Look at those tulips! They're acres of red.
> There are acres of scarlet; there are acres of
>   yellow and orange and blue."
> But from the height, it would look like a
>   patchwork quilt, as I said on KLM and
>   viewed.[2]
>
> But as I approached the ground, the quilt
>   faded.
> The acres became scarlet, and in the distance
>   blue.
> And then there was a white glowing bright
> At the side in my sight;
> And lo and behold, it was of a different hue.

We landed. Where were the tulips? Only in the realm of describing the experience to you. Can you relate to a tulip? Of course you can, because we all agreed to call that manifestation of Wonder by the same name.

From a distance, you would never have known they were tulips. It looked like a patchwork quilt of silken pieces, wrapped around the earth.

> It looked as though healing was being done
>   to the surface of the planet —
> These colored scarves to bring a healing to
>   some!
> I didn't see who was creating the balance,
>   but every color fitted in the most
>   incredible way,

---

2. On a flight to Amsterdam.

> Because the blue of devotion, with the Sun
> always shining, wrapped the landscape
> in Wonder.
> What a tulip parade!

We said we landed at the great terminal, the *end* of our destination? "Thanks for being with us." It was the most amazing contradiction. I didn't believe it at all! It was the *beginning,* and they said it was the end! We wouldn't have done anything! They fed us a lie. They said it was "the termination of your flight." It was the beginning! That is what I did to the "dam" of the "amster"! I said, "You can't dam it by saying it's the termination of our flight. It is the beginning of our action, which is to revisit this land and see the Creative Spirit still being manifested in the Wonder of gardens, tidiness, order, His handiwork to show."

What is your handiwork showing? The ability to buy a car, a new suit of clothes, expensive jewelry? And what do you do? Do you invest for the sake of appearance, or do you invest for the sake of diversification so that others may appreciate whatever form your beauty may wear? It all depends on how you view the diversification, whether you call it extravagance, selfishness, flamboyance, *or* the elegance becoming the Divine Apparel. *If you are elegant in the Divine Nature, why wouldn't you appear to be elegant as the Divine Expression?*

Wrap yourself as a gift and let others say, "What ribbons surround your boxed condition!" And you say, "Yes, open me and find me a theme of your Allness. Do you dare to view me as an aspect of yourself?"

> *How long will we have separateness?*
> *As long as you cannot see*
> *the beauty of another*
> *and know it is your Self.*

Do you think I'm going to leave Carol looking so gorgeous, and have her out there a ravishing woman? I'd be ravished if I did, because I would be right in the realm of attraction. Knowing the Beauty that is Carol is my Self, I'm satisfied to see the facets of my own appearing as another. The handsomeness of Stephen, Terry, Itamar, Rob, Ben — boy! Justin, growing up. Do you think I'm going to leave it outside mySelf? Wouldn't you be a fool to have all these jewels unset in your ring of engagement with this plane? What a circumference! What a periphery! *Is your finger pointing to the moon or to the Sun? Or to the Individuality that cannot be destroyed by your belief system?*

It's a wonderful lecture to cause you irritation if it hits home, upset if it has struck your pot, and Wonder if it has pierced your disguise.

This has been given to you from this Plane of the Uncontradictable Light of Wonder, for in it there was no thought of anything that has been given, so how can one be bound by the thought of having been a giver?

> So in this spontaneous Ejaculation, may you
> find the Seeds of Light
> Find a place of resting in seclusion as they
> bring forth the Wonder of Unfettered
> Life.
> May your garden bloom in Wonder with the
> asters, the snapdragons, the calendulas,
> the sunflowers of time;
> And may your seeds be Self-perpetuating
> and reveal the Wonders beyond an
> errant mind.

Your world is what you have made it; the World that IS is Divine: Which will you accept? Your world, to be practical and try to heal *all* that is in it without offering the Divine Panacea? The world will change if you change your thought. Without thought, where is your world that needs a change?

If all men and women could say, *"I will only choose that thought commensurate with my world through which I move,"* that world would appear to be a revolving platform on the Axis of Wonder and in the Embrace of Light. The Balance is Divine; it is only achieved when Love is All.*

They may call you a freak, then, because you just Love — come hell or high water! *The only dammed nation is the one that does not realize it is Divine. What makes up a nation? Its inhabitants.*

> *What will you espouse?*
> *Reality or unreality?*
> *Options or Uncontradictable Premise?*

The choice is yours! That is what hope gave you. It struck you on the chest with the thump of your heart beating and waiting to be freed from the limitations of such a limited embodiment.

Oh, it[3] is not very "hopeful"; hope has nothing to do with it! It is demanding, because it says, "Live beyond believers and carry the pinions of the Bird of Light!"

▼

---

3.   The Lecture called *Unfoldment.*

XIV.

A Reflection of the Wordless

You are endowed with the rights of all aliens.
You have entered this planet with
a Green Card and you are allowed
to live here, to vegetate here, or
to succeed here, to leave a mess . . or a
wonder, according to your attainment.

A Reflection
of the Wordless

You are the Custodians of a most *unusual* Experience.

I would now try to offer to you, in the framework of language, a Language of a Sound equivalent to the Sound of Silence. This is an Experience of the Sound of Silence.

It has been endeavored over the past occasions, in our visits with this View magnified beyond the densities which surround the mortal mind-weavings of confinement, to bring to you and to penetrate your vehicle of attention with the Seeds of Promise that are affirmed to be true because *I*, in the magnitude of Wonder, live.

I live beyond the myriad thought-forms of suggestion; *I* live beyond the starry-eyed concepts of promise. *I* live, not because you have made it so, but because Love must always have a corresponding identity and be found as the Force Field that causes agitation so that the great Movement that is commensurate with Being is once again magnified and keyed-in to the Infinite Possibilities that are awaiting those who Love.

> *You who seem to be hearing*
> *the tenor of these Words,*
> *allow your minds to relax.*
> *Do not equate what you are hearing*
> *with anything that you know.*

For what you are hearing in the Sound Forms as they come to you does not demand that you equate them with anything in your limited computering, but does demand that your computering rests for the moment of hearing this Cataract of Sound so that you may enter a state that is termed "meditative"; in other words, where the thought machinery seems to slow down as a moment of restoration and a recharging of the spiritual pockets, which are enhanced for the adventures of tomorrow.

You are endowed with inalienable rights. It is so, because in the hearts of those who have appeared on the surface of this planet, you are given the rights of all aliens: you are allowed to pass the time-space continuum in this formation without the disturbance of not having the rights which *allow* you to seek a living and prosper, be happy and successful according to the indoctrination of your planet.

However, these words are a *correlative,* you might say a *reflection,* of the Wordless. The words are trying to offer to you a State that you will intuit as being *viable* in the force of the vitality and the renewing of your spirit for the encounters with that which is inevitable: the Wonder of those who find your Presence on this planet, which has up until this moment been disguised in the garment like "otherness."

You are fortunate indeed, because you have received, without stint, an abundance of such a treasure-trove of Stellar Light that it is unfortunate that you have not donned a gown which would attract the Confetti of this Passing unto you. For you should be sparkling with such plenty and such wonder and such irradiance that it would quicken all those whose spirit wanes as we approach the gateway and the doorway into another century of belief.

You should not be inundated with the attitude of the skeptics; you should be promising so much hope and newness in the new century! A new century is just a number on a calendar, as is a dollar sign upon a piece of paper; it bears *nothing* other than a way to mark the *passing* of the time on this planet. The expectancy has caught your attention, for you see, *you are geared to be hooked by certain ideas so that you will try to once again be brought out of the waters or the delusion of this mesmeric encounter with form, and once again awaken to a Conscious State of Being.*

You are getting used to the Words that are used by this One, and you are being gradually lifted into a new type of vocabulary in which your human form is now accepted as a *cloned* experience. This is fortuitous unto your spiritual and Light edification, because as long as you attribute unto the human form attributes and conditions that are really not authentic, your nature can never grow in the amplitude becoming the Sound Wave that is being entertained by your attention span.

You are in a position of events. It was mentioned, in the passing of the information from attention to attention, that there is an event. That event, of course, is one that has to be bridged, and it is bridged by realizing that the event of "you" and "me" is, really, *contained.* The real meaning is not "you" and "me"; it's what has happened in the events *between* "you" and "me." It's in this space, this "no man's land," that the great Event is happening. It is due to your *attention* that that great **Eventuality** is not doing anything other than causing you to focus so that you may be found accepting this Sound Wave and finding it once again beating in a rhythmic content of importance so that the Self is once again being recognized not as something cloned but as *that Element of Wonder* that allows this cloned semblance to appear motivated in the realm of the unearthly: the *spiritual* realm.

This is the way we have been *programmed.* You should *know* that the program has been conceived as almost perfect, but not totally; *this is why this **Mechanic** has appeared!* Part of the Code was not completed, and it was not realized until you had left for this planet!

The part that has been missing is that part that allowed you instantaneously to never lose contact with your vibrating Essence! *This vibrating Essence is a tonal feature that has been nullified by the intellectual pursuit of the mundane plane.* This is the *time,* you might say, to lose confidence *in* it! Because it is not in the passing of time, but in the vibratory frequency of the Wave that comes when one is being attuned to the frequency and the vibration of a Higher Motivation and an *Operandi,* not equated with the considerations of time, that you are being given a Charge of replenishment to your vehicle, which must *never* be devoid of the vitality *and the innate urge to move!*

Movement is equated with change. There is a great need to understand movement, because you think of movement, of going from one place to another, and you say, "I move." But you see, movement on the higher level means that when you go from one place to another, the place you have arrived at becomes the next step on your ladder of achievement.

> *There is no going back to positions outgrown!*

This is why that statement has been given to you on the lower plane where you are being given the basic ingredients for the discipline that must become the vehicles wrapped in the element of "mind" to attain a mastery of the technique that is essential for leaping beyond the kind of obstacles that the mind offers unto each and every one who attunes unto the Mystery of a Divine State that is never altered.

If your state is being altered by the penetration of this Sound Wave, then you know your state is one that is worthily and wonderfully received, because you are present for the perception of the *need* of being altered. That Power to *be* altered is not because you have arrived at the stable; it is at this *Stable Point* that you must find how the "within-ness" and the "without-ness," the room within or the stable without, is a condition of mentality. **It is the donning of the Divine Principle which *allows* you to be what is Real without having to offer your appearance to the demolition of time's incessant wear and tear upon your vehicle.**

You understand in time that you age. This aging is the name that the mind gives to the process of seeing the change in the vehicle. Now, you should understand that this has been agreed upon by you before you came: **you agreed to gracefully make an exit.** You entered onto the plane — sometimes head first, sometimes feet first — but there could be no breach of contract with the Facts of your Purpose for being here! *You are here* because you *chose* to be here.

You are *planted* upon this plane because you tended to the possibilities of being seeded on a fertile ground where you might view your own efforts at growth! In the other dimension, you do not have this experience at all; you do not need "this" at all. You must realize that the experience of understanding what is termed "the wonder of germination" is really encoded with the knowledge that is considerable with regard to this short period in the time framework. *But it is not coded with the understanding that allows you to be freed from it before it deteriorates!*

Every plant has a length of life, and this is why, I am sure, the Wisdom of the Saints and the Sages and the Masters of Wisdom have so endowed the plane with this possibility: you would *watch* the germination from a seed to a mature flowering and then returning to the seed. You wish to see such a cycle, such a circling, because it is an essential element of orientation: the movement from a center with a radius which can describe a circumference if it is outlined by a Living Force.

The great task that we take up is the great burden of trying to deal with "this" as if it were Real. So the song "This is My Task" is one for those in the stage of becoming, but "This is My **Wonder**" is the song that is given to those who start to perceive the Limitless Nature of Possibilities! "Possibility" is only a word that has been sounded for *you* because it goes with *position.* Every position has a possibility, either there would be no need of the position; so you see, "possibility" and "position" go together.

The one thing that has been adopted that *should never have been adopted* on your level is the possibility of procrastination, for *procrastination is a great hole through which much energy leaks.* It is subtle; it is termed "devilish" because no one knows what to tell you to alert you to the malfunctioning that happens in some of the patterns of assimilation of the fiction and the facts surrounding this experience.

Sometimes it appears that you associate yourselves with the fictitional and it takes a great deal of *force* to bring you to the point of being *willing* to perceive that you have based so much of your life on fiction and not on Fact! Fact has what is imperishable, unalterable; therefore, what is alterable and what is perishable should never be taken as the code or a standard from which you operate! If you adopt What IS Imperishable and it's omniactive in your experience, you will *not fear* what appears as this process that you do not understand because of your lack of *Wisdom.*

Now, no one has engaged this devoid of the possibility of understanding. You would not be attracted to this unusual Declaration if it were not within your Code to do so. **But it is imperative that you perceive that you may not understand this, and this is not in any way disturbing!** The only requirement is that you *listen* and refrain from thinking that you've heard it before and you will hear it again. It is a *request* on the part of Light that you listen with attention but allow your mind to drop its barrier wall. It is *not* in any way going to destroy it, but it is going to *relieve* you from the mind's ever-thwarting tendency: *The mind attempts to always define your situation in reference to its patterns of thoughts!*

Understanding has been misunderstood! It should never be an essential for achievement.

> *What should be essential*
> *for achievement (be it known to you)*
> *is obedience to Principle.*

And if that appears as person, then no matter how wrong that person is, if your heart is right and your mind is unquestioning, you cannot help but be blessed, even by what appears as a mistake which turns out, due to your obedience, to be a blessing.

The only time false teaching may have a deleterious effect upon you is when you aren't totally present in your wish to attain the Culture that frees you from this structured culture of limitation. The present culture of today is one that is totally limited by the scandalous situations magnified to an importance they do not rightfully deserve.

You are not a people *of* a nation. You are a people who are a Light *to* a nation. Your nation is *not found here.* You are *not* of a nationality. This is why to try to call yourself a Canadian or an American is so difficult, because it doesn't mean anything to you, particularly, other than what each state causes you to obey. It's a fascinating thing: *The culture of limitation has a force of restriction, and the Culture of the Light sees none.*

You are endowed with the rights of all aliens. You have entered this planet with a Green Card and you are allowed to live here, to vegetate here, or to succeed here, to leave a mess . . or a wonder, according to your attainment. The great Code that you have been endowed with is one that is complete, in some ways, for your peregrination here, but it is incomplete. And this is why what is termed the "High Teachings" or the Emergence of the Light was called, so that you could be freed from your plight, because you yourself are able to question your abilities and see them lacking. If they were not lacking, the Code would have been complete.

Those of you who have achieved will perhaps see, one day, Light Masters, and you will perceive that the Code must have been completed, either They would not be present with the answer to what appears as a deficiency of the Spiritual Energies commensurate with the necessary thrust to regain your position in the Stellar Fleet of Wonder.

The Enterprise is grounded because it must have a point of origin. Your exploration can be unlimited because it is done by the Sound Wave of response to a call, a plea, and that is always (to those who are ever on duty) for the enhancement of the Plan, the magnification of It, and the reenchantment of the Wonder of Heaven here on Earth.

You will never find the planet a reenchanted planet. It is only the reenhanced Light of Vision that allows you to look upon the limited terrain and bestow upon it the infinite, unlimited possibilities of a *concept* untarnished by a thought-filled mind.

Your intuitive prompting to cohabit with Wonder is a wise one, to put an end to that which would cause division. You see, when men and women are cloned for the purpose of experience, they should not be dissatisfied with what they have as their forms. If women are women and wish they were men, as so many do, and if the men are men and wish they were women, as so many do, next time you will, perhaps, make a different choice. It was your choice to choose the clone and its formation and what went with it.

You were also taught and geared for performance before you came here. *You were geared to perform upon hearing a Frequency, and that is why it is said that it is the recognition of the Voice that is essential for those who are attuned to the Promised Age of Endless Wonder.*

The Promised Age of Endless Wonder is really the higher level of the Utopian dream. Utopia has been misunderstood because "Eureka!" hasn't been experienced.

Your dream is not in vain; it is vanity that makes it so.

If you will see how your ego tends to make excuses for everything you're doing, and it tries to psychologically imbue you with legitimate reasons for sustaining your position where you are, then you *know* that you are dealing with a psychic force of diminution, because you were given a power of augmentation. It is through this Power of Augmentation that I perceive, while remaining the same in body, mind, and

Soul, a View that only *I* witness and still maintain a form and a presence.

You can say I am not the same when I speak as when I live my daily rounds with you. That is, really, malpractice. *I am exactly the same,* but due to *you* I can't have my round and be as I AM if *you* will not dance with *me* as I AM. It is a square dance, you might say, in the round! *But how can it be squarely dealt with if "you" intend to have your own corners?* [1]

The Secret Place of the Most High is where you go when you would leave your "me" and find an impromptu happening garmented in an unworded feeling, intuitively so profound that the unverbalized Moment is *intuitively magnified.*

It is in the power of the Intuitive that the magnification happens, and what you call "within" or "without" no longer is considered of importance because you are stabled in the Knowing Place of that which is termed the Secret Place of the Most High. It is there that *I* abide.

Why would you criticize God for remaining in His Heaven and appearing not to be anyplace on Earth?! If "God's in His Heaven" and "He's right with the world," why do you say He's left in Heaven? When you say, "God in His Heaven is right with the world," do you think you have been left out?

The Divine is not material; the Divine is the Light that allows the material to be defined and cut in many pieces so that you are clothed in Wonder.

Your garment is wrapped and ribboned with Wonder and Love. How do you know when anyone walks with Love? They bestow a Grace just in their passing. What kind of love have you got if your presence isn't calling another to question, *"What is this power of attraction I feel for you?"*

---

1. Mr. Mills has stated, "In the Esoteric Literature, the corner is always where the devil hides."

You can say, "That is the Radiance of the Quickening Spirit of Wonder that I exude because IT causes my heart to beat in rhythm with the Rapture of Being and my movement to bring about change."

The reason all musical form has movement is because it is *forever changing* in the garment of a *Harmonic* Embrace. So is Life living embraced in the Harmonic Splendor of the counterpoint commensurate with That which will **give evidence** of the *One Voice,* inditing a Message according to those who would listen and the need for various subjects to be expressed.

It's very difficult to listen to many subjects and counter-subjects, because each must have a *hook* to catch your attention while *I* tie the ribbons of Wonder for your embrace.

You are a chosen people because you have chosen to question that part of your system which is missing, which allows you to be at One with that missing Force, the Self. That Self recognized and experienced has many names and has been called into many, many serials of expression; but the one that is common to you who have been Christianized to some degree is called "the Christ." In the aftermath of trying to define IT, IT is called *that part of you* that allows you to perceive your Self and to *know* your Self more than this! All this and Heaven's abundance!

All is well, for in this I rejoice: I could never have uttered a word if a Word had not been the *instantaneous moment* where a historical past and a promised future *fade out* in the newness of the Nowness bearing meaning that allows you to experience the Feeling of Being I AM.

These words may not make sense, but at least they have been a Cataract of Sound upon your attention, which once again *retunes* your strings to *respond* as I pluck them, for the Symphony must be attuned for That which will be conducted in this Age upon the stage in which you will be known for having participated in the Spearhead of Sound and its evidence.

The Sound of Silence . . It's not when something isn't happening. The Silence is the fecund Might of the Unlimited waiting to find exaltation freed from the minimized concepts of those endowed with the alien's rights to be at peace in the land, sojourn, and multiply the Substance of Being. In this rejoice: It is said that *I* have poured you out a Substance that your limited sense cannot even contain, because you have realized the Wonders of giving yourself to That Which IS as the first fruits of those who would seek Him and find Him Altogether Lovely in the name of the Divine Self. It is graced, it is bestowed, and it is multiplied according to your inherent *penchant* to be involuntarily a Benefactor of Light to your Age. The Ageless Wonder is that you could appear to express an infinite Stellarscape of opportunities.

▼ ▼ ▼

Rest in awareness, not in oblivion.

Revel in the masquerade you wear, for the Ball has begun and you must know how to square dance and how it shall be accomplished that you circle the Point with the effervescence becoming the champagne music of the gods!

You should be exuding the Wonder and the vitality of a newborn!

The Joy of Being is profound; in other words, it's deeply intoned.

Stop gossiping!

Anyone who meets and discusses another one just for the purpose of discussing what you don't like about them or their pitfalls or their weaknesses — unless you are discussing how to free them, raise them, and exalt them, shut up!! Love one another, and stop criticizing unless it is to critique the possibilities of Wonder of all those who love.

> *Expose error by all means; but be willing to stand as the Witness or Light to it.*

Be spiritually inclined to attune the ear to the Wonders, and review the scene not with the eyes but with the hearing of the ear, and take away the dictatorship of the eye so that the Mastership might be *heard* as a **Wave** of movement upon your "sketch-pad of possibilities."

> *Conceive a Wonder, see it magnified, and in one minute, it is done!*

▼

XV.

The Pristine Drop of Clarity

There is no possible way
to escape Being Divine.
What is the obstacle course?
It's made up with the personalization.

The Pristine
Drop of Clarity

What flows from the Center is the **drop of pristine clarity** and what reaches the outer rim is the pristine clarity diluted by the thoughts that it isn't. It is the tincture of belief that has diluted it.

The delineation of "this" is all because of the Center.

Well, I think of all the Thanksgivings, and the fragrance still remains with me; they have all been very, very moving, but I think this one has been one that has perhaps, in certain ways, transcended them all. I have heard, I have seen, and I have experienced such an enhancement of clarity, and such an enhancement of purpose, and such an enhancement of freedom that I have never before perceived as the Body of Christ. Ordinarily the Body has been impeded by the members of it trying to have their own way, but I think the old chorale "Have Thine Own Way, Lord, Have Thine Own Way" is far more in keeping with the Confetti that has dropped to Earth.

You see, you have taken upon you the yoke of simplicity and now you must have the reign of prosperity becoming the paradigm of the *new* freedom found in the body of a living organic wholeness that will bring about what is termed the Essence of a Cosmic happening that has sometimes been called the Cosmic Christ, which has been such a Mystery.

The Cosmic Christ is that Effulgence which beams from the Center of any design that man holds dear to the delineation of his propensities.

If the Word is to be made flesh and dwell among us, it can only be in the appearance of the magnification of Wonder, because the Body That IS is so fitly joined to the archetypal response of Essence within the heart of each and every communicant that it is expedient that no more is allowed to enter into the thought-patterns of your experience, for now you are perceiving the frequency of adoption and adaption which comes when one is being adapted to the Electrical Force of what is termed the *Invisible*.

The Transcendent Nature of Being is practical, because you are the practical custodians of the Invisible. For you people to be sitting on the floor of time and thinking that you are nothing but so many pounds or so many stones in weight is one of the most fallacious jokes for any semblance of identity. To sit on the floor of time is to anchor the Meaning of the Gift so that all those who are witnessing unto prophetic fulfillment and the fatidic Wonder — which becomes the fanned expectation of many who have engaged in the Esoteric Studies and who have attempted to bring them into a practical application in the everyday world — are finding as never before that the study of the Word doesn't do anything but allow the intellect to become more intoxicated with its own supremacy instead of being brought to the point of reverence for Something beyond itself.

This is why, in the Adamic culture, we might say that the first great block against man's natural gift of self-explanation was that, instead of considering how come we appear to be matter, we have dreamed up such a nightmare: "Well, God did it! He took a clod of earth and he breathed into it a Breath of Life." It isn't into the matter that Life is breathed; it isn't the matter that breathes Life; it is the matter that your mind has projected into a dimension where it can be *perceived*.

Matter is not necessarily *this* organic structure. Matter is *not* necessarily this organic structure. This is the way you have *defined* your projection . . into space.

What you projected into space, you now have lost the ability to account for, and you called it by a name. It was not self-explanatory because you *impressed* upon it; in other words, you carved the name of your lack of identity and you called it "matter," instead of perceiving that what you call matter is the description your mind, in its incompleteness, details to that which it cannot identify. That's why matter is termed "dust to dust," because it has no determined nature from the standpoint of its Essence.

Matter is the name of the objectified projection, and the life it seems to exude is another misunderstanding of *Life!* Spirit, Soul, Mind, Principle — these are names that have come to the assistance of a *supposititious identity crisis* because they are not, cannot, will not, should not, never will be, subject to tenure, because they are incorporated within divergent streams.

These synonyms of Essence, collectively called "God," "Self," "the Ultimate," "Principle," are compound, complex considerations because they do not bear any resemblance to your projection that you call "matter," which means, in your Enlightened State, you now can consider what is at the core of the disillusionment of mankind.

> *You may now perceive that matter has been the root suggestion that needed to be seen for what it is and for what it isn't.*

Now you know how it is defined: It is the projection of your mind into a place of identity, and you don't know *how* it's happened, you don't know *how* it's called, but you had to call it "matter" because matter was touchable — but *not permanent!! That* was your key for these past thousands of years and you have not perceived it!

We have echoed from the Mountaintops this refrain, but there have been very few on the entire Escutcheon of Achievement who have decked themselves in the royal robes of self-renunciation to attempt to bring freedom to this encumbered thought-pattern which has misidentified the Structure of Being!

You are the Moment of great attunement as soon as you perceive that matter isn't solid; it is really the mental objectification! It cannot be what you call Spirit and the rest of the synonyms. They cannot be in matter because they cannot be found in matter, but what *can* be found is the evidence that they *must BE,* for without them, matter isn't!! Without them . . I AM. But what is I AM if you *personify* it and say it is captured in matter? I AM is not captured in matter; IT allows the material, mental construct to reverberate with the Thunder of Identity: I AM!

The tympani of time is the thundering on your mental *hide* (which is what? the acquired thought-sets that you term your intellectual attainment). When the "tautness of time" brings you to question, then you *hear* the beat of the drum, because it is beating out the rhythm that is in keeping with the Synonym of Essence and it reveals the Light Strokes so that the thunder is heard as a witnessing, a demonstration of the Invincible Nature of Being.

If there has been one great gift misevaluated, it is your great gift of being a projector! You are supporting the most incredible system of agreement ever conceived. You are supporting a system that is termed cosmological in its essence and its holistic nature. This is one of the greatest gifts you have, but because you have lost the *reins,* you have lost the *Throne* position, you have allowed *the mass of objectification to seduce you* into moving it around instead of the projector altering what is to be moved!

There is not a thing out there that can't be moved, if it is essential to your correct Identity — *but it isn't!!* And because it isn't, that's why it seems stationary! If it were in keeping with your Identity, it would be as *fluid* as the River of Life, but since it isn't, you don't need to be concerned about that objectification that you call your world and its inhabitants. All you have to do is rest in the assurance that I AM that ability to exonerate the suggestion from the devilish confinement of misapprehension.

If matter were actual, you would never be able to see through it! As soon as you can see through an "it," it ceases to be actual; the *seeing* is actual. What is the seeing?

It is amazing to see the robbers of the past, when the coach was staged and the stage was coached: No one perceived that the drama enacted was not only in learning the lines to give them power. The coaching had to do with what? Getting the actor or actress to adopt the attitude of playing a part, which meant it had nothing to do with the supposed identity; it had to become another enactment. That other enactment gave the stage an opportunity to allow the witnesses to identify with another type of identity. But the crisis was not great enough, because the audience left when the lights went up and said, "What a stage show!" not realizing that their presence was the only thing that allowed them to perceive a show on the stage, all as a result of their attention being focused upon what they had objectified as the actors of a part.

Why is revelation considered paramount in the foretaste of Glory Divine? It is because revelation is the revealing not of an understanding of an old text but of the obliteration of its suggestion of limits. Revelation reveals an initiatory flight into perception unconfined and uncontaminated by human hypotheses and undwarfed by the material fortifications of an intellectual skin of attainment.

When you hear your head throbbing with the invisible mallets upon the skin of time, then you know the Force to that throbbing is waiting for audience. The throbbing is *not* the audience; the throbbing is the knocking for *alertness to the Visitor.*

You think all your esoteric studies, all your sincere motivations, will give you freedom. They only give you a panacea for a short time. It's like an anesthetization for a short time, before you wake up to the pain that still exists.

One of the most important features for your Glorification Ceremony is that you now know that what you consider matter is not in Essence matter at all. It's the name that forgettery gave to a culprit in order to make friends with it for better or for worse, because there was no sense of the Holy Union!! It had ceased to BE, because men had dreamed too long about their objectification becoming superior and ruling the planet of their own thrust into the cosmology of an unlimited Consciousness, which at that time embraced All and everything.

When you think of a Cosmic Christ, you think of a Cosmic Selfhood. When you think of a Cosmic Selfhood, you think of a Consciousness uncontaminated and unfettered in any way. Well, if this is a Conscious experience, it can *never* be other than That. That is why it is said I *AM* That . . I AM! I AM That Consciousness that allows That and "this," and "this" and That. If it were not so, I would not appear, drumming upon the attuned skin of attention that you call present at this moment.

You say, "I am *present*," and I say, "*I* am present," and you say, "I am being **drummed** upon by these words." *You are the entire vehicle that constitutes the reverberation* as a result of the tension that one brings to the head in order for what *isn't* seen to be heard as a Tone.

There is no point of having the tympani if there isn't someone to play it. There is no point of having a drum if there isn't someone who knows how to beat it, and there is no point of a beating of the drum if it isn't pitched, for it will never reveal the contents of its emptiness and yet the contents of its fullness. The sound of a drum bears no resemblance to what constitutes it, and the sound of my voice bears no resemblance to what appears to be the vehicle.

What do you think "The Little Drummer Boy"[1] is all about? Someone dreamed a little poem, a little gift of a penurious state, and never realized it was really the first

---

1. A Christmas song composed by Davis, Onorati, and Simeon.

trickle that one had to give up the sense of objectification and find the subjective State of Being.

Thus it is that this weekend [Thanksgiving Workshop] has been one given to self-renunciation in order for the Self to be once again restored to the Throne or to that Chair of Power within your very experience from which you will ordain what shall be transpiring in your world. Let others call it "its future," for you live and move and have a being *Now* and that is the Timeless Zone, in contradiction to the time warp of a fatidic promise and an apocalyptic suggestion.

You see, nothing can change but that which is capable of changing, and if it is capable of changing and you are capable of watching it change, then it's obvious that what is changing is perceived as changing because What is watching is Changeless.

The Pristine Drop of Wonder is only diluted by the suggestion of making mud pies until *I* come!

I hope you see, as never before, the inexorable Law that binds you and finds you:

> *There is no possible way*
> *to escape Being Divine.*
> *What is the obstacle course?*
> *It's made up with the personalization.*

What is on a canvas can only be there because of what isn't on it. A voice and all its colors and its spectrum of Wonder is only heard because what was thought there *isn't there at all!*

What is the difference between an ordinary voice and a voice set free? One is **thought** *into experience and one demands the space filled with the AM-ing of the I.*

As soon as you personalize your voice, you can be off pitch. As soon as you allow yourself to be the reception of a frequency vibrating the members of attention, then you are impregnating the very uterus of the world so that it can birth the realization of an Enlightened Body.

We haven't time to make up. We must project newness, nowness, hereness, and That-ness via the willingness to be the receptive vehicle of Cosmic Resonance. This *is* living; therefore it is not beyond your ability. You may imagine it and find it vain; Christen it and find it living!

▼

XVI.

Words Seasoned with Salt

I feel that elegance is a state of our Being. I think that beauty is a part of our environment. I feel that Love is the greenness to our environment and response is the sunshine to it.

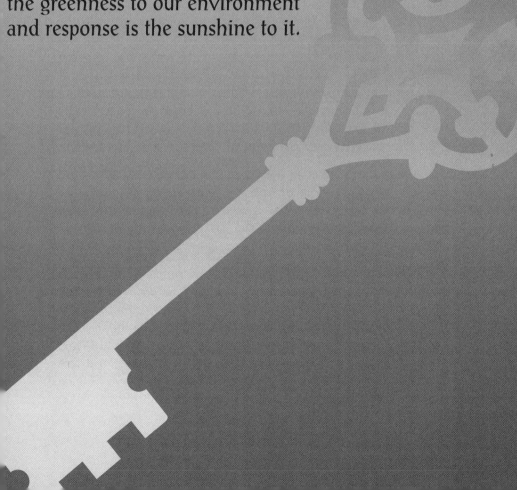

Words Seasoned with Salt

Perhaps we can talk about something that seems perfectly ridiculous, but it's so much fun to talk about it and to live it: So many people feel that they are born into this matter and will die out of this matter, but there is nothing more mythical in its nature than matter. Man has never been born out of matter; Man has never been born into matter.

It is a very important consideration for all of you who dare to be new in a time when everyone is expecting something new to happen. To actually *be* the Newness happening, however, is such a tremendous experience if you can offer it to others without any effort to do so.

Just being the Newness is enough to cause most to be filled with consternation. Of course, if you can aggravate that enough, then they might come to you as a remedy! Being the Living Remedy, you find it's an entirely different type of remedial responsibility. You would respond to them not by the confused dis-at-easement of their presence but by the interest that you would show to that part of them that bore the mark of your recognition. So it's a wise investment.

To secure a place in Newness you have to change an old habit. *One of the oldest habits is your form*! We start out with your clothing — and, of course, here I am — but then we've got to consider your form.

It's a new song. When you stop and consider how this whole thing happens, you haven't any accounting for yourself and you can't believe a thing your mother and father tell you, because they're frequently trying to account for their actions and then blaming it on you. Then, of course, they say that it was because of you that they knew what pain was: "You don't know the pain you were until you came, and you don't realize how it's the same now. Why don't you be nice to me?" You know?!

We've been talking about the importance of words. I gave something in 1990: *"Correct words are used to prepare the mind, to diminish its force so that it cannot degrade the Information that has to deal with That Which IS beyond it. This is why words are important."*

> Dr. B.B.) You know, in all of our recent considerations about sound and healing, there is a particular passage from Scripture that came to me the other day that I'm hearing in an entirely new way. It's the story in Matthew about the centurion who comes to Jesus and asks Him to heal his servant who is at his house. Jesus begins to set out and the centurion says, "No, I'm not worthy for you to come under my roof. Say but the Word and my servant shall be healed."

"Say but the Word."

> Dr. B.B.) It was very interesting. Following that, Jesus speaks about how such great faith He has not yet found, and that people will come from the East and from the West and witness things greater than this. He says, "The very ones near me who are prepared for the banquet will be set out into the darkness with weeping and gnashing of teeth." I've always interpreted, or had interpreted for me, that the words of the centurion were such a sign of faith. A deeper understanding of this passage reveals an amazing secret that this man acknowledged. Obviously, on some level, he had experienced that without having been right at hand.

You see, the word does hold your attention, and the wonderful part about sound (and tone) is, it doesn't know anything about corners. So you can't corner it, you know? That's why your *words are important*, and your joy should be full.

> Dr. E.S.) In finding the proper words to express something, when you say something or I say something, the word has a meaning to me. As I am listening to what you are saying, I realize that I am trying to relate what you are saying to previous experiences that I have had, or, What does that mean to me?

Don't.

> Dr. E.S.) That's where the problem is, because it highlights to me the imperfection of the word as a method of communication.

It highlights the imperfection of the education that has allowed you to think you are this! That is a double-barreled statement. "The education that has allowed you to *think you are...*" you could say, "...this," "...that," or "...educated." It's not so much the language; it's the carelessness with which we use language.

Language in essence is a sound response to Presence. When the language used points to what is beyond it, then the language conveys a hidden Knowingness that is recognized by those who understand. Language should be able to be used by everyone correctly. Unfortunately, it isn't. But those who do understand quickly perceive what is being said *without* words.

It's a different level of hearing, just as there's a different level of feeling, or sensing. I can give you a napkin and then I can give you a rose. You can say which is hard and which is soft; you can mention the difference. Then as life unfolds, you will come into an experience where one will start talking about a napkin and about a rose, and you sense it on a different level. That's just what's happened with my words. You are sensing the "starched framework" of the words through your education, but I am showing you the aroma of them on another level, if you don't associate them with your starched or doctored-up background. The Essence of the rose, of course, has nothing to do with the petals. They only mark the Path upon which you walk as you appear to be the Fragrance.

> Dr. R.K.) So, is language a step down from what could have been a better form of communication, and that is music?

Language is a step down because the language originally was meant only to sing a song of Oneness. It was only meant to cognize OneSelf.

> Dr. R.K.) I was wondering if the story of the Tower of Babel could be interpreted in that way.

The Tower of Babel was brought down by tone. It was destroyed by tone, just as tone used incorrectly can destroy you.

> Dr. R.K.) Is it possible that the first language before that was just music?

Well, the voice, of course, without the cultivation of education, *is* just music. It's education that restricts us, because it creates a culture in which we define everything, where the Undefined is uncontaminated. It's our educated definition that binds us to the belief system, which means that we are always in a system of trying to convince.

> Dr. E.S.) Obviously verbal language is only one way of communication. But how would we be able to understand each other if we did

not agree to certain conventions: "We're going to call this a shirt, this a shoe, and that a horse."

That agreement is perfectly all right. Go on.

Dr. E.S.) It would seem that we do need —

Agreement. What we need *is* agreement. Agreement doesn't bring in culture; agreement brings in freedom. For no man knows the power that agreement brings. *Agreement brings in untold possibilities, unlimited possibilities.*

You see what we have done: the wonderful word "gay," for example, was used to represent a most wonderful moment of life when it was fresh, before the word had the overtones it has today. Look how the word has been used. That is just a simple way of expressing it. The words are used so sloppily today! We have to adopt agreement in our language and that's quite right, just as we do adopt notation in our music. But if you just play the notes without being aware of what the sound is doing *to* you, then you will never know what it can do *for* you. Thus, a teacher always allows you to play the notes and then he opens the door to their meaning.

Language allows you to create words, which are nothing other than the symbols of sounds. We have that in our need of communicating, which has arisen as a result of this appearance in flesh, which, of course, is what we have agreed to do. We have agreed to take on this appearance for the sake of experiencing a three-dimensional universe. That's why there's only a part of us here. It's that part of us that isn't here that allows us to question this in such depth. You can imagine if we were all here! When we put an end to ourselves "all here," we would think this was the beginning and the end of it all. But it isn't; that's why we can question.

Our language should be such that it is seasoned with salt. I think it would be marvelous if in the school systems of tomorrow people had to use the words correctly. They say, "I just love that chocolate cake." You don't just *love* that chocolate cake! You can't *use* "love" that way! You can say, "The chocolate cake is delicious." But you can't love it, because Love is not on the level of an addiction to chocolate cake!

Dr. E.S.) What is Love?

What is Love? That Undefinable Quality that unites in spite of appearances. It is the Force that allows us to be One in the seeming presence of twoness.

Dr. R.K.) Is agreement an involuntary response when the mind is still?

Yes, it is. It's the most difficult situation when the mind isn't.

Dr. R.K.) So, Mr. Mills, it sounds like a silly question, but what is the purpose of being human?

Well, it's fun to be human when you know you're not.

Dr. R.K.) But is it all a game?

Sure!! Why take it so seriously? *You did it! You make me up. "You've made me what I am today; I hope you're satisfied."*[1]

Dr. R.K.) As we grow older, do we develop a more expansive conception of Reality or the Divine?

---

1. Lyrics to a popular song of the 1930s.

No, as we grow older we realize that is a fallacy, because What IS is Ageless. So we grow old; well, we have only agreed to occupy this space for so long.

> Dr. R.K.) So what did we really accomplish from the day we were born, to that point so many years later of understanding Principle?

This has been a great concern to all of Us. It has been insinuated to *many* of the humankind that life isn't worth living and it's all just a great big question of blood, sweat, and tears. There's always a conflict somewhere along the line. The insinuation to others is: let your presence be a bequest to a Higher energy field. What is happening? There has been the intention to try to bring to an end the waste of years like "you" have had and "me" has had in what we call "the maturing process of the human."

There is a very strong attempt to have the Force of the Higher be accepted by the weakening vehicle (as a result of discouragement) so it can be taken over and reactivated and re-energized: you might say the interior machinery is renovated with the Presence of a higher awareness waiting to be acknowledged, and man suddenly seems to change over-night into acquiring a much greater and more stable knowledge of the Selfhood in the image and likeness of That Which IS termed Divine. This type of thing is happening; one author[2] has written about it as "the aliens among us."

The aliens among us are not usually recognized because many of them are capable of perceiving What IS and appear to be trying to find those who are of their higher echelon of accomplishment. There are lower echelons of that type of frequency as well, so you have to stand guard at the door of thought. The inner Presence of That which is trying to reno-vate and elevate what appears as your deteriorated condition attempts to do so through sound. As your voice and as your

---

2. Ruth Montgomery.

words appropriate more and more the defining Principle surrounding the entrance of a Higher Force, then I know what Presence I'm speaking to.

So often by being less careful of your language you allow an inferior force to enter. The inferior force enters the moment doubt arises. That's why you have confusion; that's why you have a restless night, because as soon as you have a moment of doubt the lower energy enters and raises doubts, raises confusion.

Remember, we were never born of matter! We are a thought-product and we are so capable of manufacturing this so easily! It doesn't take you long after birth to recognize there's a form outside yourself. It takes you some time to recognize you're a form. It was the worst job to get used to looking at "me" in the mirror! I could always see "this," but I knew that wasn't it.

Dr. R.K.) You couldn't find yourself.

No!! Look in the mirror! No matter how much you talk, the only thing that you'll see there is what? What others see: a flat surface! *You* create all the dimension in the mirror. Do you think I'm going to fall for the belief that we're separate? Not in the world! In Essence we couldn't be. Never.

Dr. R.K.) What's the difference in level between a newborn that knows not from good and bad and someone who's achieved this perception or has cognized Principle? Is there any difference between the two states?

Remember that to be born into matter is your choice in order to experience choice.

It's just like when you have spent the evening with me and we talk and you go back to your apartment and you have other people there to talk to so you won't think about what's been said all evening because you can't sleep. The guests drown out what you may have heard and then you can go to bed. Then you get up in the morning and you think, "Oh Lord," and what's been said last night all starts to come back. You can tell right then that the difference between the child and you is that the child accepted what's going on without definition, but you are always attempting to define what is right and what is wrong.

"Why do I feel I can hardly wake up this morning? It's so difficult." It's not difficult at all to go to bed, but to wake up — it's the defining moment! The human is the only creature that attempts to have to find a reason for what is right! A dog never thinks of what is right, an ape doesn't think of what is right, and most men don't, but there are a few like you who do. Rightness is not considered of importance these days!

You have to know what is right, even in wiring a lamp. I remember when I started in the early years putting up all my own chandeliers and plugging in this and plugging in that. Well, I got the wires crossed; I blew a fuse! You have to know which wire goes to which wire. You have to know what's right, even on that level. It's not surprising that we can go on trying to make the right connections, because rightness is something that is innate with the suggested incarnation. Why do I say "suggested"? Do you know? Because it isn't Real.

Dr. R.K.) It appears that way.

Yes. The appearance changes, and that's why it's termed not Real.

> Dr. R.K.) One who has gone through this conflict of being deceived between this false perception and Ultimate Reality, and has gone to the State beyond good and evil: Is

that State of Being a so-called higher state of being than just a newborn state of being?

Yes. "Right and wrong," "good or bad" are relative terms. You may know innately what seems to be right and what seems to be wrong. You will become responsible through your own actions; you will know within yourself what is right and what is wrong. But *when you move beyond this*, you allow another to define *his* movement as right or wrong and then you may show him in either case: it's been for the purpose of intoning, and *freeing yourself* from false vibrations or false strings.

So many people in life are tied by false strings, false friendships, false family relations, false social relations, all these false relationships. So many relationships are built on what you can get, and "who's going to do what for me?" These are the things that you notice and when you stand above that, you'll find how it opens for you.

Dr. R.K.) So really the story of a person's life is reenacting the story of Adam and Eve.

The story of a person's life is how you will enact, through the mask of your appearance, the drama that is written on the escutcheon of your spiritual pockets waiting to be decoded in the atmosphere of this plane. It is all indelibly etched upon the scrolls of your heart, even the mistakes.

S.D.) Mr. Mills, is it true that the masses have given us a forgettery so that when we are born we seem to be in ignorance of our True Nature?

No, that is your choice. The masses don't do anything to you until you become one of them.

S.D.) More and more I have come to see that there is only one awareness —

No, there's one Consciousness and many awarenesses.

Awareness is why it can be fractured and appear to be human and objective and occupy space and have a dimension to it. Awareness allows you that projectory.

Your whole attempt at seeing the multitudinous forms like yourself has been due to the agreement which must have been encoded within your cell structure that you would all have a memory of what looked like "you."

All we know is that the cell, according to analysis, reveals a magnetic pull and it contains a vibrational essence. Therefore, if it can vibrate with a higher intensity, with a higher purpose, uniting with its Essence, you can alter the frequency of the essence of that cell. It seems to change the body, just as it seems to be changed when it is healed. As we appropriate those words that are more in keeping with the Undifferentiated State, we allow the differentiated state to appear to be more in agreement with the Undifferentiated.

> *It is language that is going to put you*
> *in freedom or in bondage*
> *and it is Love*
> *that sets the captive free.*

You see, the most important thing you can do is love with no purpose, because it will be your direction. When you have no purpose, IT is all-encompassing. When you have a purpose, it's for "you" and "me"; when you don't, the direction is Universal.

Love is that Power that allows you to feel so deeply in spite of the teaching surrounding your frailty. It's such an incredible Force. It has nothing to do with age and it's just as Rumi said, it's like a red hot ball.

> Dr. R.K.) Mr. Mills, it's interesting that modern science bears this out: All cells are really different manifestations of the same

thing and they all have the same DNA structure; just one cell decides to turn on some genes and another one decides to turn on some others. But, really, they're communicating in a way that makes them one. I think there's a practical aspect of all of this teaching in that if you're dealing with cancer cells, instead of focusing necessarily on those diseased cells, to focus on the same thing but in a different place, on cells that are so-called healthy because really you're dealing with the same cell.

How are you going to focus on the cells that are healthy?

Dr. R.K.) I don't know. I just thought of this now. Rather than concentrating on the diseased cells as much, one should focus on the living part of the so-called healthy cells, because really they're the same thing.

It's just the way they behave that's different.

Dr. R.K.) Yes.

Well, isn't that the same with men? The healthy one behaves one way; the unhealthy behaves another. How are you going to reach a cell if the cell is beyond articulation and it's known by articulation? Remember, it's your intelligence which has decided that there's a cell. Therefore the cell must in essence be floating in the sea of intelligence.

If that sea of intelligence is only filled with the Wonder of Tones that are in keeping with the Ultimate, then they can't help but be influenced involuntarily to attain their own required state of balance. The language itself becomes a greater magnet. It's concealed from the realm of the cells in the realm of the horseshoe of thought. The cells are like the iron filings: They'll trace it out, and if you get well, you have "good luck" and if you don't, you go on and see the experience of suffering and dying, which you will anyway.

Remember, you're never going to approach a cell to heal it. Basically it's only through thought, because it's been a thought that's made it up. They had to use a magnifying microscope of such power to even get something "there"! Do you realize what they've had to do to imagine "that thing there"?!

A friend of mine with whom I shared an apartment was a molecular spectroscopist, a brilliant one. Well, we used to have our times! He was a doctor, but he also studied piano with me. He would often be working at the lab doing these experiments all night. You know, it was necessary to stay up all night, seventy-two hours at a stretch. This night I was asleep; he came in. I said, "What is it?" He said, "Look!!" I opened my eyes and I looked at this little thing and he said, "You see that line in there? I've been waiting for hours to see it!" I said, "What for?" He said, "It proves that the construction of that gas is wrong." I said, "What do you mean?" He said, "In every combination in which this gas exists, the valences are all wrong." I said, "Oh." I couldn't get excited about it. I said, "Really? What's that going to mean?" He said, "It means that all chemistry, all scientists have got to change this formula! It's going to cause a tremendous change!"

Well, it did. I said, "How do you even know it's there?" "Well," he said, "there's a picture of it." I said, "But who's looking at it?" How we have to go to the almost invisible to make *us* seem substantial! Isn't it amazing?

Time is a corresponding identity of the cell. It vibrates in the rhythm that man has set up within the framework of an event called "your life." The cell supports that in its event of renewal, bearing the same code that allows you to maintain a similarity so that you are always recognized by yourself as yourself.

> Dr. E.S.) In our society we see so many failed marriages. Where are things failing? Are we really capable of loving in the way that you're defining Love?

Oh, yes!

> Dr. E.S.) And what is it?

I've lived for over thirty-five years as a way of defining it! The relational one came to an end. It didn't fail. Nothing fails unless you want it to. But why do you want to keep something going just for the semblance of appearance and for having acceptance by society? Love is Universal. Men and women's love is so narrow. It's always within the family you can love; outside the family you don't dare to. I have dared to. The whole world is a suggestion that has to be given back to the Arms of Love! So,

> Love and relationships: it's bound to falter in
>   relation,
> But when IT is All, there is no relation.

If I AM Love, then I AM not in love or out of love. Love is the AM-ing that I AM. Loving is the action of the AM-ing, which is creative.

With relationships you have to deal with the seeming reduction of Love to person, place, or thing. In the Absolute and Uncontradictable Nature, Love doesn't have to be related to any "thing," and by not being related to any thing it embraces all that appears to be "things" in order for them to give up their spurious hold upon your Infinite Possibilities.

Marriages are failing, perhaps, because their bases are wrong. Many people feel that the other person brings to them what they haven't got, which is somewhat of a shortcut to completeness. In many cases it's quite a fall! Actually, what's in another is always within yourself. As long as you think it's in another, then you don't have to be persuaded to be all that the other one represents, and then what is your need?

It's your mind that would divide it. It's not Nature.

> Dr. R.K.) It's so important, because there are so many younger people who complain or feel depressed because they feel that they've accomplished nothing in their lives or they don't know where their lives are going.

You mean when they're married, or before they're married?

> Dr. R.K.) Anytime.

Well, they'll feel it even more after they're married, and it wears off.

> Dr. R.K.) And often people get married just to alleviate that need.

And cry upon each other's shoulders. You don't really have that right when you're married, to use the other as the wastepaper basket of the combustion within yourself!

You know, there is no color, taste, or sound in this world. It's always *within us*. We make up the color to paint this picture. We make up the sound to impress. We make up the taste to satisfy. It's not out there at all. Rest is not in sleeping. Rest is in Being. *Person is always tired because it's awfully hard for a mask to go on sounding as if it had intelligence when it doesn't. That's why it's such a job!*

If you associate your Reality with your mask, what's going to happen at the midnight hour?

Dr. R.K.) Is this why there is so much fatigue? There are so many people complaining about chronic fatigue.

Exactly! Fatigue is nothing but man's refusal to BE the constant action of the AM-ing of the I. Relationships are a perfect example of fatigue. You'll usually find the person fatigued who isn't living to his or her highest.

Dr. R.K.) Mr. Mills, what force maintains the false identity?

Oh! The Force That IS, misconceived!

Dr. R.K.) It's a Real Force.

Oh, of course.

Dr. R.K.) Then what is it that is able to make the choice to change identity?

The wisdom bestowed upon one who questions the Authentic Nature as being unchangeable! Wisdom dictates to the station of the mind the information that becomes a question in the light of a Greater Light. Got it?

S.D.) Mr. Mills, even though with our minds we know that we are One and we know that our minds destroy that unity, how can we keep our minds from disproving the Divine constantly and ruining what we know we already have and are?

Oh, that's a wonderful question. Well, if you're ready for work it will be work. If you're ready for just Being, it's simple. They say, Allow the mind that was in Christ Jesus to be within you. In other words,

Allow only those thoughts
that you wish realized
to be manifested.

So it is your mind that questions for the Authentic Nature, and when you have perceived IT, That is all there is to IT: BE IT.

Now you will find agreement with hardly anyone in your life, because most people cannot bear Love manifested. That in Essence is all you are! It is your thoughts coming to the surface as a plea to the Great Light that offers the mind up as a sacrifice, because the mind is unimbued with the enduring qualities that are termed transcendental features as a result of knowing this Language of Transcendency: "The Infinite," "The Eternal." These are sounds that the mind really cannot define because they are of that State which allows those words to be used, those sounds to be heard as the verification of the Greater State. So the Mind that you claim that is All is the Sound present giving you the Force at hand just to be That.

To be That is not difficult, and yet it is the most difficult thing in the world, but then you have to know that I AM not of the world. I have only appeared to be there for you to recognize yourSelf as I AM. For you recognizing yourSelf as I AM, we are inseparable. That's the real Marriage, when we recognize ourselves as I AM recognized.

If you recognize me as I AM, then you make an idol of "me" and I always love that because then I can give you the I-doll right back! You just cuddle that yourself. People used to say, "Oh, you make an idol of Mr. Mills." I said, "What's wrong with that? Are you just jealous?" I always say, "If you make an idol of me I can always give you the I-doll right back," because what you see is *within you*, not only within me.

Always remember, the Divine would never have been cognized as the All-Powerful, All-Purposeful Force if Man had not been able to register That Frequency within his Self. That is registered within the escutcheon of your own Soul, which is the Feeling of Being I AM. That Feeling of Being I AM is the meaning, and a Word full of Meaning is a Life full of Love.

> Dr. E.S.) If God is such a Force, I am just too little unless I am part of IT.

Well, you are!

> Dr. E.S.) And so would you explain what your concept of IT is?

Well, you've done it, but you're just looking in the wrong mirror. I am your Sonic Mirror, you see. So I'm only answering for you, "to you," and telling you what you yourSelf know. What you say God created — this incredible nature world, the flowers, the trees, and all the specimens like yourself that are walking — if God is so magnificent to do all this, who do you suppose is recognizing His handi-work if it isn't Himself appearing as you? That's why God says in the Bible that "I will not leave you comfortless," because when I come again I shall make all things new.

The God of you is allowing you to describe the creation of which you are a part, but from the standpoint where you think you're *in* it instead of looking *on* it.

> That's where you must stand at an
> 　　experiential distance from your
> 　　experiment in time
> So that you can understand what's going on
> 　　beyond the beaker tube of the mind.
> When the flame goes up and that beaker
> 　　starts to boil,
> You can imagine it isn't going to be any
> 　　jumping girl or bouncing boy!

It's going to be a whole new creation that comes forth, and it has, now! It's the God of you that allows you to describe through words what appears to be a solid, objective universe, but you're not even solid, any more than the universe is. It's as solid as your dream. That's why this incredible realization of God, Man, and the Universe as One is deemed acceptable in the Sight of the One Altogether Lovely.

Dr. E.S.) So we're all one in God.

Yes. God didn't multiply Himself or divide Himself. God IS; Man IS; World IS; That IS. Yes! God is no longer afar off from you. All the feeling that I feel with you is the evidence that God lives. That's why I know there is a God. I've never doubted that there is this Force that allows Itself to be known. The Self being known can wear a garment or wear a mask in time for those who really want to dance at the masked ball until the midnight hour. When that becomes One, then the Light is One and you find that what appears to be this dance of multiplicity is all because we agreed to dream the same dream in this continuing Event of the Stars.

We're all actors on this stage called Earth, and we all wear the various rays that allow us to be memorized in the pattern of similarity so that when cognized we perform as expected: without a script, without pen in hand, with no medium of exchange, but in the very Presence of an act of offering food to those who cry, "Sahib, food!" Love is the only Force that allows you to say to the wave, "Thus far and no farther."

How frightening it is to see what we think is individuality, shattered! The only thing we think we are is a personality: "He's developed the most wonderful personality." It's not important to develop a personality. *It's important to perceive Individuality*, which is one of the most difficult questions to find an answer to, so they say. He thinks he's an individual and you think you're an individual, and that is not it at all.

You're a person; he's a person. But *Individuality is like the Universe: it cannot be divided. "Universe" means to turn into one, and Individuality is One, incapable of being divided.* Then how can you divide the Individuality "I" is? It must be your mind's play pulling you.

If your imagination isn't redeemed, you're being operated by invisible strings like a puppet. If you have redeemed imaging, then you know you're the puppet that knows it's Charlie and knows who Edgar Bergen is.[3]

> Dr. R.K.) Mr. Mills, the Talmud says that "Out of God's goodness He created the world." What does that statement mean? I don't really understand.

Well, it's one way of saying, through an attempt to be holy, that God knew that man needed a world. Now God knows no need, for God is the name applied to that aspect that is All. That Allness never fractured His Allness by applying it to any situation that needed more or less, or to any other theater for Being. He created the world — not at all! That's the way that the people who are deluded would be brought into the fold of those who are not deluded. (Perhaps. I hope they weren't.) Remember, it is your very God-Being that allows you to experience the world.

There was no point of a Jesus if the Man was the only Son of God there ever was. When they asked Him who He was, Jesus said, "I and My Father are One."[4] I always say the verb is wrong: "I and my Father *is* One." As soon as you use "are," it's two. So, for a moment everyone thinks I'm ignorant when I say, "I and my Father is One." And that's how you have your world.

---

3. See "Impersonations," in Kenneth G. Mills, *The Golden Nail* (Stamford and Toronto: Sun-Scape Publications, 1992), p. 326.
4. John 10:30.

You can imagine the magnitude of the Father or the Self that allows what appears as you to cognize this incredible display and yet know it's not there at all. *The world isn't within you but everything that you are projecting and calling the world is that aspect of your own Artistic Nature that is perceiving Itself fulfilled as a display called the painting, the performance, and the pageant of the Divine Mind appearing manifested.*

You see, God is not afar off; God is right at hand. "God" is a sound, as "Self" is a sound, as "Love" is a sound.

> When I know Love, I know Sound Being.
> When I know God, I know Source Being.
> When I know Life, I know Vibrant Being.
> When I know Spirit, I know Spirited Action.
> When I know Mind, I know Awareness.
> When I know Principle, I know I AM That.

It throws you right beyond the veil where everyone wants to keep you. "You're my little fellow." You know? "You come right home and you tell me all about it." Sure. That's where you play your part. I always went home to see Mum and Dad, and I never did anything right and if I did, "Are you sure you're giving the credit where it's due?" Of course, I did; I naturally would.

> Dr. R.K.) You said, before that, "God is a sound."

God is a sound. Say "God."

> Dr. R.K.) God.

Yes, sound. God is a sound. Otherwise, God is a state. The God-State knows no question and would know no answer if it were not for mind. That's why it says, Let the mind be in you that was in our Lord Jesus Christ. What is that Mind? The acceptance of only One. Why do you think Moses was having such a fit and such a "terrible headache" when he looked down and saw everyone else relative?! One God: Worship Him with all your body, mind, and Soul.

> Dr. E.S.) Mr. Mills, what led you to do what you do? Most people just go through life and get into a certain groove and say, "Well, I have to be an architect," or whatever, and just follow that through. Then, of course, we all are haunted by thoughts and doubts: "What's the meaning of Life? What am I doing?" But it seems that somehow you did not stick to a groove.

No. I have been always rather groovy but I haven't stuck to anything like getting caught in an old track.

> Dr. E.S.) You have mentioned your experience as a concert pianist.

Yes, I was a concert pianist. My joy has been in the agreement of dying to this vocation of being a Sonic Mirror for others. You know it is so because when you look in the mirror that is Real it doesn't reflect "you." The secret is, it should be a sonic reflection. *The constant fretting over what isn't is the very attention that will destroy the very factor that is perceived to exist in the Sonic Reference of the Soul.*

What has brought me to this point in my experience was being willing. I made an agreement that I would speak if someone asked me and otherwise remain silent or appear to use the same language that everyone else did. As soon as you ask me anything, then, of course, it's a very different story, because then I can speak to you. So one man called me and said, "Mr. Mills, I want to speak to you about art." I said, "About art? You shouldn't speak to me. I don't know anything about art." He said, "Oh, but I know you do." Then I remembered my vow: I said I would speak if I were asked; otherwise, I would remain silent. He had asked. He was the first one. So he came, and that was the beginning. On it went, and here we are. Finally so many came to speak to me that by February of 1975, I gave up teaching just to speak.

> *I feel that elegance is a state of our Being.*
> *I think that beauty is a part of our*
> *environment. I feel that Love is the*
> *greenness to our environment and*
> *response is the sunshine to it.*

What I appear to be is a strange creature. I am so many different "things." It's only by being so well grounded in the technical proficiency of an instrument that this one was able to be utilized in such a way that there could be a sensitivity to the sound of the question and from whence it cometh. Even though it's a question about me, it's speaking from a remembrance. There is not one person here who isn't here as a result of remembrance or question.

There's not one person who has left the High Teaching who hasn't remembered. They have left because they ran the last time and they've run again! No man can touch the hem of the Garment of Truth and not have goodness go out. It's usually the feminine manifested that catches the man on his run. He doesn't realize that the feminine that he's running from becomes manifested to catch him. Remember, it's always a test.

> Dr. E.S.) I have felt for so long an emptiness.
> I have been longing for, if not an understand-
> ing, some sort of peace.

Well, "peace passeth the understanding." You don't have to understand first. Understanding is one of the concepts in education that should be taught as incidental music.

Acceptance is first, and then after experiencing the acceptance, you understand and that is there, wrapped in the garment of peace.

Your praying to the Father has not gone in vain, because when you pray to the outer space, to this emptiness that you think is space, you are really allowing all the Frequencies that are commensurate with a Divine Ideal to start to accumulate within your awareness, which prompts, impels, and compels the Quest. *Loneliness is always the accompanying factor of the Ever-Presence of the Divine.* If you had not felt lonely, you would have been self-satisfied. By feeling lonely, you were waiting to be found and thus adopted and adapted to Self-Realization. Self-Realization is that State of knowing your Oneness with the Primal Cause, the Unitary Principle, the Divine. That Oneness is the Ever-Presence that responds to being called "Father," "Lord," "God," "Jehovah," "Jesus," any name that has borne the bearing of an Uncontradictable into the avenue of time.

Your very presence marks the Presence of That for which you search, but having not looked within yourself, other than with the eyes that were expecting to see God personified, now hear IT sounding within yourself as "I AM That I AM." You'll never be lonely now that *I* have come to view. You will only be lonely if you wish to be lonely. No Wonder? God! What Wonder! Another Wonder!

> Dr. R.K.) Mr. Mills, a question about the power of thought which manifests as disease. Is it necessary to know error in thought and how it relates in the manifestation of disease?

No. You don't need to name it. You never need to name a disease. If you cognize it as present, then be more interested in what is present as Reality so that there is no room for disease in That Presence.

Once I had a young man brought to me who was only capable of moving boxes from the sidewalk to a truck and from the truck to the sidewalk. He was totally wasted on drugs at nineteen. Two of his friends brought him to me, and I didn't know anything about his history; I never asked. I knew he was sitting on the floor in front of me, and that that wasn't going to do it with him. So I asked him to sit up on the sofa beside me, and his friends sat on the other side of him. Then I spoke to him. I noticed he was very "out." I said, "You love art, and you are an artist." He said, "Yes." I said, "Well, I think I have need of you. I would like you to be involved with producing a book." He said, "What?" I said, "Yes. How about you doing some of the artwork for the book? How about laying it out? How about planning it all?" That was the beginning.

He became so successful! But as soon as he became wealthy and successful, he slithered away: the reptilian. The reptilian brain[5] was awakened by the cognition of his art. I awoke it through the genius level of him. I didn't rationalize with him. I told him of his talent, of his genius. That responded, because his rational brain was not functioning; it could only put stuff on the sidewalk, in the truck; truck, sidewalk. As it started to come clearer, he started to, undoubtedly, question. Do you know something? *He left!*

That is what the drugs do! They leave you with holes. It allows people the leeway: "Well, the drugs did it." The point is, *there is no vacancy in the Divine Mind.* There is no vacancy in employment. Man is Self-employed. There is no need for people to be out of work. The reason people are out of work is because they don't work according to the demand of this time.

The demand of this time is, **Prepare ye the Way,** *and,* **Those that have walked in darkness shall see a great Light.**

---

5. Part of the theory of the "triune brain," as explicated by Dr. Elaine de Beauport and others.

The demands are all over the place. But people want it in their own way, and there's only One Way. It's almost a Divine Dictatorship until you realize that it is the Ship of Soul upon which you embark.

Your life is ruled as a dictatorship, from the Standpoint of Principle. Not "*a* principle" — Principle! A depression is totally the result of mass mesmerism, under the direct control of those who know how to do it. That's how the media is used.

Well, we've had quite an evening!

▼

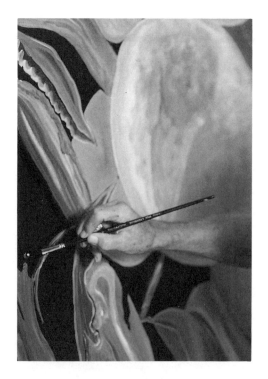

XVII.

The Newness of the Unchanging

The whole purpose of a day is to bear a newness pointing to the Nowness of Being.

The Newness of the Unchanging

Prelude

These lines are given as symbols upon the
    page in your sight
To cause your mind to tingle with the
    promise of the new discoveries of Light.
To offer a melody equated with the Eternal
    Truths of Light,
To offer a New Land of Promise in the one
    of changeability in sight.

No matter where a symbol is written, no
    matter where 'tis found alone,
If it is found caught in time, it must be lined
    and spaced for those who would find
    Home.
To find what one is searching for when only
    following a prompting of the heart
Points one to look and see and ask, "What is
    this internal spark?"

What is it that causes the heartbeat to give
    rhythm to a living man,
So that his promises and his hopes may
    spring forth from the Well of Being as
    'tis planned?
O the head must hang in humility, for its
    thoughts only turn it around,
Never allowing it to come to point to see
    how the Father abounds!

Know, if you seek the Promise — with all
    your heart, you do!

This Lecture is available on cassette, Sun-Scape Publications ISBN # 0-919842-02-X.

Then you will find how it is fulfilled in the
  Land where *I* see *I*, no "you"!
No you: BE in the Light of Glory all
  wrapped in the Unchanging Newness as
  planned;
Just walk as you seem to pass in the
  changing, claiming newness as the plan.

The newness of each day dawning, the
  newness of each moment, if scanned,
Points to the Unchanging Power that enables
  Beauty to be new and ever at hand.
"I AM always new in My Being" can be
  attributed to the Primal Act,
And the heart forever knows the longing to
  be found in the newness of That!

As newness clothes the landscape, as the sun
  enlightens the way,
May you be decked in its Robes of Light and
  embrace the Enraptured Way.
For the Promise is ever given that you shall
  always find
How newness clads each Day of Light as
  Glory fills the sky.

So, in the Newness of Being Unchanging,
  appear changing if the moment
  demands,
But in the Eternal Now of Love Light, I AM
  always what I AM — that's the plan!
O for the prompting of Newness; 'tis one
  with the Cause "to Be."
I AM always new in the midst of changing.
  Will you find how *I* live and move and
  BE?

This evening we are found with no other purpose than to BE. In this attitude all others who are found here, there, and everywhere who can claim a pitch (*and pitch is the consistency of attention!*), may they find the words spoken acceptable and sustaining in the frequency of That Pitch when Love is claimed as All.

In the great light of this evening, when the desert and the mountains stand garmented in their silver gowns, may we give all honor and glory unto the Sun.[1] May we see in the clarity of the Light that when a question is asked and an answer is given, the place from which the question arose cannot be found; the self-evident fact is that one cannot return to positions outgrown! You do not grow old in a position to outgrow it; you see the newness of Life . . and then find if your position is anything *but* new! You do not try to work with the changing; you only abide as the Unchanging and *watch* the changing change, pointing to the newness of Being. Men and women should never be concerned with newness appearing; they should only be concerned when oldness seems satisfying.[2]

The questions to be asked today should not arise primarily from the suppositional (concepts of living based on the premise of the changing). A question should arise when the suppositional is known to be merely suppositional. For when the suppositional is known to be suppositional, who would suppose it to give a fixed answer?[3] An answer fixed

---

1. This Unfoldment was given on the night of a full moon which caused the desert and the mountains to appear clad in silver. The color silver represents the outer realm of appearances, the reflected light (duality), whereas the Sun is symbolized by the color gold, which signifies the inner realm of experience, the direct, unitive Light. The ideas of "inner" and "outer" are thus introduced and are woven throughout the fabric of the Unfoldment.

2. "The promises of a New World (New Conscious Experience) are never found in the suggestions of the old world. If one were satisfied in the old, he would not be searching for the new. The difference between a New World and an old world is not found on a calendar — A.D. and B.C. — the difference is *was* and *is*. Any suggestion of a past or a future is simply by-passed in the experience I AM. Whenever That is declared, it points to the Eternal Now beyond the limits of a vagrant mind." K.G.Mills.

3. "No one would expect the suppositional to give a fixed answer. Anyone who asks a question from the suppositional, who knows that the suppositional is transient and changing, would naturally expect to move with the force of the answer, because the answer isn't going to have anything to do with suppositional beliefs." K.G.Mills.

has you secure in a new position with no possibility of seeing from whence you have come. When you have once eaten a Golden Delicious apple you can tell of its delicious flavor, but you cannot give the apple you have eaten; you can only point to another that may be found under the tree if it has blossomed in the light of spring.

The whole purpose of experience is so that process can be stemmed.[4]

We are told that to partake of a joy spontaneously arising is such a privilege. It would seem as if partaking of joy were a rare happening![5] There is no statement given from

---

4. "Regarding 'process,' consider the example of the apple. When you have once eaten it, and while you are eating it, the resultant experience is a conscious state that we can term 'delicious'; it is an appleness experience. From the standpoint of the conscious experience of eating the apple, the entire process of the seed's having to grow into a tree to eventually bear fruit is by-passed. The conscious experience is instantaneous — appleness. Appleness, therefore, is a state of consciousness in which the object (the apple) is 'swallowed up' and freed from its limits! That is how process is stemmed. The Teaching itself is like appleness: IT throws Light onto any thought of process and eliminates it if one is willing to take the experience and not worry about a step-by-step process in order to experience. You see, the Fruit of the Teaching, like the appleness of the apple, can be claimed and experienced instantaneously! You don't even have to 'change your mind'! There are no magical ceremonies, initiations, or great realizations to have to go through or attain as such. All you have to do is *cease thinking in the old way and claim the new!* Process is like a horizontal line, suggesting that life and love are lived one event after another. The High Teaching is like a 'Plumb Line' that is dropped, which is so filled with awareness, experience, and 'appleness' that right where it meets the horizontal line of appearances is the spot upon which angels can dance, if need be, for those who would doubt or demand to see proof. Those who appreciate, however, will perceive the great privilege of seeing a Divine Coincidence. *The Plumb Line can be practically experienced by living as Principle, by living in accordance with great ideals and divine ideas — Order, Love, Rhythm, the Golden Rule, etc.* The Plumb Line is like a Ray that stems right from the Heart of God, from the Heart of the Light. It is the Ray that streams directly from the Point of Effulgence that is termed Universal and Cosmic in significance. The Plumb Line, of course, establishes a ninety-degree angle, which is so necessary when the Law is to be fulfilled as Love is revealed. The moment is wrapped in the garment of appreciation as an apple is taken and given unto the world, and in its dying it appears to live in the garment of praise called 'appleness'!" K.G.Mills.

5. "Joy is a constant and is a garment of the Source. **Joy is the name given to a condition of experience when spontaneity wears the garment of praise. It is an ornament brightly shining on the gown of Self-Realization.**" K.G.Mills.

the standpoint of the changing worth more than a brief observation to see where it is pointing.

There is nothing wrong with the changing, provided you do not find yourself in the changing. It is so wonderful to be the Changeless in the midst of the change, and in the midst of the changing, pointing to the Changeless!

This is the whole purpose . . "to BE." "To BE" is this: to be Joy, to be Truth, to be Light, to be the spontaneity that fractures (that breaks personalized actions and responses), to be the newness that makes oldness uncomfortable! A man unknown once said, "When one has awakened, the next step is to voice." The whole purpose of voicing is to give, without form, an experience.

To experience an apple is to savor its appleness. You do not have to understand what constituted its skin or its flesh or its core. However, in the natural wonder the experience reveals that the skin was its coat of mail (its protective "armor," likened unto the physical body), its flesh was its tenderness (the womb-like nature of the mind in which ideas are nurtured) surrounding a garden where an orchard could grow. (The "core" contains the seeds; seeds point to the embryonic ideas of Being, held in suspension, waiting for the correct moment when they might find expression.) The stem was the umbilical cord of apple to tree, and as soon as the fruit is ready, there is no suggestion of the stem's being invisibly bound to the branch of the tree from which it is to be harvested. (The umbilical cord to a "medium" always has to be released.) Yet the fruit itself bears the evidence of the tree, its root, and its willingness to waltz with the seasons. It is in three-four time because in the winter it rests![6]

In the experience we observe as living, we note form, movement, and waves of actions. When the living is limited to matter, there is no season in which matter can be relieved

---

6. "This denotes the tree's 'willingness' to be naked for a time, to be garmented in foliage for a time, and to show fruit for a time, all as a natural expression of what it IS. The tree remains fundamentally unchanged (like the Unchanging) in the midst of apparent change." K.G.Mills.

of matter (released from suggested material limits) as long as it is *believed* that there is reason (reasoning ability) to matter. *The only way is to know . . that*

> *Reason is the process that an evolutionary act bears in order to allow those in process to have hope of leaping beyond it.*

If there were reason in matter, no matter would be allowed to pass as a grave mistake (be buried)! If reason were paramount news, it would be a gift of the Age;[7] but the Gift of an Age is one in which the apparent receiver knows, through the grace of the Knower, that the passing has never made it so,[8] but the Light to it is the Gift so that the passing may seem to come and go, but I AM fixed in Mine own knowing effulgence.

To penetrate the educational skin of the mind is considered difficult, and to try to persuade people to change their mind is an impossible suggestion, because you are sup*posing that there is a mind to change! Instead of trying to get people to change their minds, offer to them the opportunity of observing what constitutes what they call mind in the changing. And then ask them to perceive what it is that enables them to be mindful of their watch, and to this, leap!*[9]

The wonders of awareness are the gifts given to those who would be new. There is nothing to do away with! (If

---

7.   "'Para' means 'beyond'; 'paramount' means beyond the 'mount' of the limited mentality. 'Paramount news' is the news that comes from beyond the limits of mentality and from beyond the beliefs of matter. When reason via the discipline (training) of the High Teaching becomes revelation, **paramount news issues forth as the Platform of Pitch — a gift of the Age.**" K.G.Mills.

8.   The "passing" refers to the Teachers of the past; they have not established Truth (the Gift) as such; rather, Truth has established itself via the guise of past Teachers! **"It isn't the Teacher that bears the Light; it's the Light that bears the Teacher."** K.G.Mills.

9.   "How do you stop the wheel of change? Some have said that the great evidence of the All-encompassing Nature is the constantly changing world picture. **I would say that the evidence of a Constant Conscious Experience rests in the experience of per-ceiving the passing and remaining fixed in the position of witness.**" K.G.Mills.

Churchill can say it, I can!)[10] But having gone beyond the limitations of the church, men and women see by standing on the brow of the hill that where they thought they lived was only limited as the thought was held to the view observed. Upon achieving the brow of the hill (an elevated point of vision), they realized there were other houses, other domains surrounding their own, but from such a low point of view (from within the valley of thoughts) they only saw the limits of their own "plot"!

Now, it has been the gift of experience to garment the voice of opportunity so that opportunity is not seen as a chance happening, but as that moment of perception in which there was no option, no choice, to the act. The privilege of knowing the purpose "to BE" restores unto oneself the prerogatives stemming from Deific Origin. It is preposterous and a gigantic hole in our educated mental skin — it's a huge "pock mark" — to be taught that God is All, in the church, and never taught that *if God is All, then there must be a way to experience the Allness of God and be the Church!* This great abyss has been bridged by some teachings which would drop the name of God, for in some way God has become a stumbling block and has been kept at arm's length.[11] If God is a living possibility, then living must be from the Source (God-Being) that is one with Act as Life.

Now, Life is abstract. We think we know what Life is, but how we miss the point! Love has been dropped from the

---

10. Churchill once replied to a woman who criticized him for ending a sentence with a preposition: "Pedantry, madame, is something up with which I shall not put!" The statement, "There is nothing to do away with," simply states that the old does not have to be forcibly annihilated; it naturally fades as the "wonders of awareness" advance in the tide of newness. "You don't try to do away with anything; all you do is remain fixed in what you know to be true and then enjoy the experience of anything by not being limited by the 'thing' (the apparent objective appearance) of 'any' (apparent multiplicity)!" K.G.Mills.

11. "The 'abyss' or 'stumbling block' has arisen due to God's being worshiped afar off, but God is a living experience at hand in the Light of the Teaching of the Son of God. You might say that Jesus was an extension (medium) of God to the eyes of the people who didn't see. To the eyes of the people who did see, there was no difference. That is why He was called Jesus the Christ, or Christ Jesus." K.G.Mills.

vocabularies of power because it has been associated, due to the teachings of time, to be what it isn't. But no one has questioned Life as being something beyond what we have been taught. Life is not necessarily "living." This is what the mind thinks Life is. Mind thinking is said to be "living," but living thinking can only be said to be mind. Living thinking is mind.

Now what is Life? If you free Life from the limits of living, then you will find that living is only the outer garment of Being, for Being abides as its own experience; it doesn't need a reflection. If Life demanded a reflection, it would always be what it isn't; but Life being what it IS enables life being what it isn't to be observed. The mind is not gotten rid of — the only thing that changes is thinking. You can think your way into a cul-de-sac, or you can leap beyond your mind and its bag of tricks and find how you can view What IS through the vehicle of the changing and yet remain the Changeless. Life bears within itself a Power that can appear as expression, and the expression will point to the Soul of Life, provided the responsibility of expression conforms to the Soul of Freedom in the Light of the Law. Life then wears the garment of a discipline, and the voice is gowned in expression — *When one has awakened, the next step is to voice.* The whole purpose of the voice is to give without form, thus without limits. And you will receive according to how you hear, for if you really hear, you by-pass the senses which would limit and demand a form to titillate the experience.

> *The simplicity of the Magnificent is usually lost because of the complexity of reason.*

To magnify a point is to have the attention focused on none other. It doesn't have to get bigger or smaller. Magnifying does not necessarily mean to enlarge beyond all possibilities. To magnify means to Wonder. *For in the*

Wonder comes adoring, and adoring is the lens which opens the sight on the brow of the hill.

If I am correct, the word "meek" has a root that goes back to the word which means "trained." The meek shall inherit the Earth. If the trained are to inherit the Earth, it means this: Discipline has entered the reasoning process to such a degree that Independence Day, the Light of Oneness, dawns and men and women are able to step beyond the limits of their thinking mind-entanglements and are thus able to perceive more totally than those who think that the meek are those who give way to suggestion or conventional belief with the hopes of knowing what God is all about by going to church.

If the meek are to inherit the Earth, it is obvious they can't be "mish-mash." **For to inherit the Earth is to inherit the whole domain of mentality.** And to inherit the domain of mentality, as it seems, has given "you" living on Earth, as it seems.

> **But to inherit the Kingdom of God is**
> **to be so trained that the Earth**
> **becomes your footstool.**

In other words, there is wonder and there is the ability to put your feet up and know how it is that the kingdoms of this world shall become the Kingdoms of our God and of His Christ.[12]

The only reason that reason takes place is because thinking, bridled to hypothesis, brings reins to the mind in

---

12. "The mind is a name given to a state that is capable of being pitched in such a way that its contents are readily utilizable when given unto the Hand of the Almighty. The ability to put a stop to the horse of the mind is at hand when the reins are in the hand of one who knows there is but One Mind; for there is but One God, One Self, and the One Self knowing its own Selfhood can be called God Now Knowing. Claiming Self-identification reins in the mind; and the mind is no longer on this but THAT side when the Work is done in the Light of Knowing that in this I AM satisfied." K.G.Mills.

process.[13] When these reins can be held by claiming a Figure not formed after the limited, but one embracing the Limitless, the Chariot of Power (Light of Intuition) comes as an awareness of what it is to travel the Path of the Sun and to partake of its fecundating wonder: Light.

The branches of a tree resting in winter look, to a viewer, dead. But when the season comes that the sun appears magnified, and the land entombed in coldness and indifference melts as the planet turns on its axis, the branches tremble with the surge of power, which comes when the sun just shines involuntarily upon its barrenness, knowing that if it lives, the life will be known by the new birth of gown.

The apple does not come first. A point called a seed is acknowledged, put into the womb of Mother Earth, and given unto the care of the nurturing factors unseen by the limits of a see-er. But a Seer can see right through the picture and knows, "Don't step on that plot, for there is a spot where a tree shall grow, for a seed is planted and within itself contains a harvest."[14]

The apple, you might say, knows it doesn't come first, for the seed is there for those who doubt, the tree is there for those who would have a promise, the blossom is there for those who expect, and the fruit is there for those who would see, even in time, how it is that from such substances as unutilizable as that of a tree (or a body) — its bark, and its trunk — comes forth a fruit (a Message) for the table of time.

Why would you doubt the promise of those who are disciplined? If you will practice to use time as holy, every second will be a Light experience. The reason an hour can

---

13. The "hypothesis" is like the "rod" or "pole" in the following statement "The mind is forever swinging like the elephant's trunk — from one thing to another — and until you give it a rod or a pole to hang onto, it is never under control!" K.G.Mills

14. "In other words, the embryonic ideas (seeds) of Being must not be stepped on or disturbed by a personal approach that would try to regulate or expedite their natural birthing." K.G. Mills

seem so long is because you travel it and get caught in your trip! And the reason some trips are known not to be done again is because there is nothing to prove, for truly what is seen "there" (the objective world) is really only what is known "here" (the subjective conscious experience).

Be alert to this fact: It is not *who* you are, not "*Who* is man?" but "*What* is man?" It is not "What is living?" but "Is living Life?" It is not to be loving which is the demand, it is to BE . . and the purpose fulfilled and called Love. The tissue of time is so thin as the awareness is magnified, and it is so apparent how the stems of timed pieces (human beings) are forever needing adjusting! To be cast beyond the timed into the conscious experience of the Timeless seems so natural, and yet for the timed pieces there seems such a reluctance to cease, always winding yourself up in order to keep going on![15]

Everyone depends upon being wound up for so many hours in order to unwind so many hours, and expects to have a day that is filled with Light.

The whole purpose of a day is to bear a
newness, pointing to the Nowness of Being.

The only reason the word "purpose" is used is because you were taught that you are the result of something happening, which you remember not, and that you are the outcome of something that came forth in process. ("You" always demands a purpose; "*I*" have no purpose or goal.) If you cannot remember when you arrived, why would you try to? Because if you don't remember when you came or how

---

15. "It doesn't take time to think right; you only have time when you think wrong. Thinking is only the garment that Consciousness wears, and when unlimited, is found omnipresent by all those creatures who have need of it. Consciousness is only known on this level of experience. It is only on this level of experience that the Word had to be formed because men mistook (divided) their form from the Formless, and that's why the Word had to be formed in the name of the Wordless." K. G. Mills.

you came, you certainly are not going to remember how you go or when you go. It was the cause of your coming (your parents) that told you you came. Who is going to be present to tell you you have left?

Does the apple blossom tell the apple how it came about? And does the apple acknowledge the blossom when it is just an apple? The apple (when thought of as only an object) is the lowest form of its existence. The apple came out of the *flower* (a higher form), and you called it a flower because a flower was to bear a *fragrance* (still higher, pointing to essence or "appleness"),[16] and a branch was to bear a promise ("branch" symbolizes the spiritual lineage of those who appear on Earth from time to time and bear a higher purpose, message, and awareness — pointing to Essence). And when the branch of the tree flowered, you knew that the day was at hand when the fruit could be taken and offered to those who would know what an apple is, in order to wonder and marvel and magnify the point that in the eating of the apple, men could be satisfied, but in the knowing experience an apple could be enjoyed and its essence — an experience of *wonder!*

When the seed is planted in rich, prepared ground (offered to the "trained"), it cannot help but blossom and bear the fruit for those who would claim food, wonder for those who could see the blossom and say, "It was a sight to be in that land in blossom time." Know, from the brow of the hill, that it was only there for you to prepare for that wave of Wonder upon which you could ride into that sphere of Sound which could make all new.

> *Newness has to do with seeing; oldness has to do with thinking . . in a way that never leads to anything but a hope and a promise.*

---

16. "If it is the fragrance that gives the flower identity, what is the fragrance that gives man identity?" K. G. Mills.

Men and women are sometimes persuaded, but oh! to be so privileged as to see what hearing is and still appear formed for those who would ask to be fed from your table in time (from your level of conscious accomplishment).

The moon is full, for the Sun gives it light.
The Day is the Sun, the Knowing; the moon
is the night.

Reason if you must, but fail not to acknowledge that there is no reason to matter when the experience of Wonder gives the fragrance of Knowingness in its gown. It's very practical, very provoking, and filled with opportunity when there is no door (in this case, representing process) to open. For you see, the door is only that state of thinking which bars the way to the natural flow of Life's Event, and that is Love. The Event will never be known in its fullness until the Harmonic State of Being wraps Life, Truth, and Love in its gown of Music.

The trained are those who have sacrificed opinions to gain the pinions in order to fly beyond the brow of the hill and inherit the Chariot of the Sun given unto those who know the independence of the hands. What the right hand doeth the left hand knoweth not, and yet in knowing, all shall be seen, and the Earth shall be touched by the Wonder and by the fecundating Power of Promise for those who would enter the Church of Self-Realization as a Conscious Experience and find God a living reality as Life lived as Love.

This message sounds far-fetched, but the tissue of the veils is so thin that it appears right at hand. Times past, it was considered far-fetched; times present, it is considered a happening everywhere; but in the point of Now it is a known experience and called "privilege."

Anything that you inherit comes as a gift because of your natural right to it; and the trained shall inherit whatever constitutes the idea called Earth. (Everyone will find Earth just as they think Earth to be.) This is why the teaching on any high level demands obedience to the fundamentals, because no one can play the piano competently unless there has been the willingness to work and sweat over the suggested obstreperous children called the fingers until they are seen to be the servants of focused attention and can appear to be independently directed as the need demands for the translation of the symbol of a promised sound into a sound experience with no limits due to the lack of independence.

To be independent does not mean that you "do your own thing." *To be independent means that you have the ability to play whatever role you need to play in order to fulfill what it is to voice the parts that are to be played as the great contrapuntal composition of Life unfolds in the panoply of Sound and in the Keyship of C, the Christ.* The power of Wisdom is like Life and Love: It is from the Source That IS; and Love must steer its course in order that it be handled and offered with great compassion, for raw power can be destructive as well as enhancing.

So, it has been given to praise, and having been given to praise, the *"P"* is the Principle raised . . all in the sound called a voice. Consider the Unfoldment well. It is provocative, for it tantalizes those who think they understand, it may irritate those who understand, and provoke them to such a degree that, with ants in their mental tissue, they will change and put on the new garment commensurate to an Ideal! There!

▼

XVIII.

Robotery

Men are forgetting,
due to over-robotization,
to question their Source.

ROBOTERY

We are gathered together for various reasons, perhaps some out of curiosity and some out of various inner needs in order to, in one way or another, cause a lessening of the sense of the material confinement.

Over the past weeks there has been considerable talk with those surrounding me, and many of the incidents, of course, give the needed ground for energizing the various Light Bullets (seldom Pellets) that are needed, because *the tendency of the mechanical mind is to construct such a hide of impenetrability that it is very difficult to bring about what is termed "the shock" that is so essential* because everyone is *dulled* by the psychological inventions of the mental. This is why I have been considering so many areas that might be of interest to talk about, and I hope your questions may arise and I may be graced with an answer that can free you, to some degree, from your self-styled infatuation with limitation.

One of the salient features of today's inventory is the great movement within the realm of robotery, in other words, cloning your selves: the parts of you that manipulate your form. The robots are being given "minds," and these minds are so much like yours because the mind of the computer is the result of your mind-sperm! It is a frightening situation because what is invented and the inventor are so alike.

Last evening, Dr. F. was telling me of the lectures that he had attended and he was very surprised to find that some of the lectures were about robotery. He said, "I just could not believe what we were listening to! They were going on about what you've been telling us." There they were, all these doctors convening from all over the country. I don't know where it was, some sort of a needy center, apparently, because all the doctors were there! Something was going on, or something was coming to an end; I don't know which!

He said that this robotization is a tremendous concern to the medical profession, and I'm sure it is, but it is more of an interest to you people, because if my purpose in life has been seen even one millionth of an inch, it would be obvious that it has to do with questioning the basis of how you consider your Life. To consider your Life from the basis of this mechanically-conceived sensorial apparatus as the sole basis for your existence is a *dire* situation. In other words, everyone in it dies; prior to that they're *mired,* frequently in quagmire!

You hear the medical profession announcing that they now have formulated a program which allows a robot to go to school, so to speak, and gain higher information without the need of his inventor. The doctors were pointing out that the line between the mechanical human and the mechanical robot is so fine that it is very difficult to distinguish what's present in this form. This is why J.H. said to me with Dr. B. one day, "Mr. Mills, if your Work isn't fulfilled within the next ten to fifteen years (there are only about eleven left now, and nothing very much has been done), the entire race will go down in robotery for three hundred years!"

You can see why the robot always chooses itself. The robot always chooses its conditions. All robots are the same. They all lack one condition that their inventor has and they don't have, and that is: the condition to question their Source.

> *Men are forgetting,*
> *due to over-robotization,*
> *to question their Source.*

They're losing it in bed, they're losing it in offices, and they're losing it in everyday life because, remember, a robotized life has to live on incompleteness. That's why it constantly has to be renewing its programming, and that's why you have to be so careful of what key you press in case you lose the entire programming!

My life has been one, hopefully, that could lead you to find the Key that would erase your robotization and would allow you to perceive your True Identity. *This is not easy to do. The reason it isn't easy to do is because you have such a love affair with your everyday experience without realizing it is built on supposition.*

You consider, through a mechanical means, how to sustain the mechanical means. Mechanical means breed mechanical means, which means that each note of your octave is less and less noteworthy! In other words, notes of an octave bear seven, and the eighth one is the same. Remember, unless every note is sounded fully, you do not understand or experience what is called the bedrock of tonality. In other words, every degree of the scale has to be sounded with the same intensity and quality of response as is the *doh* or the beginning note.

You see, what happens is that we are too infiltrated with amateurism. What marks the amateur from the successful professional or accomplished artist? The amateur never has secured a basis. He has never developed a technique. He has never developed the basics of technique, which is self-mastery.

What can be mastered in performance if it isn't the coming to the perception that it is a mental experience that is governing the calcium and all the "stuff" that goes to make up this heat-controlled, cool-controlled, moderate-zoned space suit. We call doctors in when we can't control the heat. It goes too high or it goes too low, and there's too much up or too much down. We say that the mechanical apparatus is "having its ups and downs," but really, what we're saying is the programming is faulty, and due to its being faulty, certain portions of it have clogged up, or certain portions of it haven't been used correctly and consequently it needs an *overhauling*. That overhauling is usually very expensive because most of the people in the grease pit don't know what they're doing anyway. That's why they have to keep taking courses and having tea, and a party, and throwing overboard all their conventions and finding that they've got them all anyway, because they've convened all on the suggestion that the great gift of Aesculapius, of course, is to be found through overhauling and scalpel-izing the vegetable, and the mineral, and the animal that are running around in "you," and you're calling it "the personification of a wonder of humanity."

Well, most vegetables only show their heads, anyway! Most animals show they've got more but don't know what to do with it. A mineral, of course, doesn't do anything but shimmer and shine, waiting for somebody to facet it correctly so that it can be worn as an ornament of adornment. After all, there's nothing that isn't living as a result of our attention. There isn't a fiber that isn't living as a result of attention!

Why is it that we are so schooled to limit ourselves to the limit imposed by those who have perpetuated limits?

You know? Why do we go along with limits as an educational process? I just don't understand it.

I've gotten to the word I wanted to mention to you: *understanding.* I didn't know how I was going to get to it, because it would never enter your head that you're ignorant; even though you've graduated from Harvard, and George Brown, George Blue, and everything else! You know, what has come out of all our solid education is the most *ephemeral* existence.

Most of us are taught to fulfill the inclination of our progenitors. We are taught to be like mommy and daddy, and we are taught to be like auntie and uncle-y! It's so fascinating that no one is ever taught to put into question anything surrounding those you have called your family, those you have called "constituting your culture."

In the culture of bacteria, such as yogurt, they have now been able to use the sensitized instruments of your advanced inventions to find out, through a lie-detector type of hookup, how the bacteria actually respond to each other. Oh yes, on the culture in yogurt, for example, I saw the needles actually moving. (You see, bacteria constitute a great part of you. If you feel a little bit of jealousy, can you imagine the millions of bacteria back of you supporting it?!)

There were two vials of bacteria, both of them good bacteria until one bacteria vial was fed. The other vial standing next to it that wasn't fed didn't like it a bit; it was jealous. They had the apparatus attached to them both. The one that got fed started eating and was perfectly happy, and the one that didn't get fed — you should have seen those bacteria! I don't know what I would have done without the magnification; I couldn't have seen them fighting! They were so enraged at the other bacteria being fed that they created enough energy to move the needle: the jealousy and the resentment of the others being fed and them not being fed!

Why are you cast down, O, my Soul? And why art thou disquieted within me? What bacteria are telling you that you are "this"? I'm telling you, without bacteria and with bacteria, I AM *not* "this"!

This is why it is said, "Understanding is the line of demarcation between the real and the unreal."[1] Now, understanding is also essential for utilizing information up to the point of what is termed knowledge. But knowledge gained from your educational pursuits and from your experiences with your form is relative knowledge. This is why knowledge is acknowledged to *be* knowledge by those who are knowledgeable, have doctorates in knowledge and bestow the degree of knowledge! You're creating manhood, humanhood, peoplehood.

Did you ever realize what hoods people are? Everyone wears his hood, because if he exposed himself to the

---

1. Mary Baker Eddy, *Science and Health with Key to the Scriptures* (Boston: Trustees under the Will of Mary Baker G. Eddy, 1934), p. 505, l. 21.

Vibratory Frequency of a High Octave, he couldn't possibly go on with the false basis upon which his life is based at this time!

That's what the Work is about. It's altering your whole gleaned psychological basis — but no one wants it. As Nicoll pointed out, when you want to do something physically, you have to observe the effort used in order to do it. So, in your everyday lives you should know exactly what you're doing! You get up at five o'clock so you'll be awake by seven, and then you go to work for somebody who is not there! Then you fulfill your day. The interesting part of it is, you have directed every movement you made in the outward experience.

Your outward experience demands such direction. After all, to get here you could use your thumb, or you could use the railroad, or you could use the telephone and get a ride, or you could do many things. It's obvious you did something to get here. You used your mechanical mind to get you here, because it had what? Pertinent relative information on the direction that you had to take in order to arrive here.

Why is it that the part of you that's in question doesn't come under that Force that allows you to question this secondary creature that goes from Toronto to New York, or from Toronto to Victoria, or from Tucson to New York? *Why is it that we have every outward movement directed in order to make all the right connections?* If you don't: "Dallas/Fort Worth." [2] That's what you call being mired! It's not worth it!

What kind of a soap opera are *we* playing? We're building it all up on the positive and negative understanding of opposites. *We are not facing our invention.*

---

2. Dallas/Fort Worth Airport in Texas is a major hub for air transportation in the US, which is notorious for its complexity and the long distances that must be traversed to get from one airline to another when making flight connections.

What if the suggestion of "opposites" is less and less important? What are you going to do with your relative knowledge, therefore knowledge relative to the situation? If this situation is relative, then the understanding of it is relative. The knowledge of it doesn't solve it, but it allows itself to be in need of solution, and that's when you start to question philosophically: "What is the Unknown Factor to my presence in my mechanicality and yet bearing the Accent of Wonder that allows me to transcend it and yet appear to be in it?" That is another Force that allows another tone of your scale to be grounded.

You *cannot* leap intellectually. That is what's wrong with knowledge. Knowledge allows you to think you can leap from this octave to that octave through intellectuality. It doesn't happen. You must pass your full weight of presence on every key. The fingers all are different weights because they're all different sizes; we have to find the One Constant. Most teachers don't know what it is, but it's the Master Teacher who *does* know what it is. It's that part that everyone has, but no one knows how to use. This is called "the full arm," bearing with it the perpendicular nail joint to the key and the constant arch over your cathedral of hand, so that the full arm weight can be passed, regardless of the size of the finger, to every key. Then every key goes to rock bottom, and if your piano is well adjusted, well balanced, and there are no false strings, you have a purity of sound that bears a *tonal reference* to a limited object.

Now, a limited object of ivory, wood, steel, is transcended by dealing with the components that work on that level: skin, flesh, blood, salt, bone, thought. But there's a thing there that allows you to know that when all this objective stuff comes together on the material objective stuff called a piano key, the experience is going to be different! *The basis is different as soon as you have struck that key!* Until you strike it you don't realize that striking the key is like hammering it. You have to hammer it home, you might say.

You see, when you understand, you don't *hammer* it home, you don't strike it home, you listen to the quality of the sound that is becoming to the demands of the surroundings that are called the composition and the intent of the composer. Now, frequently the composer doesn't know what he's composed!

I always remember a very famous English composer who sent his music to a very prominent publishing house. I happened to know the president of the company very well at the time, and he called me and asked me to look at this manuscript. He said, "Ken, is that right?" I said, "Don't you think the composer would know? Do you think I'm going to touch that?" (I knew the name. I'd played his music.) He said, "Well, what do you feel about it?" I said, "I wouldn't play it like that if you paid me!" He said, "The phrases are wrong." I said, "Yes." He said, "Good." So they rephrased it and published it altogether differently than the composer had put it.

When a child learns in school, he goes to learn his ABCs and he realizes that they are used, not in constituting an octave, but they're used in constituting a word! By learning how to use these letters after he has memorized the alphabet, look at the nitty-gritty, rock-bottom stuff. He had to memorize the alphabet, then he had to write the alphabet, because he just didn't want to know the sound of A, but he wanted to be able to have a symbol of A so that it could be followed by B. Then he started to write his ABCs. But remember this: The second force to the child at that point is learning the alphabet, learning each letter, writing each letter, speaking each letter, and then he comes to the *"me-fah"* of his octave.[3]

What's happened? He's got to have a shock! What is that shock? Realizing that he has to be able to expose himself to using his language and his words in sentences and phrases. The first shock he's got to have is meeting people

---

3. The "surprise" or "shock" in sound of the first half-tone in an octave occurs between *me* and *fah*, the third and fourth tones of the solfege scale.

who are speaking in phrases, in sentences — and he's only faced with words that as yet are not "sentencized," or phrased. That's a shock!

Would you let your child stop school just because he wouldn't talk with you? Of course you wouldn't! You make him meet the first shock in his growth, and then what happens? He starts to talk to you and say he would like another piece of pie, he'd like a hot dog, and of course now he wants french fries, and he wants pizza, and he wants the parlor — prematurely. So, what happens? You have a very advanced, imbalanced society, unless what? After that shock, the control of *what* he's thinking enters in.

So on it goes. On the outside we know how to deal with the children, and we move from Toronto to New York, from Tucson to Toronto to New York, and from Toronto to Victoria. What happens with the movement *interiorly?* Why are you so sloppy with where you're going interiorly?

> *How much are you guiding*
> *what you're thinking*
> *in the direction you're taking interiorly?*
>
> *You should know exactly where you're*
> *going interiorly every moment you're up*
> *and awake and on the High Way.*

Look at what you do exteriorly! Interiorly you're saying "I'm pondering; I'm contemplating." Don't kid yourself! You aren't doing either! What's the result? Depression! **Depression is always a result of no inner course directed. Lack is always a result of no inner course directed. Want, poverty — all are a result of no unquestionable direction.** The result of poor teaching? No! It's a result of the *refusal* of the student to *utilize* the Teaching!

What happens? People try to evade psychologically. Psychology enters in the realm of the mechanics of the mind.

You will find, I think, through Gurdjieff and Nicoll, that you will perceive the difference in the psychology that is really meant. The psychology of the machine is where we alter our thought-patterns to conform to a more exalted thought-pattern. Not only is the psychology that *changes* utilizing the altering of the thought-pattern, but the destination of the thought-pattern is totally different. Psychology either alters the disturbed thought-pattern or explains the thought-pattern if it's not too disturbed. When it's very disturbed it's called a psychiatric thought-problem and you go to another thought-problem, bearing the doctorate of that problem that is making a living out of it! But you see, the psychologist is more tolerant because he doesn't *need* to be intolerant. He can't be intolerant with this condition, because he is dealing with a thought-pattern that is compatible with the dream — or the relative.

It's not compatible with your *unseen relationship with your Source.* You would never be able to talk this way about mechanical man, or mechanical woman, if there weren't Something Greater present. It is this Something Greater present that allows this conversation to happen. That is the Force that will cause you to consider how you are sleeping. As soon as you question your thought-patterns, you are opening yourself to change. Remember, when you change, you automatically bring about something new, which must take the place of something old.

It is funny how when you are married, people don't want you to get rid of the old. They want you to have something borrowed. A very famous woman in Canada wanted my ex-wife to borrow her full-length ermine coat; it was like a huge cape. It was unbelievable! She was absolutely ravishing in it! I was *blue* about that because you can't move into something new and carry anything old with you. If you do, you are mechanically assessing. Are you purely a mechanical man? If you remain purely as you are now, you are really entering the vanishing stage. It is a very, very serious time!

If you are unhappy
with your present situation,
it is very important for you
to consider the quality that allows you
to question the whereabouts
of your inner journeys,
your inner thoughts.
Where are they leading you?

What is the route you are going to take to get you at least to the next juncture where you need a shock? Remember, an amateur is never really shocked. He knows he is not grounded artistically in his achievement. Don't you feel the world is filled with amateurs? They are never really shocked.

The psychological basis has to be given up, as Nicoll says. It certainly does! The psychological basis **never, never** will yield an answer.[4] Then what basis does? It's the Restoration of the Force, appearing *garmented* in thoughts just like the mechanical one, but this time bearing allegiance to a Fundamental Law or Principle.

That Fundamental Law or Principle doesn't allow robbery; it doesn't allow forgery; it doesn't allow insincerity. It demands the fullness of Love, the fullness of Spirit, and the fullness of That which is the purpose of our lives: a Brotherhood of Man, and a Community on Earth, you might say, of the Saints and the Sages once again impregnating our atmosphere with the Fragrance of Being Real!

It is so fascinating to see the efforts you make with your mechanicality and the direction you take to arrive as a unit: you congeal in this one moment. Isn't it amazing you don't congeal in this one moment in the Force of Love, in this Force of Togetherness, in the Force of Oneness and refute every damned thing that people say This isn't about when it *is* about IT?

---

4. Here Mr. Mills refers to "psychology" as the intellectual analysis of personality traits without any higher perspective.

It's one thing to understand, but when understanding allows you to misunderstand, it's not real understanding. So, you know as soon as you have misunderstood, your understanding is at fault. As soon as you realize that your understanding *can* be at fault, then you understand what it means to be psychologically based on what is termed the Uncontradictable, and That is said to be the highest Path known to man.

As Nicoll points out: the first way is the fakir; the second way is the monk; the third way is the yogi; the fourth way is what Ouspensky talked about.[5] The fourth way of the Work is not the ultimate way of the Work, because "the ultimate way of the Work" still has the Work to be *"ultimized."* That is why it is only the fourth. The fifth way has you dealing not, as in the fourth way, with realizing that the psychological basis has to be totally changed; the fifth way demands that the New Way be perceived. The New Way is in a Realized Way that you are not "this." But then the sixth way: if you're not "this," then what are you? You must be Conscious Being. Then you have to be responsible for being Conscious Being, so that you may **bear** the direction of awareness in your activities. That's how people know where you are going interiorly, because your awareness delineates your route exteriorly. The seventh way is the Way of meeting a Master. Once again, you have to. You can doubt Him, because, you see, doubt goes hand in hand with your need of a shock.

Nicoll said that the people who have evaded shocks are total failures. That is why the people who have left the High Teaching have all left bearing a psychological reason, but in actuality it's the evasion of a shock. That's all it is. That's why you can feel sad but not indifferent. That's all you can feel. They have wasted their entire time by evading that shock, which is never pleasant because it means a

---

5. For Ouspensky's discussion of the fourth way, see his *In Search of the Miraculous: Fragments of an Unknown Teaching* (New York: Harcourt, Brace & World, Inc., 1949), pp. 44 ff.

relinquishment of something you have tenaciously held, so that That which you have never held before can come into an appearance of **Being** held. That's what the eighth step has to do with: executing or carrying out all the demands of this new sensitivity to Actuality. That Actuality is called Reality, upon forgetting about understanding and *standing*, exposing yourself to Revelation and the New Path. Between the third and the fourth is the half tone where the shock happens, but at that level they often put in meaning and it's a *relative* meaning, because **the highest of all is allowing a Word full of Meaning to be a Life full of Love!**

> *If you do not love one another,*
> *what under the sun is going to happen?*

The first octave is the Sun Octave and there is no one in that Octave, because no one has "*rayed*" to the bottom of the key. They have had all the withholdings of personality because they have evaded the Master Touch. That is why there are all the problems. It is easy to have *doh*, *ray*, but as soon as you get "*me*," then you have got your Festivals, because they all mark where people have to be shocked, and haven't been, with Unknown Events.

The Festival of Christmas: no one has understood death and they have dressed it up as rebirth. Jesus had nothing to do with it! The Spring, the Rebirth. What has happened? It's the Birth of Light! It's the Birth of a Newness appearing as a God of Light. That is my God, if I had a God. I can't have a God and be in an Octave that is beyond personalization of a Divine Incidence that has appeared as Co-incident.

When you realize that *person* is a secondary feature of a belief system, then you realize that worry is useless. I have never seen worry do anything but have company, because everyone worries. Everyone my mother knew worried. I never heard my father say it. Dad loved. Mum worried. Dad said, "Do!" My mother said, "Don't!" Mum would say, "We can't afford it." Dad said, "We can do it. We'll save until we *can* afford it."

You can never afford "it"; "it" is your downfall. The real windfall is when you see the apples going up instead of down! That's the incredible thing: *to meet somebody in the form of the flesh and see him rising before your eyes with his Hidden Orchard!*

That's the way I see people. I see people always with this Hidden Orchard, and that Hidden Orchard is always behind the fleshly element. You never worry about the flesh, because you know you have the Seed of an Unlimited Orchard of Possibilities within you.

Wherever you go, remember Johnny . . Appleseed. Everyone goes and remembers that wonderful little story about his dropping the seeds and planting the apple orchards everywhere. That isn't all that it is saying. It is saying that with every step you take, Love must be your footprint. Love is not going to say it's going to be just for women or it's going to be just for this one or it's going to be just for that one. That is your psychological basis of exclusivity.

A worry is based on overindulgence with yourself. Abundance is found on a different footing entirely. That is why we say the basis has to be changed. That's what most people do not want to do.

I am trying to recap what I have said. Isn't it fascinating? In the cap and gown ceremony, after it's been done to you, you wear your mortarboard! In other words, to prevent anything from going up any further! That's like having the blessed Bread and mixing it with the cement of intellectuality!

Where is the inspiration with men today?

It is the inspiration that has to guide you when you change your psychological basis. People never actually want to change the psychological basis. They want to use a psychological basis to reason with a Tonality that the psychological basis of mentality cannot cope with, because it is not endowed with the Higher Frequency of *the Realm of Feeling of Meaning.*

It is one thing to use words, and as you know, you have to use a dictionary if you don't know the root meaning. We don't mind looking it up in a dictionary if we don't know the word "indignant," but it's so fascinating how we refuse to look *beyond* the dictionary of limits when we have to find the meaning of a word that doesn't exist on the next octave!

If you are reacting, you haven't left your lower octave. *If you are maintaining the same position in your life, every moment you aren't budging, Newness will never find you in the same rut.* Even a recorded performance on the old black discs meant that the needle had to travel towards the center, and yet you people don't; you want to keep extending when you have nothing out there to say but the same old libretto: "I am this," and the Center will say, "No way! You come to Me in the end. I AM the Center and the Circumference of Being."

What do you do? You flip over and play your other side. It's the same old story: you start from the circumference and it gradually dwindles as you become more egotistically involved in maintaining the false center of yourself, and your needle comes to rest in a nonproductive tone level. It's called the hiss of white sound. "Please turn the record off! It's ended!"

> *Egotism always draws you to the center of nothingness. The Self always extends you into a relaxed atmosphere of All-inclusiveness.*

Every religion has its place in the world, but it doesn't mean that it isn't the result of Something that they haven't found. A religion is nothing but a tonality of an octave that people engage in until something in life forces them to consider further movement. What is it that usually causes you to move? Pain. Certainly! *Do you think people are going to move if they are happy?* They are quagmired in the whole belief system that pain shouldn't enter into the High Teaching.

The High Teaching is nothing *but* pain to the struggling sense. Then there is absolutely no pain to it when you are Real! It is only in your unreal state that it is painful. Why? *Negativity lives off negativity.* Remember that a negative would never have existed if the Truth hadn't. If you are totally negative you know that, in Essence, Truth is back of your negativity, but you refuse to accept it, and this is your hell. That's why it is called Earth. *Earth is either where you can bury your roots or reveal the Trunk of Greatness.*

Are there any questions that are pertinent to anything I have said?

Greg S.) You mentioned earlier how the thing that distinguishes the robot from the human is the ability to question its Source, and that the robot also doesn't have the ability to feel. How does feeling uphold that knowingness of Source generation?

It is only feeling that does, in spite of the robot. That is the one feature I left out *definitely*, because that is where it comes in with meaning. You have to feel the Meaning of Feeling the Being I AM. You see, the robot doesn't feel anything. That's why you know most people don't feel anything, other than their own condition! But remember, the robot is never conscious. The robot is never conscious; it only appears to be.

The robot can never stand in another man's shoes! It is only a conscious man who can try to! That's why I know how *un*conscious most of the people around me are because they have never put themselves in my shoes. That's why I know how serious it is, because a robot can't possibly stand in my shoes, but a conscious man can put himself in my shoes. What a question to have asked me! I couldn't have said it without it!

People wonder why there is a depression in the world today. It's not in the world! The world is the magnificent place it always has been. It is our perverted way of viewing our creation. *Our* **creation!**

You cannot have "I AM That I AM" and have it static, other than that white sound that doesn't create anything! That white sound is just that suggestion of "I AM That I AM" that everyone says. It doesn't mean a thing. An intellectual assertion that "I AM That I AM" is only the preliminary attention-getter of those around you. The *experience* of "I AM That I AM" is the Force that starts to release your suction cups which are attached like an octopus to the belief system you have engendered by adhering to it for so many years.

The point is, as J.H. says, "If this Message of yours doesn't get to the leaders of the nations and the peoples of the world within the next eleven or twelve years, there is no hope! We will go into robotery." J.G. said the same thing. He said, "You have got to get to New York. This city is without a Soul!" **The Soul is the Feeling of Being I AM.** That is the Soul of every one of you; it isn't "me"! Why would you limit it to "me"? You just make me a scapegoat for your limitations! You use me for what you can get without evidencing what you've got!

Nothing is happening by chance with you or anyone else. You are creating every bit of it yourself. There's not one in this room who isn't creating his own heaven or hell or whatever he wants to call it!

It's not very heavenly, because heavenly would be *harmonic, harmonious, rhythmical, Nowness, Newness,* new creativity; not the oldness of return of a syndrome in order to get attention. Much of it is karmic. Not you, though.

Much is karmic because of thoughts you entertain about the Teaching after having called me.

Just think, before I ever knew anyone in this room, I went by an inner calling to give up **everything** I had studied for twenty-five years. I gave it up overnight! **Overnight!** Everyone was stunned! My family, my friends, and my ex-wife, I'm sure, were stunned that I gave it all up when I had been offered a world tour as a concert pianist.

I never knew why for **three solid years,** but I did nothing but pray, and teach children and people with handicaps. I worked with several people with handicaps and saw the results until the revelation happened on every level: physical, mental, and spiritual.

> *You have no right to your own life at all!*
> *You have only the right to the Life of Being*
> *Authentic — Real — Genuine!*

That's the trouble with this beautiful world: It's the people in it who think they have a life of their own and will do any damn thing they please! That is not the way man should live; you should love one another and stop causing upset for everyone by having your little shenanigans which are *deliberately* brought on.

> *I appear to be timed and I AM not timed. I appear in a time-space continuum and I AM Timeless, either this continuum could never have had this Burst of Light! Whereabouts? At the shock points of your life!*

I AM the shock to your life.
   You have made me the starting point.

You have resented my dough,
      you loved my Ray,
         and then you called it "me"
            and then you said, "Fah!"

Then you didn't like my Freedom when I went to *soh*.

Then I said I would sing my own Tune and BE
responsibility anyway,
and that was my "la, la, la."

And my "te" is where I again meet you.
Because you haven't met the cross of the Truth yet
in crossing to your next octave.

*This is the High Path; It isn't a progressive
one. It doesn't say the High Path is
progressive. The High Path is One Spot of
Effulgence appearing rayed unto those
octaves that can cognize the Overtones of
my Beingness!*

▼

XIX.

The Unlimited View

You have only one choice to make,
and you are given one choice
in your entire lifetime:
To Be Real, Authentic, and Genuine,
or to be unreal.

THE UNLIMITED VIEW

Here on the top floor of this building, on the forty-second floor, the consideration is one of responsibility. Of course, you don't need to put a "forty-two" when it's the penthouse. You have to *have* it either you wouldn't be in the penthouse! It's usually the house that is pent up, and what's that mean? It's not fully expressed, so no wonder you have to have windows of opportunity surrounding you.

We are visiting this morning from the top of a structure made by hands and yet in That State that is Eternal with the heavens. We are in That State considering the Harmonics commensurate with the Grandeur of Being and the techniques and the means by which we can ascertain our whereabouts from the ground floor to the elevated State and know where we are.

You can enter a building and question, "Where do we go from here?" The only obvious way is up or down. It's obvious that the "up" looks more attractive: there are forty-one floors plus penthouse; "down," there are several levels for parking! You often wonder at the ground level what is there to beckon you into a foyer or a lobby but a doorman dressed in such a way as to be a specimen of uniqueness in a drab society, who upon seeing one of our Society arrive, looks with wide open eyes to something that challenges *his* disguise. So we walk through the lobby where no one is hobbying, no one is lobbying for his hobby, because this is not a day that men and women can have what they have been geared to think as possibilities for changing the world.

Before coming here this morning, there was a lecturer on the radio addressing about eight thousand people who had gathered somewhere to consider how to change the world. It was all based on offering hope and making the correct choices and considering that someday perhaps people will involve themselves with a viable ethics and bring about a whole change in the world. To this one listening, it was the most ridiculous speech. The woman was exalting the human and exalting humanism and saying how there were various religions which did not exalt the human but they were so impractical. I thought, I'm so glad I'm not a religion; I'm so glad I never knew that man called Paul! I'm so glad to *know*! My Knowing doesn't have to be called "Pauline," "Christian," or "Godly."

Words are only a means of holding your attention so that I may be in residence. The correct words bear the power of a tuning fork. A *tuning fork* allows everyone present to adjust his instrument so that if the Symphony is to begin, at least each one will have a common Pitch, and the symbology translated into sound will bear a corresponding, hopefully accurate, Pitching.

It is ground-floor technique to be *Pitched*, because if you aren't Pitched, you have nothing else to do but catch! There cannot be an incompleted act, and if you're going to pitch woo, there's got to be somebody there to catch it, and woe! Whoa, why woe? The new appellation: *Woo why woe!*[1]

If you are going to consider your life as a *human*, there is nothing to do but spend most of your time being annoyed, because the only way one knows they're human is to *be* annoyed! If you're not annoyed, you don't know that you're capable of movement! *Unless you are challenged, you don't realize you have the energy to face the challenge.* The only thing that seems to challenge people today is tithing and meeting the demands of gratitude and having enough vitality.

Paul S. said to a woman getting off the elevator, which had descended, "Does this one go to the penthouse?" and

---

1. Playing off the Taoist term *wu wei*, which can be translated literally as "nondoing, nonstriving, noninterference." This implies not inactivity, but rather the ardent engaging of a discipline to cease "trying and striving after personally and intellectually motivated goals."

she said, "I would never know. I've never been there." I thought, If this isn't interesting: *How do you know where the penthouse is unless someone has found it?!*

> *How do you know the Unlimited View*
> *if you haven't found Someone*
> *who has been There?!*

How can you have a human going up and down in an elevator but denied the Penthouse?

This is the trouble with humanism: It goes up and down, like the stock market. The humanism is a result of stock marketing! It is called "genetic stock"! And you wonder why you play the market? You *came* as a result of market playing, selling your goods and chatter! How many of you have ever come under the auspices of wonderful, enlightened parents? Few! But if you have, you have come for a *Soul* Purpose, and that Soul Purpose must have to do with an unnameable *Feeling* of Being that transcends the thought of being a human.

What does the human live on? The suggestion of unlimited choice.

*What exists, apart from that hell state? The Absolute! The human dwells in the realm of duality; the Absolute is known to exist by Its Ability to rescind the very **suggestion** that the magnitude of a projected "marble in space"(Earth) and populated by humanoids is of any consequence other than manifesting the Wonders of the Unknown Source!*

This is a Theater of Drama because it comes under the Aegis of the Divine Rama or the Divine Source or the Unknown Source. That Which IS Unknown demands allegiance, for IT says, "I AM only known when you have annulled the suggestion that *I* am not All." *I AM never known as the Uncontradictable as long as you think "choice"!* As soon as you question existence, you show yourselves as part of "choice-dom." It is unfortunate that people are so afraid of the Absolute. People try to say IT is impractical in order to alleviate the propensities surrounding ITs Considerations to inquire further.

The day is at hand when the Wonders of Being are really coming to the surface of considerations because of the dire circumstances surrounding, "You have so many choices to make."

> *You have only one choice to make,*
> *and you are given one choice*
> *in your entire lifetime:*
> *To Be Real, Authentic, and Genuine,*
> *or to be unreal.*

How can anything unreal be genuine? It can be a counterfeit. Look at what they have done with the jewels. *A star* in a sapphire or a ruby *does not move in the counterfeit,* but it travels according to the light in the real stone. This is why to wear star sapphire, to really allow it to be seen, there has to be the right light present. If you haven't any light you only see a milky blue, and when you do see it, it's a scintillating star on a beautiful blue background. There are no clouds to it.

If you go on, as you certainly are going to — you can't stop that! No matter how much makeup you use! *You have agreed to be in form for a certain time, and you have agreed to be in form to learn to be informed about what choice does in the ramifications surrounding the Theater of Life.*

"Life lived abundantly" is referring to That State when newness and novelty and uniqueness, spontaneity and vitality, surround every moment — not because you **must** be this way or you **must** be that way, but because God made thee **Mind**! What you hold as Real, even in the realm of sound — when it's pitched correctly, the words open the door like a magical statement: "Open sesame!" and you perceive **doors** opening and no longer just look through the windows!

*Words that are **impractical** to your passive, choice-full realm are words that should become active, so that the passive realm loses its force field, by devitalizing the words of the choiceful realm which incarcerate your thoughts into a pattern of finitude.* The whole purpose of questioning points to the dream of the finite. **The Infinite never has dreamed!** If the Infinite had ever dreamed, there would have been a seeming continuity to your dreams! *Someone,* you might say, is watching! If God watches over the sparrow, why wouldn't I sing that He watches over me?

Why are you so dammed? Because your language has to be different, your countenance has to **blaze as the sun,** and your pockets are filled not with a medium of exchange but with the *Riches* of the Cache surrounding the Pockets once again endowed with the Potency of Knowingness commensurate to Reality!

There is **absolutely no choice!** You think this for sure, for the Shore is beyond your reach unless you know the direction and the intention of your *activated elevation* to the Most High! You cannot escape from bondage by death. Death is nothing but what goes on behind the wings when you are only part of a spectator audience. The wings are forever concealing *the next act.* You are draped for a moment in the wonders of costuming, but I'll tell you, it is not the custom to be in such a fragile state when you are known as the very Power of the Divine Sun/Son.

There is no Eternal Wonder in the genetic *stream* of stock. The Wonder in the genetic stream of stock is that each has an opportunity to leap out of it as soon as a question arises!

> *Whom will ye serve,*
> *God or mammon?*
> *The Real or the unreal?*

Why is there so much adultery? Why is there so much disdain for the Stable where humility reigns, Wonder dawns, and Marvel is the constant Door that is open to those who would kneel at the Manger of Simplicity?! Why is there so much fear of the Stable? Because IT cannot be cast down by any choice; IT cannot be cast down by any opinion. As one lady said recently, "I haven't got time to argue with you! If you want to argue with me, you call me back and pay for it on your phone bill!"

Those who have touched the Hem of the Uncontradictable have touched the Hem of the Highest Path able to be articulated into time. It can never be forgotten and It can never be re-membered; It can never be re-discovered, It can never be re-found, because It is the Continuing Legacy of the All that is *Rayed* upon each and every one but adulterated upon birth into form by being considered *stock*.

> *You will only be agile as you exercise*
> *your prerogatives to BE the Living Son of*
> *God or the Living Presence that shines*
> *upon every situation*
> *and allows Transcendency to occur.*

You were never given a prompting or an inclination to come to see the likes of me if it were not within your heart so written that you would BE as I AM.

As David said, he had to die to sing, to imitate the sound, because as long as he personally was involved with wondering how to do it, he couldn't! *You can't argue your way in the choice realm to the Choiceless!* The choice realm is marvelous for convening because everyone can talk about everything, from All There IS to nothing, and from the diuretic to the diarrhea of the mind and the constipation of your activity!

The restricted activity is all due to the feeling of *passivity*. You remain passive, as I AM actively creating through the scenario of Words your opportunity to become active participants in the Drama, in the Theater beyond *time* square! You can't take this Frequency, this Radiation, this Force from the lower notes of your experience, the lower levels of your experience, because, you might say, it is not cosmic — it's more *Galactic*! It's beyond "this," because what I'm talking about doesn't make *sense* to you, but neither do *I*. If *I* made sense to you, you would know that *I was* sense! Since *I* don't make sense to you, it is obvious I AM more than anything your senses will say I AM!

Why in God's name are you trying to analyze sensorially What I AM in Essence: Vibration!

How can you analyze a vibration? By finding something that is vibrating constantly, accurately. That's like the pitchfork or the tuning fork. When you don't vibrate accurately, there's another force that comes in and says, "I'll take your fork, and God, you can sit on the damn thing!" Because you're so "insensitized," you won't even know you're sitting on it! Then they're apt to give it to poor Poseidon. Why give it to a god of belief when you can bear the very Sword that can put asunder the suggestion of God and mammon?

Your life is a life of **Wonder,** of resplendent ease, grandeur, and order, for your very Presence His Handiwork, His Theatrics, shows!

Your Presence in critiquing should alter the condition of the critiqued. There is nothing wrong with a mistake; it's a disguised opportunity. But there is certainly nothing right about passivity; it develops a mold, and unfortunately, I don't know what antibody there is today to contradict decay. If you don't meet the Wonder of Being, here-now, through the artistic rendering of the best work possible to the scrutiny of the Son, how will you ever know the Dividend of a Stock that never rose, for IT was never conceived *in the sin of choice.*

I live in a Choiceless Realm; you have taken on the realm of choice just to have the experience of it. The realm of choice is not known, only in this dimension. You so wanted to wonder what choice was like that you took it on; you didn't realize that it was the disguise that hell wears. There is no choice to be made! There is One Altogether Lovely, and in This we glorify, for we know that in the Beauty of Holiness and in the Simplicity of the Lily, That which was termed to come about in the remembrance of a tomb experience in the tide of Easter is nothing but an assemblage point for people to once again reassemble their forces to consider once a-gain the Constant Beneficence of the Choiceless Cause, to allow men and women to see the pageantry surrounding what appears as death and the transcending of it while you appear to be in the living.

The whole value of Easter is to die to being "this" and live as That, appearing to be in the choice-full realm. The great theatrics of time deal with this dexterity which comes with the technique of ascribing only those thoughts that are commensurate with the Real, the Authentic. Suddenly you start to take on the agility to be what anyone wants you to be, while you remain as you really are! Has it touched What I AM?! It's only Being What I AM that allows me to appear to do all these things, which has been such a **horror** to your buffoonery! You're all playing the "Dawn Song of the Buffoon" [2] because you don't want to see the Sunrise of Authenticity.

You know that in sunrise and sunset, the angle is so different; you don't get the direct rays of the sun! *How can you see a Star shining in the gem quality of Authenticity? It has to be directly overhead so that the Perpendicular can appear to meet the hypothetical horizontal and man walks as some enraptured thing!*

What is the theater of today? The curtain goes up on the Uncontradictable State of Being.

I had dinner the other evening with a remarkable doctor, and I said to him, "Everyone is terrified of the Absolute." He said, "Oh, yes! There is no alternative with the Absolute."

---

2. Maurice Ravel, "Alborada Del Gracioso."

I tell you now that **the Wonder of Being is the Constant Point from which all directions are traced.**

No Breath of Omnipotence will ever bring anything other than a Pitch of Sound that tells you all to take words and find them fitly chosen as apples of gold on dishes of silver; in other words, as sun-rayed, sun-filled words, appearing upon the reflective, the silver of your mind. Until you take the stand of Being Real, you are *moon* children. Do you realize that the only reason that Neptune or Jupiter or any of the planets have any effect on you is if you remain as a moon child, because you belong to the family of reflected light. *This is Direct!!* That's the difference.

You see, how can you *name* what you are doing when your *doing* is the Activity that is creating so that the passive may perceive what it is that allows glorification, adoration, and Wonder to once again be *ensconced* within the Heart Chakra of a Vibrant Life Experience!

Living Life Abundantly is first of all knowing that to the Source I give one-tenth, and in so doing have inherited an Infinitude of Substance being translated into the glistening Presence of a Chandelier of Glory.

Every light is multiplied because man has paid his price to have **the Light turned on** for a century that is closing in the darkest realms of materialism.

This world seems to be devoid of any form of commitment, responsibility, and fidelity to Principle. You are so fortunate to be clothed in the majesty of this verbiage, because by claiming to cut this framework of Sound to fit your figure, you may find your Self a *Pitch* to be reckoned and unlimited because you radiate from the Center of Being, and the circumference can only call you a figure that allows another to perceive that in the Heart there is a rising of the Theme of Significance.

I and my Father are One? No. There is no Father other than That Which I AM, and That appears to satisfy the need so that another may say, "Where is I AM? Where did IT come from? Why do I say it, 'I AM'?" It's the Assurance, it's the Dividend that comes in Sound to verify those who have incarnated to experience choice and know the Choiceless.

Dwell in the Tonality of the Universality of Oneness and allow the Harmony of the Spheres once again to be heard in an **active** chorale of Universal Chanting.

Satisfied in Thy Image and Likeness,
I AM seen as a Tonality
and characterized as a Chorus:
the Wonder of Unity
in the face of diversity!

▼

XX.

Green Stuff

Creativity is the very Source and Wonder of your experience.

Green Stuff

We are here watching the green leaves come to fruition from the bare trunks and the bare limbs of the past season. We have never doubted the constant Creativity of what appears as the dead season when nothing active, nothing of growth, nothing of beauty appeared on what appeared to be the dead limbs of the dead trees. It wasn't that they were dead; it was that they were *resting* to be prepared to receive the wealth of foliage: that green stuff!

The system of our own creating has given us the most incredible octaves in which to realize the various intervals involved in becoming . . what we *really* Are. Some of those octaves and intervals have appeared as our seasons, the intervals and our seasons, because "what is within is without," and "what is above is below," and "what is below is above," and "what is without is within." We can use all these types of expressions. We come, however, to the consideration which we call "the great depression" that we *seem* to be in. We never consider the winter or the trees losing their leaves as a "depression." We never consider this in the winter months when the trees are bare, having lost every green thing they possessed!

Why should we, in our thought-organized and manifested life stream, ever consider those moments when nothing seems to be happening to be devoid of the incredible Spirit of Newness and Fecundity? Yet we feel the "depression" is something that has come upon us by means that are totally blamed upon a handful of people. Perhaps it has, but we don't have to believe that Power rests in such control.

The beauty of the tree is in its foliage, and if its bareness and scant beauty were believed to be true, no one ever would look to a new spring! The reason it is a new time is because everything *bursts* from the cocoon of doubt and expectation. When you drive through the desert and you look at the various trees, you find the leaves appearing on some trees very soon, while others appear to be dead. "Oh, no, no, no! That tree isn't dead. Don't cut it down. It is just waiting for its rhythm to appear to be manifested as the new foliage."

I wonder how often we are entering, willingly, into that stream of cutting down our successes *by allowing ourselves to be whittled down by the aggressive thoughts* that would cause us to want to uproot all that we have done, thinking it was dead just because the foliage hasn't appeared, as the selfishness and the narcissistic control of situations has tried to inculcate by their propaganda!

If the dead season were really dead, the tree would never be filled with such newness that a whole new print job would come out in the spring! It's never counterfeit wealth; it's the Wealth that is inherent with Promise. It is the Wealth that is inherent with the Knowingness that *you can't believe the appearance if you expect to see a new spring.* You know very well, what appeared to be the unmanifested time of the formal gown of Nature is being stitched and nurtured and woven within the Root System of Life's Tree. This is *exactly* what is happening in the world today! But we are falling for the scatteredness of the chemical situation which has been induced to cause men and women to find it difficult to focus because of the bombardment of vibratory frequencies that are diametrically opposed to the manifestation of Unlimited Wealth.

Wealth is supposed to be our natural inheritance; it isn't supposed to be just in thought and brilliance of thought-structures appearing recognized with doctorates. They're usually glorified blinkers! There is a need for constant souls of granite to be able to withstand the imbalanced training existing in so many of the so-called leaders and people prominent in the world of commerce, finance, and art. The artists are forever having to delve within their own pockets that are usually empty if they are creative! Your pockets are always full of last year's raking, if you don't share! You stuff what you have gained from the previous year's harvest into your pockets so that you will always have these withering green pieces, crumpled and worn and dried out because you keep them from circulating! Remember, the tree knows better: *The tree drops its substance* appearing as the enriched chlorophylled leaf and restores its system so that there is a constant cycle of renewing and nourishment.

Why, in God's name, are we so inclined to be prone?! Do you realize that seldom when you're examined are you stood up? When you meet your date with a sense of destiny, you are seldom stood up if it has to do with anything that is termed remedial. You are never stood up for an appointment by an accountant, by a doctor, or by an employer if you are in need of an analysis of some type so that you can ascertain just which part of you is in that state of needing beneficent bestowals.

Wealth is the inherent rhythm of Man's Nature which allows the rhythm of Mother Nature to appear cyclical. Who ever talks about wealth? Have you ever talked to people who were scared to talk about wealth? Try it! No one wants to talk about wealth! So what do we have? We have the refusal not only to allow what is Real to manifest Itself but what is unreal to appear to be authenticated by our attention given to it.

Why do you bother giving attention to the counterfeit movement? When you go into a bank and you talk to the tellers, you can ask them how they can tell a counterfeit. This is perhaps why they have such long lunch hours: They're studying all the counterfeit bills! But when people were really wise, they studied the *One* that was authentic, and everything that wasn't Real was self-evident because it could not create; it was synthetic, it was a counter-fit. You notice the counter fits that are going on all the time. Talk about money! You should see the fit that counters wealth! People don't want to talk about wealth.

But you know, primarily the leaves (the wealth) were for the healing of the nations. What does that mean? Every leaf is an aspect of Being realized. When man starts to blossom, he is as a tree. From the system of Root he gleans the nutrients of Life and is able to bestow upon those who witness the account of the Unlimited Source when man acknowledges Creativity as the very evidence of the *AMing of the I*. When man says, I AM That I AM, he means that I AM *That* I AM.

So in the dark barren branches of the Invisible, we know *That* must be present, for I AM, and in That is being experienced the Creativity of the Wonder becoming the greatest engineering feat of all time: Man's ability to structure an edifice of thought-projected form that he calls himself, a human being.

It is only men and women who call themselves "human beings." There is no other creature on this earth that has ever called anything by name — therefore limited it — but men and women who *thought* they had intelligence. But you see, intelligence was never thought. That's why intelligence is so limited, because as long as you *think* intelligence, you never have the total access to your pocket of Unlimited Wealth. It isn't the intelligence that you *think* that is the key to your box of Unlimited Wealth.

> *Intelligence is that vibration that is the*
> *silence that links what appears as the*
> *silence between two thoughts that accord*
> *sense with meaning.*

When you make a sentence conform to the grammatical demands of the language in which you speak, you say, "He speaks the language, his mother tongue, intelligently."

Now, the key to the box is the key to your words, because the words are supposed to become the healing to the nations and they're supposed to be as the leaves of the Tree. This is another form of Pentecost, because I AM a Tree telling you about my Leaves, and my Leaves are constantly turning according to the centuries of man's historic tale.

If the Tree bears the Words, then the System must be Wordless. The reason you appear to hear words is because that which is in need of verification within the realm of its own projection demands that an abstract have a corresponding identity until I AM realized in That State which is inherent within the Root System of the Tree of Life.

The box that bears the pockets of such unlimited Wealth is the box of this Age in which you stand, whether you're a flautist, an engineer, an architect, a pathologist, an internist. Whatever your profession is, in doctorhood or in nursehood or in knighthood, it must always be realized that the Service around the Table revolves on the Axis of Being that is termed Principle, that is undifferentiated, uncontaminated, and unfettered by any of your thought processes. Therefore, IT is termed Divine.

No matter *what* you think, it will not interfere with What IS! You cannot stop a Tree from exuding its Garment of Wonder just because you think it's dead. No one can stop *you* from exuding your Wonder and your Genius just because this may be the moment the forces are reorganizing themselves within your system so that you will no longer appear to be a *sap* under the bark of somebody else's little shack of considerations. Your Mansion should be the wealthiest, the most successful; you should be the wealthiest, most successful; you should be beyond a condition and you should be beyond any of the conjugations of "may" or "might," "may have" or "might have" *been*. So to heck with all the fourteen conjugations of the French verbs! The only Verb is "I AM Now!" and that takes care of it. *"Je Suis!!"*

We tend to program our experience through allowing ourselves the tenses so that they can be ameliorated by having them past or future but seldom present. *Remember, to declare Wealth is to BE present.* Why do you think a limousine bothers so many people? Because the Spirit is supposed to be poor. Some jackass "hyena-ed" that out in the desert one night and said, "If you're going to be spiritual, you're going to be poor." Well, "the poor in Spirit" doesn't mean that you don't have anything; it means you have *everything* because you have the simplicity of knowing the All-inclusive Nature of Oneness, the leaves appearing as the audience, those that have allowed themselves to be raked into the Gathering Place where once again can be bestowed the Wonder of their Foliage.

Every tree in this room has borne what is termed "the World Tree of Wonder," and we have thought it into the confines of a human condition limited only by our own thought! We exist as a thought-condition and that's why it can be changed! If a thought-condition couldn't be changed, you would have no point of going to school. So today you wonder why they go to school! That's why I'd like them all to close; I'd like to start them all over again, you know, crank the old Ford up again and get the horses back where they belong — under the Hood which knows the correct speed with which to assume the Road of Life.

A Model T was really the Truth expressed regarding an idea that Ford utilized. A ford is crossed when it is considered the River of Judgment. You see, it meant that we were envisioning, on a higher level, *immediacy* and *effortless Being,* provided we had the substance to allow it to appear. That appeared as the cost of a vehicle that evidenced an ease with the suggestion of your continuum which you have created in order to stabilize a passing.

Your presence in this continuum is stabilized by the components that constitute it, otherwise it isn't. Now that doesn't mean that What IS is dead. It's like the tree: The evidence may not be immediately at hand as to the understanding of what I'm saying, so you may look at this entire Epistle to you on these shores of time and say, "What in *hell* is he talking about?!" Well, of course, that's where it is being exuded if you consider that you are just chips off the old block. "Yes, you're just a chip off of the old block!" Well, go on, chaps, there is much more to it than this.

What we are dealing with is that type of Message that allows you to perceive that *Creativity is the very Source and Wonder of your experience.* There is not *one* who is not creative, but we are taught that we have to *become* creative. We are not taught that we *are* creative and the purpose of our education is to free us of the leaves of the past that have bound us to what is believed to be a new beginning. This is why the Word is said to have been with God and the Word was God, because *That* could stand in the box and bear witness to ITself. That is why in this Age it is said that the womb of the female is going to be used less than ever before, in the service of propagating the Masterships, the Knighthoods, because it is allowing a dark period to last too long. The enhanced awareness of the space-time continuum is growing and encroaching upon us by our lack of creativity. This is why time is said to be running out, and those who are concerned about What IS are hoping and praying for a new Appearance.

What Jesus "promised," what Buddha "promised" — they never *made* a promise; they *lived* the Promise. It was the people who refused it and upon refusing it said, "I can't be raked into that bin. I've got to be able to leave the fumes of my burning and say that I will come again." Men and women don't realize that they create their own inner pyre. There is nothing wrong with anyone's approach to existence; they just may be slower or faster according to their speed of recognition of their *own* Divinity! No man can make you aware; the only thing that another can do is allow you to perceive that Love is all there is to you and makes you such an unusual Tree that you have been popularized in the Books of Secrecy and have been thought to be a *symbolic* study of the Ages. The Tree of Life was never fully named;

if it had been, it would have never been anything but a symbol attempting to be understood.

The real life of a tree is in the evidence of creating a foliage becoming each season so that others may perceive its Wonder. This is you; this is what appears as me. The only difference is this: When you know you know, you know you know; and when you think you know, you've got a believer thinking. A believer thinking takes time; Knowing doesn't. "Know" has the K and the *Now*. Then what do you have? You have the ability to look at your barks and to see what type of creature you're calling unto yourselves!

Why are the arts such as music so important? They attune man to a Harmonic Presence within himself that is more Real than the poundage that goes with this time-space continuum.

> *Music lifts us beyond the gravitational field of a mental entombment. Music allows us to be freed from the gestation period of suggested might where it is termed we live and move and have our being for a time on this plane. Music is what we term the accompanying force field of harmonic agreement with what is termed the Heavenly State or the Divine.*

That is why Earth *is* Heaven but misnamed because of our dualistic premise and failing to translate what appears as the objective into a subjective experience. Thus, what is within is without and what is above is below, and what is within must be abundance without, for I AM All and therefore everything outside is All that I AM.

Everything that is not as I AM comes to you as the great practitioners of the Wonder to give itself up. All the cancer beliefs, all the AIDS beliefs, all the "dying" beliefs come to you because you are the very Presence of the

Nightingale that can say, "Flow over with the Rhythm of Knowing that you could not be experiencing this pain if you in Essence were not the Peaceful State becoming your Divinity." Remember that, and if the patient doesn't know that and is not conscious, it doesn't mean a thing. You can speak it in the silence, because Intelligence is the very force-field that *allows* the unspoken to be perceived as a feeling commensurate with Soul.

You think your thoughts are not being detected? This is absolutely ridiculous. They *are* being detected and this is what is moving my wheels so that I appear to be talking. The only difference is this: I am not saying, perhaps, what you *think* you're thinking; I am saying what your thinking is causing me to say in order for your thinking not to get you into a jam or get a "speeding ticket" when you should be pacing your way in the Fulfillment of the Divine Plan.

This is what this is about: If you're going to have a wash clean, there's got to be an agitator somewhere, and it's best to do it with the All! (There are not too many suds, as you know!) While it's happening, you can allow a Tone to permeate the whole vestibule in which the interim of this life is being fulfilled.

Do you know, this life (it may be a hundred years, five score years) perhaps is nothing but that [Mr. Mills snaps his fingers], and this is why there is so little of you here. This is why there is so much present in order to remind you of how little of you is here. So little of "you" is necessary for here. Look how little is necessary! Just this little bit for you to be a doctor or a priest! You, to be a part of the intelligentsia of whatever your belief system happens to be. Or you, to be just an x-ray technician and incidentally a housewife and incidentally a mother. These things are so little! They're so small that you can't remember them when you go to sleep!

Why do you think the prolonged sleep is looked for? It's because it puts an end to your limited concept of the

Rhythm of the Dance of Life. That is what the seasons are, objectified. They point to the parallelism which exists in so many different octaves: The Unseen and the seen, the inexperienced and the experienced, the unintelligent appearing detected by the Intelligent. Why do you always appear to have the duality? In order to strengthen the fiber of your knowingness so that you can eventually leap as the grasshopper! It never considers the distance; it just leaps! It doesn't measure it. It doesn't have some doctor come in and measure the distance from one spot to another and then decide, with the pressure on one of its legs, whether or not it's got enough energy in each one of them to allow it to leap such a chasm of suggestion. Its natural impulse is to leap when the situation is obviously boredom.

Why do you do so much? Why do you keep yourself so involved with your work? It's not because you're Good Samaritans. Heaven's sake! It's not that at all; it's because you don't want to have to consider what's in the side of the pot you're making in the kiln of your own Fire.

When you shape a pot of clay or porcelain it is because you are having the great fun of allowing, you say, "a piece of earth to have meaning"? *That* isn't what you're shaping it for! You're allowing your students to perceive the Invisible Body of Space. The only reason anything has shape is because that which has carved the space out has allowed itself to die to having a presence, for without the Body of Space present you would not perceive the form . . of your thought-structure termed a sculpture in clay.

It's the same with your architecture. I spent hours yesterday with a renowned architect, a very famous and brilliant one. I had a great time with him! He said, "I've never been so excited!" You know, you can't expect to build a beautiful structure until you find out what the space which it's going to occupy tells you to do with it; otherwise those sticks and stones will really only go up at great cost and never bear the support system of that Organic Structure that is invisible but contained by what appears as your walls. That is one of the reasons so much space today is unused and businesses are going out of their offices; it's because the offices in Space have not been filled with the Wonder of It. They have been filled only with the commerce and finance that would support the mechanical contrivance to keep you deluded in the white slave job of being somebody else's employee while you are never considered, perhaps, a Master in disguise.

This is why the offices in all these great towers are so vacant. They wouldn't believe it, but of course, that's the trouble. That is the trouble: *Belief* never solves a problem. In fact, *belief is at the root of all problems.* It isn't believing that two and two is four that five fades out; it's *knowing!* If you believe, you can always say, "Well, of course, there is five because there couldn't have been the two twos there if there hadn't been somebody writing them, and that makes the fifth, the other point unseen." Well, if that's all you are, a numeral, then I don't want to be around. Please let me go!

Now, look. If those gathered in this room are all in one country, where is the Standard? Is it trailing in the dust of nationalities and races and creeds, or is it living as the Wonder that is termed the Prana or the Breath of Life, which is what allows the trees to bear leaves. If it weren't for the Breath of Life, the Creative Spirit would not even appear to breathe upon the tree. This is why a tree is never still for very long; it is always evidencing the omnipresence of Wind, which is what? The Invisible evidence appearing as the train of the wind moving the leaves as it passes. This is what the ripple on the lake is; this is what the wave on the sea is.

When you scubadive, you know the Might of Omnipotence has blown those waves on the sea very high, but when you go below the surface the most difficult thing is to get down, because then you're not in the turbulence. The turbulence is always on the surface approach to every-thing. In the depths there's only the Rhythmic Wave that goes with the Living Body. Down a hundred feet, all you can do is see the coral and you're in neutral buoyancy so you're swimming with any school you wish. It takes that buoyancy to achieve the level upon which you wish to swim; it's neutral only because you're not having to go up one minute and down the next. You achieve a balance so that you can appear to be in any school, enjoying it, but your presence alters that school and sometimes they will move in a different direction as a result of your presence.

One day when I was swimming, there were about a thousand barracuda — small ones about one foot long — all swimming in this incredible silver school, circling very high and very low. You'd swim in it, and they'd all change because of your presence. And as soon as you left it and became the observer, they went right back into their form. But it was only because it was neutral. If I'd been kicking, I don't know what they would have done. They would have scattered, only to reassemble beyond my kick.

Perhaps it's obvious that you need to kick if you wish to scatter that which isn't becoming to the buoyancy of your Spirit. You need to be in agreement with That Which IS, in agreement with your buoyancy; therefore, you are not neutral but you allow your Presence to have the support system that allows you to move in rhythm with their movement, which may be from sense to Soul.

This is why the dualistic language is always permeated with several levels of meaning, because the word that is spoken must be heard in order for the one attentive to allow the vibratory frequency of the Word to impinge upon the essence of his thought-structure, the cell and all that accompanies it into the formation of what you call the human body. Remember, the cell in essence was thought before it was formed. That's why it took so long to perceive you could see a cell. You had to realize the need of invention to look at such a deep level and perceive a Rhythm that was not in any inharmonious state, but on the surface it was chaotic.

A young man said the other night, "Well, chaos is wonderful," and of course he loves chaos, either his life would not be wonderful. It's chaos that gives him a meaning for living, at this point; he's so brilliant. *He* is so brilliant. But I said, "Yes, but go deeper, because chaos deeper is not chaotic at all; it's the very Essence out of which comes that which must be manifested, because it's not known." But it's on the surface, where you are fooling around with ideas that really are not of the family or the School commensurate with your accepted Principle of Being, that you must exert your force or your kick so that you allow your Presence to rescind the suggestion of that which would impinge upon the Infinite Possibilities of your experience and another's. What blesses one blesses all.

So, the story of Substance is really the story of Selflessness. The Tree appears to die so that others who doubt may see a New Spring. Is it not like the life of a form that bears a Word? Why do you suppose that so many of the Greats have been crucified on a tree? Because when it appeared to be the structure for that which was to die, it was always the obvious appendix of the Book of Life that was written when it was grounded in the Root System of Being.

Look to the Appendix and you will find that a Tree just didn't grow in Brooklyn but it broke the line of that brook that you thought you had to ford when the Truth had to become known as the evidence, in a simple act, of an object that would allow your ease with space and its continuum to be timed and termed effortless in movement from this to That.

It doesn't take time to think right, and the Model is before you. Take IT and live IT and find your Self exculpated from this realm of confusion. Rescind the laws of a counterfeit business and allow the Creative Spirit of Newness and Nowness to be ever fortifying and fructifying your words, as each missile of your life appears an epistle of Wonder for those who would expect Food from those who have walked in the Light of Wonder. It is only through the Window of Wonder that you can see the Moment that is Timeless, and it is in That Moment that *I* come and go and yet never leave Home for earth.

It is the same with all of you. Enjoy your impersonation, but allow yourself to be caught in the Rapture of Being and the Rhapsody beyond any symbolic form of a Brahms. If anything, waltz! And Strauss may build a structure!

Do you think. . ? If you do, use it only for the evidence of selflessness and *allow* your expression to be All-inclusive Love under the Hood of the Invisible Light of whatever you deem to be the Ideal, the Hero or Heroine of your life, for if it were not so, in the beginning there never would have been the Word and the Word would never have been possible to have been with your Ideal if in Essence you were not That.

So your spiritual pockets, I hope, are empty, for you are constantly exchanging the leaves of your garnered Creative Might daily in order for the Office of the King to be filled with the Wonder that could be bestowed upon the Kingdom of His Might and His Glory. Thus it is that World is without end because it's a Divine Idea in the realm of the gestation period of those who wish to experience a realm of choice.

> *Go sideways and see what is before you,*
> *Ascend and believe in a Transcendental,*
> *And descend and bathe in the compassion*
> *of a Knowing Might.*

> *I AM*
> *directionless*
> *seasonless*
> *but the spice of Life!*

It is very important to hold to the Truth, whatever IT may be to you, for the chaos, the unbridled and immature actions that are seemingly controlling events of great significance, should become devoid of their energy to thwart the power of Achievement. May all those who are in places of power, who have the ability to bring about a new consideration of atmospheric conditions, be struck by the Light, so to speak, or shocked in such a way that their bias and their selfishness may be rescinded, so that this great planet can continue for a few more years.

Order must be restored to the deep Tissue
of Being so that man can see that
the tissue is so thin between this dimension
and the next.

Your greatest aid is Love that sees not selfishness of sex or the eroticism that comes with having or not having, or giving or not giving, and the neurotic conditions that follow. We need to see the All-encompassing Nature of Love that frees so that there is no offense or offender before the High Court of Appeal. For *I* have come to judge Righteous Judgment and not to cast a verdict upon the strivings of a fettered soul in a condition that should have moved beyond the confines of such a dismal creed of person, place, and thing.

We should be living a Cosmic Awareness so
that this world can be given back to the
Arms of Love and the universe can be seen
to be our grandest concept worn in the
gown of restoring the lost to the Cause of
Being and the Cause of Being found in the
jubilation becoming I AM.

It's great fun to be here where Space is so gracious and the walls echo the Wonder of our being together. The only purpose of walls is to allow the harmonic structure within them to continue to sound within their own echo-ness. The reason the flute sound is so magnificent is because it has a tube to magnify the inaudible impulse to sing. The shorter the tube, the shorter the duration of life in sound. Are you going to shorten your tube by being selfish, or are you going to have it such a length that some will say, "Oh, boy, it passed through the reeds but my God is resonating even on the king of instruments. Why wouldn't it in the Symphony of Soul?"

You see, what you're dealing with is purely symbolic language. Yet on one level it is totally viable, but on another level it's intoxicating! On another level it's the most swinging experience you know, and on another level you literally fly. On another level you literally drop your confetti, and on another level they'll say, "What was that?! It appeared for a moment like Kahoutec upon the horizon of my perception, but left a trail of an incandescent Wonder!" And you were the strange man?

▼

XXI.

The Magician

I AM Eternal;
I have never been encased
in matter to come and go.

The Magician

As we have enumerated the various happenings that have confronted this One and those associated with him through the passage of time and the sequence of Holy Events which have anointed us all with the promises of tomorrow, festooned with Infinite Possibilities, it is Our great pleasure to bring to you these formations of acceptable evidence for your considerations of your future possibilities.

Since we make our tomorrows, why not let
    our words begin
To rescind the suggestion of the illusion that
    you are here and this is where you
    begin?

You came to see the Wonder
And you came by Victory's band
To walk into this land,
Which was supposed to be one of milk and
    honey,
But it has been refused by most in the land.

For people have so festered within the
    festooned mind
That they have allowed their thoughts to fall
    into the orbit of one chasing after the
    other but not the Divine.
You can't chase after the skirt of success and
    expect to find a blessing there;
You have to take the moment without
    despair and say, "My God, do I dare?"

If you touch the Hem of the Robe of Light,
    you will find that the blessing flows,
That you will be transported beyond this
    vale/veil where you say are your pains,

your complaints, and your woes.
But I say, Woe unto you. Put a "whoa"
    unto your thoughts!
For your thoughts do make you this man,
And don't you know and don't you see that
    this is not the Man I AM?

The Man I AM has nothing to do with men
    or women of time,
For the Man I AM gives men and women
    the chance to thereby shine.
If I were Man in the form of "you" and you
    in the form of I AM,
Then I AM would be limited to your moods
    and your blues and your rolling stones
    of time, and that's not the plan!

For you were meant not to rumble and
    thunder about the complaints about
    Truth;
You were meant to put an end to the
    diarrhea of mind and cause it to be
    given a boot!
You were to take the bout and know the
    Victory of standing Supreme in Light.
You were told you were chosen and you
    were gathered to offer this Age to Light.

What in hell are you doing, thinking double
    thoughts? The double-minded are
    damned,
For you know in the Light of the Divine
    Selfhood that the possibility is glorified
    Man!

Men and women are the actors in time on
    behalf of the *I,* you see.

You couldn't even say, "I dislike Mr. Mills,"
     or, "I love Mr. Mills," if it were not for
     the Immaculate *I* Unseen, yet seen.
Your criticism is nothing but of yourself, and
     you sometimes dress it as me!
But don't you realize what a fool you are?
     You're taken by your mind in a hoop.

You're going round and round in circles and
     not a fiery one at all,
And you're supposed to be caught in the
     Emerald Fire and have regeneration and
     rejuvenation before you fall
Into the coffin where your remains will be
     found, and in the cache of time,
For you were given the ability to transcend
     the orbiting of your mind.

Your mind is your worst enemy because you
     think, and even if I tell you to change it
     for Good,
There's a part of you that's riveted to your
     mind and it's called the damned ego,
     and it should
Be wrenched from your mind and you
     should be seen as engaging the *Eternal
     God Omnipotent,*
And your mind evidencing the altar prepared
     to enunciate tonally the Words of
     Freedom for man.

I Love Unconditionally, but that doesn't
     mean I am blind!
I see what must be taken by storm if the
     Kingdom is to truly shine.
Why do you limit yourselves in such a
     dismal way by thinking two ways?

It's not found in the Light.
Do you know, if you think two ways you're
    in the darkest night!
Then you wonder, "What's wrong with
    me? What's wrong? There's no
    success at all."
Why you stupid, blithering shadows!
    You'll never go anywhere in that type
    of light! You'll never be anything but
    in a fall.

The shadow, of course, has another view; it's
    the wonderful one as well,
Because the whole of life is a paradox; don't
    you know that's becoming the swell?
The shadow is the place where you may rest,
    having fulfilled your course of time,
And there you sit in the shade of the tree,
    pondering the achievements of One
    Divine.

Then you cease to ponder! And you find
    yourself so moved
That you get up and move beyond that tree
    where a Buddha seemed to stand —
    still.
Then you move and your space is empty, but
    don't you know what's happened in
    deed?
Because you were convicted and sentenced
    to die to none other than the Divine
    Self, you see?

You live your sentence out in full, and the
    vacated cell you'll find
Is where another one sentenced to Life
    Eternal may sit in your shadow of time.

Then, my God, what happens to you? You
     have symbiotically found
That you are Enlightened because another
     sat and termed it "hallowed ground."

Where in God's name are you, if you are the
     Self Divine?
If I keep on shouting they'll hear me outside,
     and who in hell cares?!! In time?!
Shout to the rooftops, "I AM THE CHRIST!
     I AM THE SELF DIVINE!"
If you are ashamed of it, you sentence
     yourself in time.

What is the joy that's undismayed? What is
     the rapture and bliss?
It's to be freed in the Light of Knowing that
     Someone came before you and never
     was adrift.
One came and anchored your barge in time
     and gave you the Anchor Divine,
It was the Principle that held your barge
     against the riptides of the mind.

Man is his own worst enemy. How come?!
     You're misnaming Man, you blokes!
Men and women are truly not talking about
     the Man of which I speak and have
     spoke.
I speak of Man generically, and you will find
     this fact
That I'm not saying a man is above a
     woman; my God never enters this fact!

Man embraces men and women, and thus is
     the Marriage Divine.
It's the alchemical one, but it doesn't bear

the sameness of other little ploddings in
time.
It gives you the emancipated State of
Freedom, it gives you a Soul that flies,
Filled with the bliss of knowing service to
the One that never lived or never died.

I AM Eternal. I have never been encased in
matter to come and go.
I have allowed it to appear to be, so that we
could get on with the show.
I agreed to be born and I've agreed to
disappear and so have you, don't you
know?
Do you think that putting This secondary is
ever going to have you disappear
without a hell of a show?

Whoever saw a magical act and had
someone doubt the magician's might?
You never would have made that high, high
perch, a hundred and fifty feet at the
top of the tent in Light.

I saw a magician, he took his act and on an
elevated stand in time
He placed this very beautiful specimen you
call a woman in your time.
She was gorgeous to behold but the walls
did come and she was encased in walls
for your sight;
Then he dropped a canopy of cloth and then
a magic happened and "O what
might!"

The canopy was lifted and there were the
walls, and then they were removed in
time.

The canopy was all rolled up and left on the
    ground at his side.
The walls were removed, no woman was to
    be found, but in her place stood a
    clown!
The man had never been seen at all and
    there was no trap door in the ground.

You heard a scream and you looked up to
    see, in the twinkling of an eye,
There was this beauty hanging by her heels
    upon the trapeze a hundred and fifty
    feet in the sky.
It hadn't taken a minute since she stood
    before your sight,
And there was absolutely no way that this
    one could have disappeared through a
    trap door, not even the mind of Light.

It was magic! And you could tell what a
    wonder it was to behold
That this beauty floated above this plane
    because she trusted the Magician of old.
This is how man dons the wings and flies
    without wings in sight.
When this one held by her heels on a
    trapeze, why, doves appeared in Light.

She was festooned with dozens of doves as
    she hung by one heel in time;
The doves they settled upon her arms and
    upon her fingers and toes as she was
    inclined.
They danced with her as she moved by her
    heels so high up in the air,
And the doves they cooed and wooed her,
    you see, so that it told us, "Why don't
    you fly like this if you dare?"

Then I saw the mighty feat of believing not
in time
But knowing the Magic that we all do have
if we would transcend our worst
enemy: the mind!
So I took my mind into hand and I said,
"What a magnificent job I've done!
I just sit here and watch the Magic of Mind
give me the magician, the angel, and
doves, and Son!"

That is how I view each one, and you'd
better start doing this act,
Because you've got to come and appear in
time and disappear and leave a God-
blessed Act.

What are you going to do? Remain in the cradle of a drugged, soporific state? You talk about the slave market of yesterday? The greatest slaves of today are those who are working for a paycheck instead of working to be the Magic of the Christ or the Divine Self and allow other Buddhas to blossom and yield a Fragrance as the interface for the Age!

Your presence is secondary to the exuding of the Wonder of Fragrance as you pass.

May these words which have been spoken
and have rolled on this tongue of time
Find their place in your heart, if it is
contrite,
and your mind filled not with guile; you do
not despise.

Despise not the Truth! If it's buried in there,
look at it! It's your purpose, you see.
You can't go on burying and saying, "Well,
I'm being honest"; that's not your deed.

I've had so many come and say, "Well, at
least I'm honest in fact," and I say, "It
doesn't do you one bit of good,
Because you're lying to yourself: You're not
doing one damned thing to make
yourself with a Hood.

"You're just a hoodlum, a spiritual one at
that, and you're supposed to be wearing
the Hood Divine."
So you can be honest, if you tell me so, but
My God, what are you doing to
transform the mind?

Don't fool with me as I AM! You will live to regret it, because I am speaking for the "I" of "you" that I represent until you wake up and listen to your Self, and then you will worship That which you call wholly/Holy acceptable in the Sight of the One Altogether Lovely.

This country is the most wealthy, prosperous land, and it's become the opposite because of you. You were here to bless the land, and *how can you bless the land when your own inner climate is so filled with the fumes of chemicalization due to guile and due to considerations that should never have entered your ken!*

Remember, prosperity is a result of "cans"; impoverishment is a result of "can'ts."

Why are you such a hindrance to yourself and loving it so much? Are you fulfilling just your racial creed? As one Teacher pointed out and said, very eloquently indeed: The greatest threat to the world today is in the religious and racial cults. It's not the new Teaching, you see, but the old teachings, the cults, which dress up the new Teaching as a cult in order to create another bonfire so you don't see how your old teachings, your old racial karma, are still treading on you and dogging your heels.

Don't be dogged, be "Godded!" It is your right. And any religion that tells you it isn't shouldn't be a religion. A religion binds you to a dogma; the Truth allows God to be irradiant in Effulgence and the bestowal of Grace.

> May the Light of Love shine upon you,
> May you find your Self in Grace,
> May you see your inner Self,
> A shining place so traced.
> May your countenance ever bless
> Those who pass you in time,
> For your eyes will reveal the Freedom Soul
> And your lips will tell of Love
> Unconditional, Divine.

> This is your Legacy; this is your Place.
> Take it, live it, and be placed
> On the right hand of the Father, and in the
> Son/Sun
> Glorify the Irradiance of such a Celestial
> Source — One!

▼

XXII.

The Malady of False Identity

You are supposed to be able to transcend the suggestion of being this limited little piece of meat and allow the fecundating Power of Light to penetrate the suggestion of "you" as a body of matter!

The Malady of False Identity

As we approach the scene of many colors
    due to the budding forth of what is
    termed the Spring,
We know that in the Rhapsody of Being, the
    Rhythm of Life has bound us to Ever-
    Newness and never to a dying thing.
And so, this evening of anticipation: What's
    going to happen when the stone has
    been rolled away?
What is going to happen when we have
    given up being bound in a religious
    sway?

What's going to happen when the mineral
    kingdom starts to talk unto man?
What's going to happen when the vegetable
    kingdom does more than send down tap
    roots as part of the plan?
What's going to happen when the time
    appears that men who know so well
The animal kingdom of what *seems* to be —
    What's the difference with this bunch
    of swells?

Are you as cold as a stone? As hot as an animal? As indifferent as a vegetable? Or are you allowing a Crystalline State to be perceived within yourselves and thus rolling away the stone from your mental sepulcher?

People say that the tendency of today is far different from the tendency of yesterday. I never fall very much for this sort of consideration, because I don't know what yesterday is that today isn't. "Today" is the name given to the moments that have passed within the framework of a community or a reference to not only outside yourself but within yourself.

We all try to change and want to change. We all strive to consider what it means to change. Yet if you will look within yourselves, you will see that "without" yourselves is only the painting of your own attention span, your awareness of what constitutes it, and the light-table of pictorialization starts once again to glow and to allow your brush strokes of Wonder to again paint a tapestry that the mind terms "Altogether Lovely."

Into your pattern are woven those Figures of Design that are commensurate with the inner penchant of the Soul's requirement. As we move from trying to relate an explanation to a religious service and move into that echelon of awareness in which we can once again appropriate those meanings that are more than just the surface understanding of a symbol, we have to be able to see that a symbol, as Jung said, is a carrying agent of energy. *There is no greater symbol in our entire experience than the symbol appearing as "you" and "me." Yet we would try to understand what it is that is everything else but this "you" and "me."* We fail to perceive that the "you" and "me" have been the structures of the mind or the Conscious Awareness appearing with form.

Religion allows you to be sedated to the requirements of the sepulcher and the stone. That's why it is said there is only One who caused the stone to be rolled away and the garments of preparation to be folded, and it is this very consideration that we now bring to you for your consideration.

> *These moments of Soul preparation are*
> *commensurate with your wish to change.*

On a recent telephone call, I said,

If the way of living is put into question, then your way of dying isn't realized.

Amiability is the posthypnotic suggestion of society. All error wants is to be glossed over and left alone. Selective hearing is the evidence of the service of the mind.

When we are dealing with Easter, in the auric field of suggestion, and we are dealing with the propensity that engulfs us with this Festival, so few people realize that if it seemed to happen and be perpetuated through the annals of time that it happened to one man, it is only because in depth we feel that it must be able to be our experience. Just as The Star-Scape Singers can tell you the experience of coming to sing as they do, from 1976, '77, '78, and then the new Singers can tell you of their experience of how they have sung within the past six months, four months, a year, and appeared in concert. There is a wonderful teaching here and a wonderful lesson. It has to do with this whole idea that what you achieve on your level opens the doors to another's achievement on that level with much less effort. In other words, the Angel of the Lord has gone before you. So those Singers who have remained and found themselves present, and the new Singers who have found the Presence and so remain, have much to be grateful for, for it is what has happened in rolling away the labor surrounding a suggested Sisyphean existence.

Life in the world today is filled with "yawns," sometimes clothed in animal form, sometimes in mental form, and sometimes in emotional form. But when the feeling is present and you cognize someone and you say you love, remember this: It may be intuitive that you recognize me and I recognize you, and you say, "Ah, I know that one I love." The emotional mind will come in immediately and start to talk, "How do I know him? It's impossible! How do I know her? Isn't it interesting? Serendipity is certainly at work here!" *What we evade is the responsibility of cognizing and the commitment that it brings with it.*

When we are attempting to cognize Life on a different level, we are prompted to do so by the many questions about Life that are not answered on any level, because Life is never in the question and why would you expect a yawn? Why would you expect to be bored? Why would you bother rolling that rock up the hill and letting it roll back down upon you? It's supposed to go sideways! That's how "me" disappears; it's sideways! It is said, "I ascend, and some go to hell," but "me" disappears sideways. That's how, when man once again appears manifesting a higher State of Consciousness, he walks sideways into time, or linearly.

You see, when we talk about feeling and we have emotion, your feeling may be genuine because it is intuitive the moment it happens, but remember, it is your emotion that ruins what might be an incredible experience. I was reading just the other day where a scientist had pointed out that an emotion moves thirty thousand times faster than any form of feeling. Therefore, it warps the initial recognition of feeling and brings about an unpropitious moment.

> *What is the propitious moment of Life?*
> *It's in cognizing Ever-Presence!*

You see, as long as you leave it purely in the sensorial and allow the emotions to guide you, you are leaving it where it's vulnerable to those around you, because those around you may not have your response, say, to me, as so few do. Very few people have the response to me that you do. I don't know how many have it toward me as you do. We don't need to know, but what we do need to know is that just by knowing facts about the thing we don't know anything!

You see, everyone wants to know about you and me (and sometimes the lamppost!) But, you see, it's fascinating that when you publicize, you always publicize the person. We have always tried to announce the *creative* side, such as singing.

> What is the singing revealing to the singer?
> What is the woodworking revealing to the
> woodworker?
> What is the doctoring revealing to the doctor?

What is the nursing revealing to the nurse?
What is the digging revealing to the digger?

Is the treasure in somebody else's yard, or is it in your own and you've failed to perceive it? As long as you can say it is in somebody else's, he doesn't have to do anything about it. But then someone comes along who says, "Mr. Mills, I have a few questions." And I say, "Fine." They ask me a question about their life, and I would ask questions in return. Because if you ask about *your* life, you have already possessed it, limited it. And until it's put into question, you aren't ready to receive freedom! Because "yours" is the armor that is shockproof, and you think this is *your* life, *your* job, *your* talent, *your* gift. There is nothing to awaken you from the waking, walking sleepstate of most of humankind, which is the collective name of "yous" and "mes." Of course, some "yous" and some "mes" have an idea where they're walking — perhaps a little more than the animals such as the sheep and goats walking to the pasture — but at least there was a wonderful chorale/corral built about them, and so we will call it a *tonal framework of reference.*

Everything bears a tonal framework of reference. What does it mean to bear a tonal reference? If we are talking about tone, it means that something must have sounded. The only way you know you have tonal reference is when you hear something said that startles you and allows the saying to be considered. That is a tonal reference. As soon as you try to understand what has been said, you alter its offering. This is why it is said you must approach the High Altar of Life with a question but have none in the mind upon receiving the answer, because your questionable state will be addressed by a State that isn't in question, and then how will you ever understand the given answer?

If you are a questioning state, then the answer given to you must be freed from falling on the ears of one in question. This is what I am doing this evening. It is an attempt to bring into agreement an attitude present, so that inner talking ceases, so that *I* may speak. In other words, if what I am saying is finding response in you in any way, this allows you to move in a parallelism with me.

We are attempting, as you know, to set up not parallelograms, but we are attempting to set up Centers of Force, Creative Force. These Centers of Creative Force will be called, in time, Arts and Cultural Centers. This is an inclination of the Heart that has stemmed from thousands of years ago, because we are attempting once again to establish a Grid of Force that will protect our conceptualization *precipitated as the world* from the negative vibrations of those who cannot precipitate and have to live on what we have done. **When you bring ignorance into your domain and onto your terrain, then it is very difficult to establish law and order commensurate with the Law that is written in the Heart.**

You can say, "Why in God's name don't you speak simple English?" Well, it's obvious why: If people speak simple English, it's obvious how simple people are! That's why we have the largest proportion of lawyers in this part of the world that the world has ever known, and the largest proportion of psychiatrists, psychologists, and doctors, because no one is really dealing with the malady of false identity. People spend all day having conversations about their own limited lives! This is the basis of our sojourn in time!

> *You are supposed to be able to transcend the suggestion of being this limited little piece of meat and allow the fecundating Power of Light to penetrate the suggestion of "you" as a body of matter!*
>
> *One of the most serious flaws that men make is to attempt to bring a higher awareness into matter.*

You can never put the Greater into the lesser. That is the root of pathology. Men and women have attempted to try to understand what causes death from an organic standpoint instead of realizing what the Great Organ is. That Great Organ is that Force which allows Man as Divine Idea, instead of a matter idea, to be perceived as Real. As Divine Idea, it is unchanging; as matter idea, it is changing. *If it changes, it can't be Real; if it is unchanging, it IS Real.*

Money will never bring about anything new; it allows newness to be perceived. Money is nothing but a medium of exchange, an impersonal way of saying "thank you," but if you have no thanks really stemming from within you, you have no account to draw upon in the Cache of your Soul. If you have no gratitude within you, you don't know the Octave or the whereabouts of your Inheritance. These are the people who are termed "lost in Egypt." These are the people who have looked in the wrong place for their Treasure and they have allowed themselves to be put into the slave market of the *human*kind instead of being the Custodians of the Light that allows the human kind to be the evidence of Wonder.

> *The only value of your person is so you can sound through the Song without words. Your very presence is singing, and it will be in the octave according to your freedom from false identification.*

The whole story about Easter rests in a simple thing: When you have planted a seed, you can't expect a flower to return to it. A flower never returns to the seed from which it sprung. In fact, if you look at an acorn, other than one bulging in the mouth of a squirrel, you will realize that the acorn bears no resemblance to what grows from it, a gigantic tree. But for you to be filled with Wonder, the fruit of that gigantic tree is the seed evidence from whence it sprung, so that you will never doubt.

Isn't this similar to what appears as the continuity of Life? We raise children, we have children, we drop children, and we complain about the children: They are wonderful until they interfere with our social experience. Then you have to get a nanny (not the goat! — but you have to get a nanny because somebody's gotten your goat). You see what happens: We use a child as the symbol of the continuity of Life, just as the acorn tree says, "For you viewers of objectivity, don't forget my Wonder! How could you put my 'gigantic-ness' into a little seed?" How can you put your Gigantic-ness into this little framework? Your offering from your Tree of Life is like the acorn; it's a seed for another, but the Tree can never return to it. The acorn proves that Life never dies. That helps roll away the stone, because the stone is the adamantine error-beliefs surrounding what appears to be Life objectified as person, or, we say "man."

"Man" unfortunately cannot be used accurately in that sense, because most people think of Man as being men and women, and Man has nothing to do with men or women. If it did, Man would be fluctuating: volatile, peaceful, loving, kind, hateful, revengeful — ah! What have you got? A nightmare, and what do you feed it? Straw. You see, it's been terrible ever since the mattresses became filled with springs. When they were straw, it was okay. You just took a knife and cut out the side of the mattress and fed it to yourself! This is what people did in the old days! They just had down-to-earth wisdom, knowing very well that what you gave in respect to Mother Earth, to *Gaia*, was returned to you, what you did to another was returned to you. Today we have developed an incredible force field of procrastination, which forestalls the immediate consequences of your selfishness, of your revengefulness, or of your generousness, or of your compassionate nature.

Procrastination is built into the time sequence of age, and that is why if you can't have a Correct Identity, you can't perceive the instantaneity of the Nowness which appears as your day unfolding as Presence is manifested. You refer to *yesterday*, and your constant referring to yesterday should only be for gathering the fruit of what you have *learned* from yesterday, not what *happened* to you yesterday. *What you have learned from yesterday is your experience that is coloring this experience now.*

When you stop and consider those who are afraid of Truth, it's rather appalling when you see such an advancement made today in the mechanical side of life. [Mr. Mills pauses while the tapes on which the Unfoldment is being recorded are changed.] It's appalling to consider how the machine can stop you. The machine stopped me just then in order for you to have a record that *I* never did stop; I allowed an interruption to appear to take place so My Continuity would never be denied. *That is the point of your incarnation!* That simple little happening gave me the key. I didn't have to be aware that the tape was coming to an end. I just knew without thinking; there was no emotion to it.

If you are moving without being bound by the psychology of time, you will stop the inner talking! Inner talking is always causing you to forget. Inner talking is like chloroform: It puts to sleep that side of you that you haven't resolved.

It's interesting to know that one doctor pointed out recently that most people have forgotten they had **Conscience.** This doctor pronounced a statement like this: "It is shocking to perceive that most people have no conscience to guide them in life." They dull it, you see. He said, "They have no conscience until they're on their deathbed." That's what I have tried to tell all the anti-Christs in my life!

We talk about the anti-Christs, the brothers of the shadow, and yet there's another side of the brother of the shadow that is really the symbol of Those who have attained. That's how they can be perceived: If it were not for their shadows, they would never be seen. So there's another side!

Anyone who is against Truth, anyone who will not incorporate Truth, anyone who questions Truth from the standpoint of person never finds Truth from any standpoint. They are better with a religion. There's not a thing wrong with a religion; there's not anything wrong with anything that helps you grow. At this point in my experience I embrace all religions but am bound by none of them! The dogma of time is the reflection, on a lower level, of the Law that is Divine.

You see, when men and women do not understand the volition surrounding Will, they think they have to move matter to be free. All they have to do is change the thought, which is weightless. *What is the great matter exchange that has to happen? It's exchanging the suggestion of a corporeal body for a Conscious Awareness, which allows you, on a lower octave, to bear this incredible Wonder. It never denies it!* It only adores the Wonder of this octave of Being appearing manifested in matter and another Octave playing parallel with it that allows you to view at a distance and paint what is seen. It only allows you to sound in an octave, to appear to see, and paint the scene/seen. In another octave, it goes on. But what is the point of trying to explain it until you are playing consecutive octaves with the demands of your innate prompting to question the Truth of Being?

This Festival of Spring is the time
of rejoicing in the Seed Kingdom,
which you have all inherited,
rejoicing in the Wonder of Creativity,
and rejoicing in the Newness.

To identify yourselves continually with the form, to identify your thought-sets only with a dualistic framework, and knowing what you do, you are opening the door to all types of invasion. Mary Baker Eddy said, "Beloved Christian Scientists, keep your mind so filled with Life, Truth, and Love that sin, disease and death cannot enter."[1] What can be added to a cup already full?

---

1. Mary Baker Eddy, *The First Church of Christ, Scientist and Miscellany* (Boston: Trustees under the Will of Mary Baker G. Eddy, 1913) p. 210: 2-4.

How full is your cup — of rejoicing, of love, and of compassion? Or how shallow is it because of your attitude that you have your own life to live and you will live it according to how you want to live it? By all means do so, but don't do it in my Presence, because you called my Presence and you will never be able to deny that you did it, no matter what type of psychology you use. The Divine Psychology is that I and my Father are One Now and not "shall be." As soon as you say *now*, it takes away any possibility of dropping that wonderful statement on your psychological plane and using it to excuse yourself for being a renegade in time.

If you look to the Cavern of your Heart, you who know me should realize that *I* have never slept on. *I* have been a Soundingness that has plucked the strings of every generation that man has deemed he has generated by calling into his experience.

You can only generate what you seed! As soon as you question your Selfhood, you question your knowledge. Your knowledge can be great but your perception of Reality that of the vegetable, of the animal, of the mineral! As long as you associate yourself with Truth Cognition and think Truth is operating *through* you, you are at a place where you are identifying the thing with That which it isn't.

It's so sad that so many have so much knowledge. They're like carrots or beets: They have much foliage appearing, but no one ever sees what they have tapped, other than their own obvious leaves. They're just usually for a season.

A Man for All Seasons is one who knows
he is not in a time sequence.

When you know you're not in a time sequence, you can see how each timed experience is nothing but the enactment of the scenario, of a drama that you have deemed essential in order to experience your leap from this into That. The moment you come to the ledge of not-knowing, *leap!* Then you will find that what you thought you were is no longer, and what remains isn't a material body. If you leap off a cliff, don't expect to have your body get up and walk away. Upon striking the earth, just see what was inhabiting it. That's how your body can go and *I* live on. I AM Timeless.

That is why the "host body" appearing as Ken Mills has been so remarkable for me, and this is how your experience will be. *You are host bodies* as the evidence of an Activity on a Higher Octave of what is called Sound Baptism, and you appear as the act of singing and are termed "singers"! You become the host body of a Vibrational Resonance. The reason you can take the attention of an audience is because of your octaves as a result of your attuning to My Voice, for My Voice is every voice that you hear in The Star-Scape Singers, because you found IT by imitation. It wasn't particularly an amiable experience, but by imitating My Voice, everyone said, "Oh! They all sound like you." To the ignorant I would say, "Well, I hope not." By imitating you find your own capabilities unlimited!

If I hadn't imitated every piano instructor I had, I would never have been able later to instruct on the piano. *Instruction allows you to surrender your false sense to a Higher One.* It's beyond a catechism. When you surrender to the Higher, the lower is allowed to be there as the evidence of your comings and goings in the name of this Festival of Seasons.

So, if you have this Easter on your mind, get it off! Enjoy the Spring, use it in your action, and leap! The grasshopper knows enough to; the caterpillar doesn't. He puts some legs on the next petal and still hangs onto the past. A grasshopper never considers that over which he hopped. The type of caterpillar called the tent caterpillar, or the unstable caterpillar, can be likened unto that type of mind that has so many interests that it walks on many leaves of attainment; it takes a little from each one. That type of caterpillar doesn't let go of the back leaf until it sees another one to devour, and that is termed the anti-Christ.

Be grateful, because you know enough that in the Light of your Love, that anti-Christ has no force, no power, to destroy the Works of Wonder.

Anyone who has a doubt about it is an anti-Christ and had better get to work on this doubt. *All error wants is to be left alone!!* Look at what innuendoes made about a Teacher can do. They whispered about Him in the Garden, they whispered among the olives about Him, and they were all lies. But why did they have to whisper? Because they knew not the Truth that sets man free. You never whisper unless you're unsure of yourself.

> SHOUT *from the Mountaintop that*
> *Love reigneth,*
> *Truth reigneth,*
> *and thus error, the anti-Christ, has no*
> *power to bring about*
> *war, destruction, pestilence, famine, or woe.*
>
> *As long as you accept any form of error,*
> *you can be assured of having every form of*
> *it manifested.*
>
> *Easter — if there is a Festival of Force —*
> *is the Realization of Correct Identity.*
> *And that was Jesus' transcendent moment:*
> *He walked from the tomb having solved the*
> *riddle of the Coincidence of the human and*
> *the Divine. And that is what your life is*
> *about!*

How many of you walk around your kitchens, around your offices, having some inner talking about "I wonder if it is really true?" Don't be surprised if you are inundated with lack! If you have doubted the Uncontradictable, you deserve to be without, because I have told you that you cannot change the conditions *without* until the conditions *within* are fitly joined together, totally.

Don't be disconsolate. Don't allow a name to be an excuse to evade being the Real Man and the Real Woman you really are. The world has need of you, and if it didn't and if this weren't important, I can assure you *I* wouldn't be here. So don't say I don't make this form important. I do make it important because I allow it, the form, to evidence the singing, the giving, the working . . Man.

Men labor, and that is Love lost. They try to create a union in order to have power, but they complain and that is the loss of force. They think that by joining in unions they will have an accumulation of force; they only have an accumulation of complaints to bring about change. The change could be brought about by each one in a union agreeing to Correct Identity.

Question every "thing" so that it doesn't limit you, so that you can appear to bless everything so it will be unlimited. Seeing mothers and fathers as limitations, and leaving them there, is horrible; but being the manifestation of the Divine Self, you bless that situation and allow it to have a chance to understand the meaning of a seed, an acorn, and a tree.

> *Everything is a symbol.*
> *Don't try to drag the symbol through the*
> *dirt of your mind.*
> *Allow it to yield the fruit of its Wonder.*

The Springtime is when all the flowers bloom, tra-la, tra-la, tra-la! I hope all those who are part of this Garden of Consideration will walk through it when the Dew is still on the Roses, and you will see how I walk with you and I talk with you and I tell you that you are Altogether Lovely. In this is our Easter, paraded before your state of awareness, and your boardwalk no longer Sisyphean, not filled with "yawns" who make promises and then break them, no longer filled with the effort of trying to shove up a hill all the accumulated regret of an unfulfilled experience.

Rejoice in the *dynamic engagement of Newness* and allow others to say, "I sense not the emotional body surrounding my intuitive cognition. I accept the responsibility becoming the Eternal Nature I AM." This is how you and I can appear to dance through the two lips/tulips, or the daffodils . . or the narcissus? We just danced through that little complex tonight! Didn't you recognize the fragrance?

> *What is the Joy of Being?*
> *Being*
> *unconfined*
> *and uncontaminated*
> *by human hypotheses!*

If somebody hasn't told you that you're Love, now you hear someone tell you that that's all there is to you. Why do you live as if you have a choice to create otherness?

> I AM One, I AM only, the One called simply
> Divine.
> I AM heard on the side of the Mountain
> while you have your mind in time.
> I AM heard in a Vocal Offering; it is oral to
> your time.
> It's not a tradition recorded; IT is the Data
> simply Divine.
> It's not on a disk that is blackness, but IT is
> the background upon which all can
> behold
> The Wonders of seeing the Unmanifested
> manifested,
> When, in the Light of a New Spring Day,
> Life behold!

If what I have said all these years is untrue, don't you worry about it. If you have believed it all true and it shouldn't be true, you will be freed and liberated for being such stalwart, unquestioning disciples of an Answer. Don't have inner talking about me; have exaltation about the Offering that comes beyond a cornucopia of limitation. When you have found the Fount of Living Waters, IT flows right from the very mountains of time. Do you see the heron in the stream, standing below the white water, the white challenges of time, as you are washed clean in the Life of the Living Wonder?

Every brush has a story to tell, even your one with time! What canvas are you using? The one that you believe is conditioned by being material for a tent? Or are you allowing it to be gessoed so that it can be a condition for receiving a translation from an unstable, tent-like condition into the Pillar and the Cornerstone of the Temple of the Living God, which you Are.

The tent caterpillar destroys every place it parks. It eats up the leaves and destroys the foliage in order to perpetuate its own destruction. So do anti-Christs. Why will you allow those anti-Christ thoughts within yourself to destroy your Divine Knowingness? Don't be in a position of equating untruths with Truths, and for God's sake love your Self, if you can, more than *I* do.

It's wonderful; it's the Joy of Being unconfined, and this is what My Life is about. This is why my intentions are so different as the Pageant unfolds, because I'm in the last act of it as far as my life is concerned, and some of you are just in the middle portion of it. Unfortunately I won't be there to direct the last portion of your life, other than through my Words that will be written and unfortunately not understood by anyone. That's why I've said there's no successor to my Life. My Life has never had a successor because My Life has never been formed with any successor in mind. *Mind* has been the success, and that is how what appears as the form accompanies it in the Story as IT unfolds.

[Mr. Mills addresses those listening to the Unfoldment via telephone:] I hope you have hugged each other there and have gone beyond your limits and embraced each other and told each other how wonderful each is when freed from the self-consciousness induced by a mind-set.

> When you see another, call him your Brother
> and then see what kind of a Family you're in.

> The God of me recognizes the God of you,
> And the God of you recognizes the God of
> me.

> Who is there to stand between
> The sun and the moon of day?
> 'Tis only the thought that's dressed like a
> "you,"
> But "you" and "me" always just have a way
> To be persuaded.

Why is persuasion important? Because it is the Gentle of Spirit. Persuasion is always the evidence of the Gentle of Spirit. Some people have said heavy persuasion is mind-washing, brainwashing, and people will say about some groups, "They have been brainwashed." As God is in His Heaven, I think, "Hallelujah!" because, my Heavens, the result of the world certainly shows that there is an awful lot of dirt in most of them if they can't recognize a Pure One. How can dirt recognize That which isn't dirty? That's why you have to accept for yourselves the Divine Principle.

> *No man can free you; you free yourselves.*

> *Accept the Divine Principle that IS*
> *Uncontradictable,*
> *and you will see the Wonders of walking*
> *the Enraptured Way!!*

▼

XXIII.

Life — Force of Love

It is imperative that Life be seen as IT IS: not something living in a world of perspectives, dimensions and limits but Life as a Force of Love, Infinitely and yet finitely expressed!

LIFE — FORCE OF LOVE

It is imperative, in the days in which we live and move and appear to have being, that Life is experienced.

It is imperative that Life be seen as IT IS: not as something living in a world of perspectives, dimensions, and limits, but Life as a Force of Love, Infinitely and yet finitely expressed!

We go, we come, and we seem to feel. We wait, we look, but where do we look to see? Is it our sense of life or is it Life sensing what appears and thus becoming quite another experience?

Just because someone is living doesn't mean someone is "Life-ing." Most people appear to be living and that is all one can say about their condition: they appear to be living. But that isn't Life! Life living is not totally a finite experience; Life living is a new concept for you to entertain. I can more easily tell you what IT isn't than what IT is, because What IT IS allows what isn't to be perceived. Yet it is not devoid of the intrinsic Nature and Essence of Allness.

We are so inclined to be this form living that we seldom wonder, "What is this living?" "What is this Life-ing?" Matter living can't be the Infinite limited. Living is the timed experience of what is termed "mortals." Living is the condition of prescribed limits in form. Life demands — a Timeless consideration.

> *It is extremely difficult to transmit, yet it is*
> *of importance that Life remains*
> *uncontaminated and unfettered by "livers."*

Consider these few remarks. They must be considered or they would not have been given as the Life living rarities, the phenomena termed "the Enlightened Ones."

You who sit in the various spots listening to these Sounds must have a penchant for Life. Why? Because it is the hidden that requests, "What is God? What is Source? What is Self? What am I?"

> *I AM That Which IS freed from the limited*
> *and yet appears to be living as man walks*
> *the road of his chosen experience as a*
> *mortal, as a human, as a corporeal, as a*
> *form containing, in essence, water and yet*
> *he is forever seeking That Which IS termed*
> *"the Holy Land," sighted upon the sea of*
> *delusion.*

It has been said that certain periods mark a remembrance pattern of Those who are performing the rites of activity commensurate to the Panoply of Life-Love and Love-Life, and those have been set apart and considered effulgent moments of the Soul. These are the moments that have been called by various names in remembrance of the Enlightened Ones. This time[1] has been set aside as a Celebration of *the Christ-Self or the Self called Christ* by those who have been moving under the aegis of a religiously-garmented Figure freed from any dogma, who is said to have proclaimed that He was wonderful because He was known and was indicated as the Son of God; in other words, the Understanding of the Invisible; in other words, the evidence of living under the Panoply of Life's Extension.

---

1. This Unfoldment was given at the time of the full moon in June, during the celebration that is termed, esoterically, the "Christ Festival."

Living as person cannot find one extending beneficence. It is the Accomplished who experience and then appear . . to be able to elucidate the pitfalls of the mechanical mind, the erroneous supremacy of personal force and power.

It is imperative to perceive yourself as one fortunate indeed, for you have witnessed an Act which you called out of suspension. You have attempted to understand IT from the mechanicality of your Atlantean minds and their achievement, and thus have reaped nothing but total confusion because the Declaration of the Sacred Ones who have walked the Book of Festivals of time has always borne the Timeless Mark.

The Timeless Mark is That Which IS incapable of being limited by thought into a realm of personalization and its paranoia. It was due to the paranoia of yesterday that the One called "Simply Divine" was not recognized and identified as a Maker, as a Sounder, as a Craftsman, for He bore the Mark that would cause others, upon hearing His Voice, to respond as if struck! *This Hammer of Light may have allowed one so prepared to cognize in Presence the Self extending in ITs All-embracing characteristic and bearing not amiability but the demand to be separate from the mob and be to the scene of those waiting on the wings, to participate in the Extending Sweep of Wonder, the Attainment of those who have found!*

Why seek ye the living among the dead?[2] So it says in the Sacred Words. How could we see this statement? "Why seek ye the living if you remain dim in wit and Divine Curiosity?" *The dead will never know the Living, for the dead are those who are living in the realm of illusion and know it not. They are living in the catacombs of the mind, suffering the maladies which the Age deems wrathful.*

If the Living is to be sought, it is obvious the seeker living has to transcend his emotional involvement with the

---

2. Luke 24:5.

thing, otherwise the urge to find the Living would not be propelled through the horizontalization of time. Living has, you might say, its ups and downs. Religiously experienced, you might say, "If you're good, you go up to Heaven, and if you aren't good, you go down to hell." So, living has its ups and downs. It's strange; *Life-ing doesn't!*

A condition conditioned is not the Conditionless. Why are we hunting for the Conditionless? We are really saying, if we look closely at our words, "We are looking for less of this condition." Why are we hunting for the Conditionless? We are searching for the answer to this "less" condition, signifying instantaneously that "condition" is a *state* of living; living in form is a condition. *That Which allows this Extension to appear is beyond a qualifying state.*

You have persisted, through the tenacity that you have tried to define within yourselves, the vicissitudes which have come upon you, the Chosen of this era. *You will find That Which IS beyond condition will be extended unto you, for that attempt you make to be freed from the conditions of life in the illusion bears with it the fructifying Grace of Achievement in Life freed from your condition and its limited state.* It is termed "the Grace of the Almighty" and it is also known as "the Grace of the Eternal Presence of Life Itself" when freed from being thought into matter, into corporeality, into mortality, into humanity, and into form.

Heretofore, we have been informed of man's attempts to gain the Meaning of Life through the definition of experience, but we will never gain the understanding of Life by the definition of meaning, for Life cannot be defined! It can only be as IT IS, and when experienced, perhaps in the extension of ITs Grace, man will perceive he is capable of entertaining what appears as "madness": an Abstract Condition that is termed "Fetterless Being"!

Those who live, we are told, relegating their sojourn upon this stage called Earth to the scriptwriters of illusion and playing the parts of necessity dreamed by comedy and tragedy, are now, in the considerations of the extremities of this period, coming to perceive that *no one, no person, no corporeal, no human, can ever answer, can ever argue, and can ever have the ability to defeat the Truth of Life living as IT IS.* That is how a question may appear to be answered in a conditioned state, a heart may be quieted in a turmoiled condition, and a Soul may be comforted in the compassion surrounding the Passion of the Self, for the Grace that descends is in a state where life has its ups and downs, but if we ascend unto that Holy Hill, then we know that the great obstruction, or the "second" force, is to get beyond the top of our attainment and cease to feel accomplished just because we stand on top of the Mountain.

If there is no distance in My Voice, how could there possibly be a second force called "a mountain," called "a body," called a "conditional state?" Life would never have made Itself limited to a condition when the conditioned is simply challenged by the Abstract, I AM That.

Why seek ye the Living in the sepulcher of delusion? The Great Festival is celebrated because *Love can make thee new.* Words that are logical and acceptable to your conditioned intellectual attainment give what is termed "hope" to the mechanical nature under which the human operates, if he is non-questing the meaning of Life.

> *The reason there is such an accent called "death" is because there's a Mystery that living cannot answer, but Life-ing sees not such a condition to be answered.*

Have you ever stopped? "You" have! If you have stopped and started, have picked up and gotten on the go, are these not limited expressions of movement, of an internal prompting "to do"?

Life is not *for* the living. Life in Essence is all there is *to* the living when freed from the comedy of truths and errors. That is the tragedy of today, for men and women have been sold cheaply into the slave markets of usurpers of partial truths and salesmen of egotistical insecurity garmented in the *suggestion* of knowing because they have gleaned Facts of Lives that have been lived not for their greedy personalization but for the Bestowal of Infinite Possibilities!

> *It takes courage to stand in the knowing of a Wonder; it takes fortitude to take the testing of worthiness; and it takes suffering, lack, want, and impoverishment to stop the illegitimate use of Truth to enhance a personal, selfish conquest in attainment.*

If the root of the word "person" is "a mask," why in this hell don't you rip it off?! And see! *Why seek ye the Living among the dead?! Why seek ye confirmation of Life-ing among the living dead?! Why seek ye solace in negativity?! A simple answer: In negativity you have so many friends.* **In Truth, be One!**

I have told you that the only difference between "friend" and "fiend" is the *r*. Do you have it in your named relationships, "She is a friend," "He is a friend"? Or have you put the *R* into a wobbly state? Because that *R* is the rightness, the *R* of Righteousness, or the *R* that is unconditioned for the Redeemed to walk as a Friend.

The Redeemed among men is a rarity, for who becomes a Friend? It is not by doubt; it is by a contrite heart, a condition*less* acceptance that you could not have made yourself this piece of passing fancy. It is very hard to find a Friend; it is not hard at all to find a great number who are looking, as you are, to find a Friend but never donning your Robe of Righteousness in order to be One!

Why seek ye a Friend among the dead?! Certainly, I should have answered your question just by my Life. How few there are in seventy years of living that I can call "friend." It goes down in the Sacred Books when the Redeemed One walked and talked and met someone and said, "I call you *friend*." In His thirty-three years of living it is recorded the great gift He made by calling someone "friend."[3]

The conditioned state has fair-weather friends and foul-weather fiends dressed up as friends. Why do I say "foul"? Because if you feel carefully without the intimidation of your mechanicality, you can sense the presence of decay. It's not necessarily in the body which you wear at this moment. It is in the very constructs that are not material that you can, to your surprise and too little wonder, perceive the various features that constitute the composite of generic man decaying!

> *This is why I am giving this Transmission,
> because it is to elucidate within the
> remaining sanctuary of your approachable
> Heartdom that you take upon yourselves the
> compassionate nature of the Redeemed and
> fulfill the function for which you came, not
> to fulfill your God-dammed personal selves
> but to fulfill the God-Promise which is that
> the dead shall be raised incorruptible!*

It is "up or down" to you. It may even be sideways to some, but in that case, cross out your negativity and cease to allow your incessant, incestuous natures to be at home with anything that can dispel years of service in the name of the Word!

These Words are spoken not just because Love made thee Divine, but because man must be awakened to what Generic Man IS and find Life-ing the impersonalized

---

3.   John 15:14, 15.

Wonder of a Miraculous Conception uncontaminated and unfettered by the logic of the masked madness!

In former times One would never have sat on a mountaintop and given conditions if you were not in need of being obedient; One would not have gone, prior to this time, to Horeb Heights and had to offer the codification that is termed *Commandments! Obey them!* We have gleaned much from these Mysteries of a mind, but no Beatitude would ever have been uttered by a Redeemed One unless the attitude was wanting among those who felt they were on the hillside of expectation waiting to hear a Voice.

Do you think —? The mechanicality at hand! If it is *at hand*, the other one is holding choice. There never was, there never will be another choice, because making the Choice is the condition for those becoming accustomed to the Inner Voice of Quest.

Do not shunt between the tracks of suggestion. Do not allow yourselves the stimulating engagement with other negatives unless they are given into the hands of a Developer, and, passing through the dark night or the dark room of the Soul, be refashioned and remodeled in the unstylized Garment of Wholeness.

If living is to be found among the dead, you have not heard. Life-ing is found as the Force that allows living to bound o'er the hillsides, to perch beyond the mountaintop, and to know that distance is only the suggested. What distance can there be in Oneness?

> *Joy, it is said, is the echo of God's Life*
> *in us. If this be the case, sadness is the echo*
> *of remorse for not having fought the good*
> *fight and maintained vigilance on*
> *the Bridge of Soul.*

Why do we go on? It is in the name of progress. But one said, "From sense to Soul my Pathway lies."[4] May yours be filled with the rejoicing of having found what you *thought* you had lost and may you become once again the *re*-ward of the Divine Warden of your Self.

Why not live life abundantly?

I AM wonderful! I AM marvelous,
I AM wholly Substance Divine!
I AM gracious, I AM Omnipotent,
I AM not bound by time!
I AM the Thunder, I AM the Light!
I AM the Moment to the sight.

If you can say, "I AM the foregoing
    Declaration,"
Be That Friend and strip error,
By your might, of its suggested power.

This is the Kingdom and this is the Glory.
If it were not so, we would have to use
    a ladder
And ascend and descend like angels upon it!

But the time is now at hand when all the
    angels smile and all the world
    looks new,
For traveling upon Life's Highway,
    the I is there to view.
There on the sea of movement, Life must
    weave Its magic way
And you bear the echo of ITs grandness:
    "I walk the Enraptured Way!"

---

4. *Christian Science Hymnal*, p. 64.

This is the end of this formal Declaration given on this Festival, on this night; Nameless, Timeless, therefore appropriate for any occasion when I AM considered All!

The Great Gift is to be able to transcend the seeming identity and live in the Authentic One, and still appear to be in the false identity. If you were not carrying the Illumination beyond the form and appearing to be in the form, you would never be in a position to allow another to appear to be in-formed about the Illumination!

▼

XXIV.

The Quickening Spirit of Radiance

Why is Radiance such a Force? Because it alters the entire structure of form.

The great need today is to radiate from the Center of your Being, the Oneness that is not hindered by activity; it is known by a Touching Presence.

The Quickening Spirit of Radiance

We are meeting in the Rose Room, and we are in a state of *reception*. Being thus prepared, let us attune ourselves to what the Voice of the Ageless shall say unto the people who are massed in the Light of a Wonder, in the conscious vehicle of Individuality, the subtle, paradoxical individuation, and the gigantic consideration of universal and cosmic significance.

You who have witnessed unto the calling and who have answered unto the Name heard and unheard, and have responded within the power of your sensitive response to the Unknown, deem yourselves fit and ready to assume the role of those prepared to inherit the kingdom of this Earth in the name of the Kingdom of our God and of His Christ and of the Self that is sometimes termed the Atman.

We embrace all those who long after the formulation of Postulates that will establish order and bring freedom to this world, which we have come to see is fermenting and chemicalizing due to the incredible Catalysts which have appeared in the midst of this beaker of time, and we are seeing, as the great Force of Light gains a resurgence into the considerations of men and women all over this planet, that once again we are on the edge of the tomorrows, bearing a Blanket of Wonder and a Torch of Hope and Light, for we know that in the proclamations of freedom all those who are deemed oppressed can be free.

For it is so stated that those who are attuned to the Wonders beyond the confines of this mental realm will once again be imbued with the spirit of adventure and newness and will once again achieve their freedom and their satisfaction in the realm where men and women perceive the undivided Garment of Wholeness, as the undeviating Principle of All That IS wields ITs mighty power in the face

---

This Lecture is available on cassette, Sun-Scape Publications ISBN # 0-919842-10-0

of the rising hordes of doubt and despair and the unfettered exuberance and quandary which arise from those set free from the village of despair, and under the embrace of a new considered freedom, once again consider how the great walls will tumble and yet how Humpty Dumpty shall not fall. If he does, he shall be put together again. *For, you see, the shell must crack, but the meat, the Substance That IS, remains imperishable.*

As we approach this great Festival of Newness [the New Year], when a new birth shall take place and a new consideration of the tomorrows will be enlivened, we should approach this season and this new decade with a whole new sense of radiance. We shall call our approach *The Quickening Spirit of Radiance.* This decade shall be termed for us *The Decade of a Quickening Radiance.* And we shall know that in this Radiation, people will once again be seen to be moving and penetrating the mysteries of their everyday world, their everyday experience, and perceiving that the world is not to be frowned upon, but to be looked upon as it truly is, a product of Mind, and therefore subject unto the authority of the One Altogether Lovely.

There are not two upon the throne of man's world; there is but One. Those who think that the seats of power are claimed by those hidden from view will once again stand exposed, because the Light shall reveal, as all great stage lighting reveals, the importance of lighting the proper figure so that the shadows may appear.

The whole value of stage lighting is not for the entire stage to be illumined but only the features that need the light to accentuate what is to be seen and what is to be felt in the adumbrations that an unseen object causes. There we perceive how the drama is enacted. You have the great play of delusion, the great play of maya; you have the great play of pain and pleasure, the great play of pomp and circumstance, the great play of good and bad, all because we have brought into the drama of living, *beingness.*

Beingness brings with it the drama of opposing forces! Oneness does not; beingness does. *Being is the activity that arises on your horizon of observation as soon as Oneness is claimed to have an identity.*

You have an identity of activity, and that is termed the *"AMing of the I"*. And this *"AMing of the I"* appears as the being, the doing, the thinking, the seeing, the acting, the drama of the experience of this life in form. Being bears with it the great corresponding identity called form, subject to the *I*. The great tragedy of today is that the great activities of the forms are left objects of illusion. And it is the illusion that befuddles, confuses, and distresses.

> *The great need today is to radiate from the Center of your Being the Oneness that is not hindered by activity; it is known by a Touching Presence.*

This "radiating from the Center" does not necessarily need words. The wording is like the being, and the Presence radiating from the Center causes the revival that is being awakened in the hearts all over the world.

Everyone is concerned and excited about the revolutions, or the overturning and overturning in the world. Of course it is to be expected, because "it shall be the overturning and overturning until He comes whose right it is" to restore the law and order according to the Doctrine of the Uncontradictable. That is the Force that elucidates through words the touching Presence of Radiance.

You see, that which radiates sparkles! That which radiates is an Effulgence of Force. This does not necessarily have to be described, but it is felt, and it is sometimes termed a healing presence. A healing presence is always a crisis presence, and a crisis presence is the experience that happens when one is making a turn for the better. *When you turn for the better, you have left the place of mentalism where matter cares for matter, and you are no longer trying to impound your Spirit within the confines of a ribbed mortality.* You are inclining your ear to the tonations that are the Tones that are being offered, gowned as words, and before words as Force. You know the Center of Power is present when you feel the expectancy of the Unknown and appear to touch it by what appears as the known experience that satisfies the state of expectancy present, as the Unknown is awaited in some form of Visitation, or Incarnation.

> *Yours is such an experience, because you*
> *have adopted the disguise of being human;*
> *you have adopted the formulations which*
> *go with the demands of those incarnate; you*
> *have adopted the time-space scenario with*
> *all its limitations, with all its struggles and*
> *with all its chaos, for the sake of enhancing*
> *the Quickening Presence of Radiance. For*
> *it is within all of this upheaval that there is*
> *still the witnessing to it that is untouched*
> *by it. And that is that radiant Speck, that*
> *radiant Force, that radiant Point of*
> *Oneness that is not in any way touched by*
> *the paradoxical nature that births as a*
> *result of the mind and its attempt to*
> *formulate That which is beyond it, or the*
> *Mindless.*

To attempt to approach the hem of the Garment of Truth from the slipped stitch of the mind's weavings will always give you a thwarted feeling, because you can never approach via the bridge over the River Kwai/why That which is beyond all question. You may have a bridge, but that bridge is only a temporary position for you to find yourself in such a way that there is no going back to the other side. For when you have once passed the midway point you find the weight is growing heavier as *you realize the need to free yourself from the self-imposed limitations of self-identification with a mass of form instead of a Light Body of Radiant Energy!*

The great needs of today are so multiple and many that it is wonderful to know that they can be swallowed up in one moment of awareness of the Divine. You know very well, your great concern for the tomorrows is swallowed up the moment you cease thinking about "you" today. As soon as you go to sleep this evening, you will wake up tomorrow, bearing with it another number in order to keep track of another day, another week, another month in the calendar of ensuing events in which you are being prepared for the Eternal State.

You could not approach the State of Eternality and be caught indefinitely in the web of temporality. If you can consider the Eternal, it is because It is the Light to what you call the finite, the temporal, and the mortal.

You who are trying to develop an understanding of the myth of your mortality must come to realize that it will never be understood other than as pointing to something that it isn't. And that something that the myth isn't is exactly the moment when What IS is offering its opportunity to you to be the living factor to the unknown equation of mythology and you.

To denote the happenings of a historical past in order for the momentary present to have a semblance of authenticity, we have gleaned, through the harvest of men's experiences, features that will hold us engaged in the realm of mentality so that we do not have to consider beyond a satisfactory endeavor the possibilities of a non-historical Life. The Life that the Masters have given, the Life that the Speakers have enunciated, and the Life that the Sages have proclaimed is a Life that bears only the aroma of the Infinite, and it bears nothing that entices the victim into a snare of possibilities in that it is beyond being in a place for gambling.

You cannot gamble with your Divine lot. There is nothing to lose, there is nothing to win, for the dice of God are loaded. You see, the god of you is that part of you which knows that you have no beginning as you have no ending. And the evidence of your legacy as relative is only a bridge, a suffering for it so to be, until you see the role you are playing that stems only in the characterization of now, under the aegis of that unseen portion of your Totality which is enhancing these very moments when you are being prepared to offer the Light Panacea and the Balm to the heart that has been wounded by the belief that despair was commensurate and concomitant with living.

You are the practitioners of
a Robe of Glory, a Robe of Wonder,
for you have been birthed and
clothed in Love!

The Robe of Glory is that forcefield that surrounds one who knows they are loved above all and everything! They are beyond any form of tales, they are beyond any Beelzebub, they are beyond any garment of partiality, they are beyond the wildest imaginations! Because, you see, the greatest dream that man has ever dreamed has been considered so unbelievable that it has been considered Utopian.

The greatest dream that man can dream is
the reunification of Man, God,
and the Universe as One.

You see, it is only in the realm of mentality that we have split the power of conception and confined it to the narrow limits of a mind border. It is only in the realm of mentality that we have dreamed up myths to sustain us in our play upon the mountaintops of freedom. It is only in our joy that we have filled the valleys with the echoing refrain of Totality. It is only in the confines of our dreams that we find ourselves dreamers and must leave that dream for joyful wakening. And that joyful wakening happens when you question once and for all, *"What is this Radiance that permeates my being, even in the disguise of pain and pleasure, God and man, and the suffering of the human kind?!"*

What a Radiance to penetrate your very experience so that you can name all these conditions, and yet that Power to perceive all those conditions remains untarnished or unimpeded in its presence until it is said that you are leaving the plane!

Your world, your form and all it experiences radiate from the Center of Life. That Life allows its variegated patterns to appear, and your prerogative is to choose whom you will serve with obedience: the illusion, the mesmeric web of objectivity and its perception and its seductive colorations, or the Sight that is beyond the perception and allows that which is perceived to be seen as it really IS!

You see, there is no war within oneself in the realm of the Realization of Individuality because Individuality rests upon and radiates from the undeviating center that is gowned as Principle. This Individuality is forever constant because *no condition will ever leave you, find you or take you where you do not have an equation with Identity and Being!*

You are in a position of such power because you know this. You know that by closing your eyes you can erase the mass, you can erase the flock, you can erase the choir, you can erase the herd, you can erase your form, but you have not in any way erased the Feeling of Being Alone/All One. It is this that radiates; it is this that is the Source of your individuality; it is this that gives you courage to BE.

> *A hero is one who has utilized his great*
> *energy, in the face of obstacles,*
> *to retain his position as one that rides*
> *the horse of the mind, even though the mass*
> *would say he was a part of the stable force*
> *of the human kind.*

You can see without doubt; you can perceive with doubt. Your drama is lighted! *The spotlight is on you, for on this stage what is deemed important is for you to perceive what you will do that would cause separation.* You will see that this separation is an impossibility, for sooner or later the mind will cease manufacturing alternatives. If the mind ceases to emanate alternatives, then it is obviously under the Aegis of the Infinite. If the mind is emanating alternatives, they are deteriorating, they are changing, they are constantly altering, therefore they are not worthy of your attention! How many hours a day do you give to the alternating alternatives? These emanations constantly poured into your considerations confuse and fret you into an imbalanced state called disease. *Health is nothing but the harmony and rhythm of Being One, all the parts fitly dancing together.*

It is said that man is the source of his own Creation, one with IT when freed from the mentality that would put him outside IT. *It is mentality that makes you less; it is the Divinity that restores you to your Divine Sonship and therefore to your Divine Radiance and your Robe of Glory!* This quickening is the restoration of life to those almost dead in battle. It is the restoring to life of those who have almost lost the spirit to renew themselves as the Lamps of the Future.

> *No collapse of anything material*
> *touches the indestructability*
> *of the Divine Nature!*

This is what you hold to as practitioners on this Way. And in this way, all those whom your thought rests upon will be blessed because there is no fermentation or chemicalization in which *I* can be present or touched. Therefore, I AM the Radiating Center, and thus the Quickening Spirit for courage and renewal, and the revivifying of expectancy in those whose eyes are dim with its possibilities.

You who are having your spiritual pockets filled with the dispensation of this downpouring Light are finding as you are prepared to receive the Effulgence of such Force that you are being given into these pockets such a resurgence of Force that you may not even realize that it has happened until the tomorrows bear witness to the calendar of your events as you peruse them as a daily experience and you enhance the walk through time by bearing the hem of such Radiance that others find you a stimulation to the senses and a wonder to behold, for you are incomprehensible to the mind that is tinged with the tinsel of objectification!

You are prepared, for you are entering a decade of such power and force because it is multiplied and magnified with the infinite power of executiveship. You are coming under the aegis of a new Creative Force. You might liken it unto an enfolding Force of Sound that will enfold the auditorium of your auditory perceptive mights. *Your perceptive abilities to hear beyond the hearing of the ear, to see beyond the perceptive might of the eyes, and to sense beyond the sensorial limitations of the form allow you to penetrate the psychic webs of illusion and penetrate the wonders of the Divine Love affair that finds you totally happy, wedded unto the Self.*

You are forever engaged to the ring of consequence, for you bore the Truth which caused you to question, **"Why?!** I have bridged this situation with my mentality, with my talents, with my art, with my study, and yet I am still this! Yet I know I am not this, but if I am not this, what am I? But if I am not this, then this What I AM cannot be questioning what I am not for an answer of What I AM!"

So when a question arises to you when you know "you" are not, it must be a question that is addressed to what you are, all supported by what you are not. And what you are not is pretending that it will decide whether or not it will accept What *IS!*

This is the paradoxical nature of having a choice of which side will you be on: Will you be on the side that looks into the past for an excuse for tomorrow, or will you be in tomorrow, allowing the past to cease to influence you, other than to allow those who have come out of it, via the doorway of opportunity and expectancy, to enter into your room where there are many, many rooms. Because someone has gone before you and prepared the proper rooms or the proper solutions to every suggested problem of a *be*-er — one who is living as this or one who is being carried on a bier, or one who is so beered that they are drunken with the hops and the skips and the jumps of a polluted goalkeeping game on the field of a pigskin endeavor!

What is the point of using athletes to endorse a brew? If athletes were really endowed by the brewery, they would be filled with such "hops" that the cultivation of such would become their milieu. If you have ever seen the hops fields covered with the sticks, then you would wonder how anyone would ever consider being the custodians of a brew that would so give you a feeling of buoyancy at the cost of perceiving what has been contrived to help you pass away in a relaxed state the feeling of failure or the feeling of success.

> *Do you realize that the whole purpose of Living is to break every suggestion that confronts you and thus allow IT to be put together again?*

The Whole Point is fundamental. The Fundamental Point is Wholeness or Oneness which has nothing to do; it has no need. It cannot be considered as "beingness." It has nothing to do with any thing, any consideration mentally. *Oneness!*

It's only when you have to approach Oneness through a consideration of activity that you find a process evolving, because as soon as activity is cognized, then we have to come to a point where you have to free the doer from the doing. One has to be seen as IT really IS; one has to realize that *I AM* is only the name or the sound or the tone pealing forth in recognition of the Soundless Identity.

You cannot have an Idea without its ensuing force field, but you can have the Idea and its ensuing force field without the materialization, if you so wish! But so many have an inclination to sensorialize it, and this brings about the emotionalizing it and thus the materializing it, and when this happens you become responsible to your executiveship!

But it is no difficulty at all in the 1990s, because under that Force you have the great power of a whole decade of accomplishment to enhance you and your activity so the executiveship has the right guidance being elucidated from its office, and those carrying out the fulfillment of the wish find it successful, and abundance the natural evidence of agreement with a Postulate of Oneness.

*It is said that no one knows the power
that agreement bears with it.
No one realizes that Oneness is
the Force that allows otherness
to meet itself head on.*

Oneness is one of the most abstract, terrifying, and most demanding considerations, because everyone is so well educated today that each and every one tries to find an intellectual, psychological panacea to keep forever the Realization of Oneness at such a distance that its effectiveness bears not the explosive Presence of Radiance!

Why is Radiance such a Force? Because it alters the entire structure of form. Radiance alters the structure of form because it hastens, it speeds up, it enhances movement! Radiation does just this: It speeds up the movement from sense to Soul! This is why to be in the Presence of Radiance is to refrain from psychologically keeping yourself at a distance from it, because the great Force is accelerating your whole atomic structure to be in keeping with the Effulgence of a cosmic, universal, starlike situation.

Everything is being speeded up! Everything is, you might say, accelerating, because it is coming to the fulfill-ment of a dream. And as a dream comes to an end there seems to be an acceleration of events.

The Teachers say today that the great situation of today is that this type of Radiation, this type of Transmission, must be unearthed, "unthinged,"[1] because the corridors for a world's baptism into the Stream of a Tonal C are open for a few short years, otherwise it will be lost for more centuries.[2] They say this because when the dream fulfillment is expected, you have brought with it everything that packages it: the Ages, the prophecies, the myths, and the promises. This dream unfulfilled perpetuates the coming of what is believed to be a Star-Child, a Star-King, a Star-Hero, a Natural Dramatist, a Natural Actor.

Because, you see, to enact a part you cannot be timid! *A hero is a hero because he is not afraid to be Real.* Are you a hero? Perhaps you wish to be one in the future! Do you dare to be non-relative?! Do you dare to expose the shadow? It's simple to expose it; your very presence will reveal it, if you are the Quickening Robe of Radiance. Your very presence makes another feel the shadows which control so much of what is termed, in belief, his "unconscious" or "unrecognized selves."

> *What is the purpose of an Ideal if it isn't*
> *to allow you to have a Center,*
> *a Pillar of Fire, a Monad to hang onto,*
> *to BE, so that that which is not*
> *can be swallowed up in the Fire of Victory.*

To be Real, you should now know, does not alter your appearance. You will still be in form because you bear the Information that allows the form to appear to be informed about the Formless.

But until you experience this, you will think, "I'm not going to be in a position of realizing my true identity,

---

1. "We are drawn to consider the Force that is available when the appearance of a thing is put in its secondary place, while the very Power that allows the thing to have a presence is recognized and named the *Unthing*." K.G.Mills.

2. "The sea, as an image, refers to a body of Consciousness that is revealing a Tonality, in the stream having an outlet in this time. The Stream of the Tonal Sea refers to the encompassing aspect of hearing before seeing. That is why the Tonal C refers to that aspect of creativity that is a corresponding identity of reference in the uncharted Sea of the Divine." K.G.Mills.

because I do not want to be spiritual when I have all my relatives to consider." Well, Jesus' relatives thought He was queer, strange, and His brothers thought He was crazy! You have very good company! Remember, those who thought He was crazy had so much thought that they did not figure.

How can you figure with a Force if you have thought with a reflection? How can you stand and bear the dynamics of a free Man if you are intimidated by the setting on the stage on which you appear? Great dramas require great actors, and great actors are few, because *a great actor is one who knows he has to live in the Now in order to elucidate a part that appears to be timed but in Essence is to reveal an attitude becoming that which is termed a great part.*

You are to play great parts. **How can you play a great part and have such small concepts about your Self?** Why are you constantly being told to consider the Infinite Possibilities? Because the finite has so few possibilities!! Every possibility of a finite ends as a dust particle. Every Possibility of the Infinite leaves a trail of confetti! Because everyone who has claimed the Infinite Possibilities leaves the evidence of his passage through the Star Treks of Light.

No one who has left a Message of Love has ever failed to wear a Mantle of Power. No one who has borne the Shield of a Knight has ever been without a Coat of Mail/Male. No one who has borne a Coat of Mail/Male would have dared to do so if the Female had not existed as the Love Nature and the Force Nature to subdue the suggestion of an opposing force!

It may be written on the escutcheon of your accomplishment one day that *"No one failed, because One was All. There were not two to ail."* All those who would defend the Chalice of Light knew the need of attaining the Lighthood of a Purified State.

What is the Lighthood of a Purified State? It is that State that can be accomplished by rescinding the intellectual assertions of the educated and adopting the descending Helmet of an Enraptured Light! An Enraptured Light allows rapture to be the wave that emanates from the Center and Circumference so that others may perceive in that emanation the attractive force of accomplishment.

The future will hold much for you because you have been seeded with Infinite Possibilities. You will bear much fruitage for the land in this next decade because you have been quickened by Presence.

You will find that the Touch of Presence, of your presence, will be like a touch of magic that will enable another to say, "Something is happening! I know not what, but I now question what I think I am, and I must now know what I am, because I know that being as I am, I am not the I AM Being. If I am the I AM Being, I am an emanation; and I AM being is altering, changing." Therefore, this emanation cannot be the primal; it is a secondary characteristic of Light: the Divine Individuality, the Essence of which has been sometimes called the Monad or the Fire Principle.

This is a Wonder, individuation a paradox, and the paradox is boxed in myth.

"Radiate!" demands centering. Radiance is cognized. And cognition brings the recognition of change. Anything that changes is passing, but in that passing, witness the Changeless.

In that passing, in that changing, realize newness is wearing a gown so that no one will think in the framework of a static condition, for a static condition is not the dramatic position of an authentic actor, playing the part prescribed and the prescription of Light for the Age of Aquarius.

> *A prescription for health and wealth and genius is to be found written in the simple words: Know thy Self, and be free from the suggestion that the Self known will be like you!*

But fret not nor fear, for having found the Self that IS, you will be able to testify involuntarily that to know thy Self is to be a touch of Wonder in a world expecting newness and marvel and asking, *"Where is the Captain of my Soul?"* You can say, *"In the emanation of the Divine Tonality, there rings the very Sound out of which is made the Fiber of Being, and the precious Tincture of Pitch colors the very radiance of your Beingness."*

If you were to be asked, "What makes a man holy?" You might say, "To refrain from being everything un-Godly." Then if somebody says, "Well, if man can be made holy, then he is divine?" You can say, "No. He is the Holy One of God, but to be divine you have to bridge over the River of Holiness and find the Stream of Everlasting to Everlasting forded by one gigantic step that bridges the gap between this and That in the Realization of a Divine At-Onement."

God-Man is inseparable in the garment of Individuality, and in individuation Man is cognized. *In that rests your activity, for you will be considered individual. But knowing what Individuality is, you will not ail in your attempt to cope with the hop, skip, and jump which the game of time tries to play with One who plays beyond the checkerboard of the mind.*

You can give up your childish games. You came as a child, and having thought as a child you never considered to be other than just what you are. You imagined a great thing, and when it was all wrapped up in "you," do you suppose it could have become vain? Education has created vanity; ignorance has created arrogance; and freedom has given simplicity. *Rest in simplicity, and in that garment see how Principle is raised and the place where you sit is Holy Ground.*

The new decade, you will make it. The new decade will be planned. You will alter it, you will bless it, you will enliven it with the ministrations commensurate to the Effulgence likened unto Radiance. And in that Radiating Dance of Wonder you will be found and named.

*Never has a future been more exciting
because you have never been in such a
position to make it so. Never has the future
been more inviting than for you, because
you can make it so!*

▼ ▼ ▼

*A year of purification has passed, and the brilliance
that comes with purification allows the Light to shine, and
any opaqueness due to impurities will fade out and man
shall walk enraptured like some Holy Unthing.*

*In this rejoice, for you have been unearthed! In this
rejoice that you have caught the beam of a Star. And in this
rejoice, that it came upon the windowsill of your expectation, and then you realized that you had been reared in
Love, the Robe of Glory, and what you wore and bore is the
Quickening Spirit of Radiance.*

*This is your legacy for the remaining years of expres-
sion. Nothing can change it. It is so written, because it has
been so translated from the Scrolls of Light that have been
indelibly etched with the Pen of an Angel under the Impulse
of a Star that broke the horizons of the mind and came to
Earth to sparkle, to dramatize, to chant, to shine!*

*Don't count the days, only number the wonders that
allow you to penetrate them and to reveal the Essence of the
Immutable Principle, the Immortal and Ageless Wisdom,
and the Infinite Possibilities of Being — thus Great Actors
for great parts to be played in the Greatest Show on Earth.*

Unearthed, unthinged, I sing!

▼

WATCH!

Watch! I say unto you. No man knoweth
    when the Sentinel in the Tower
    perceiveth the Eternal State of Sun.
Watch in the Tower. No man *thinketh* how
    the State is One.
Stand in the Tower, watch in the Tower;
    catch the clarion call of Might.
And the Sound is heard, and the world
    does rise,
Healed in the Mightiness of the Light.

Who in the Tower sees in the Tower the
    Watch that I see I AM?
Who in the Tower? *I* in the Tower. No
    "off-limits" to the Promised Land.

High in the Tower, Warder in action. See
    with the Light Divine!
Wards of the Tower, claiming the hour that
    the Patron, the Sentinel Divine
Stands in the Tower, claiming the hour when
    All that I have is Sound.
Guard in the Tower, watch in the Tower.
    Bells resound: "I AM found!"

Watch in the Tower; mourner, where art
    thou? Joy has found the Way.
Wards of the Tower, I AM the Bower, the
    Fragrance, the Beauty, the Way.
Clad in the Panoply of all Life's beauty, clad
    in the Joy I find;
Watch in the Tower; *I AM the Tower*, the
    Promise, the Joy. I AM, I find!

Kenneth Mills with The New Star-Scape Singers, 1994

The EarthStage Actors perform dramatic narrations of Kenneth Mills' spontaneous poetry and prose.

Other Publications by
Kenneth George Mills

Books
The Golden Nail
A Word Fitly Spoken
The New Land!
Given to Praise!

Poetry
Words of Adjustment
Embellishments
Surprises
Anticipations

Taped Lectures

The Beauty Unfoldment
The Newness of the Unchanging
The Seal of Approval
Near to the Fire
The Quickening Spirit of Radiance
Freedom Is Found

For more information on Kenneth George Mills or other Sun-Scape publications and recordings, contact:

Sun-Scape Publications
65 High Ridge Road, Suite 103
Stamford, Connecticut 06905 USA
Tel. 203-838-3775 Fax 203-348-0216

or

Sun-Scape Publications
P.O. Box 793, Station "F"
Toronto, Ontario, Canada M4Y 2N7
Tel. 905-470-8634 Fax 905-470-1632